The Baltimore Stallions

The Baltimore Stallions

*The Brief, Brilliant History
of the CFL Champion Franchise*

RON SNYDER

McFarland & Company, Inc., Publishers
Jefferson, North Carolina

All quotes come directly from interviews conducted by the author unless otherwise noted.

ISBN (print) 978-1-4766-7841-2
ISBN (ebook) 978-1-4766-3698-6

LIBRARY OF CONGRESS AND BRITISH LIBRARY
CATALOGUING DATA ARE AVAILABLE

Library of Congress Control Number 2020007027

© 2020 Ron Snyder. All rights reserved

No part of this book may be reproduced or transmitted in any form or by any means, electronic or mechanical, including photocopying or recording, or by any information storage and retrieval system, without permission in writing from the publisher.

On the cover: The Baltimore Stallions on offense with tackle Shar Pourdanesh (69), who went on to play in the NFL (photograph by John Patrick Kelly, from the archives of John W. Ziemann)

Printed in the United States of America

*McFarland & Company, Inc., Publishers
Box 611, Jefferson, North Carolina 28640
www.mcfarlandpub.com*

To my amazing wife, Lori,
and to my children,
William, Marissa and Megan.
Thank you for supporting me
each and every day and motivating me
to be a better husband, father,
person and writer.

Table of Contents

Acknowledgments — ix
Prelude — 1
Introduction — 5

1. A Tradition Is Born — 9
2. The Colts Leave Town — 11
3. The USFL Comes to Town … Sort Of — 16
4. "Give Baltimore the Ball" — 21
5. Southern Expansion — 28
6. Baltimore Got the Ball — 31
7. The CFL Colts Are Born — 37
8. Building a Team — 46
9. Football Officially Returns to Baltimore — 62
10. More Than an Expansion Team — 75
11. Run to the Grey Cup — 87
12. Unfinished Business — 94
13. The Baltimore Browns? — 105
14. Left Out — 108
15. Final Run — 112
16. The End in Baltimore — 118
17. Legacy — 129
18. Postscript — 150

Appendix A. All-Time Results 155
Appendix B. Where Are They Now? 165
Appendix C. Baltimore Football Timeline 178
Chapter Notes 183
Bibliography 185
Index 189

Acknowledgments

I would like to thank the following people for their assistance in making the writing of this book possible:

- Mike Gathagan—Thank you for your passion for this project and for helping connect me with so many associated with the team.
- John Ziemann—I am so appreciative for you providing so many photos and other material to use in association with this book.
  - Jim Popp
  - Tracy Ham
  - Mike Pringle
  - Chris Armstrong
  - Irv Smith
  - Shar Pourdanesh
  - Josh Miller
  - John Earle
  - Guy Earle
  - Carlos Huerta
  - Elfrid Payton
  - Bruce Cunningham
  - Dan O'Connell
  - Dan Crowley
  - Bonnie Downing
  - Tom Guy
  - Rob Betz
  - Scott Garceau
  - Bob Price
  - Donald Hill-Eley
  - Tracy Gravely
  - Ken Watson
  - Grant Carter
  - Douglas Craft
  - Walter Wilson
  - Michael Gibbons
  - Roch Kubatko
  - Pete Kerzel
  - Mark Viviano
  - Glenn Clark
  - Mike Rogers
  - Zach Wolpoff
  - Kevin Sherping
  - Brendan Marr

Prelude

Baltimore was extremely well-represented on August 4, 2018, in Canton, Ohio, when Ravens linebacker Ray Lewis took his rightful place in the Pro Football Hall of Fame. Lewis' 17-year career is a reminder of what Baltimore football fans have experienced each Sunday since the Ravens arrived as the former Cleveland Browns in 1996. Since that time, the Ravens have won two Super Bowls, advanced to the AFC Championship Game two other times, and have contended for the playoffs more years than not, especially since winning Super Bowl XXXV after the 2000 season.

On days of home games, upwards of 70,000 fans flock to M&T Bank Stadium for tailgating, hours before kickoff, before cheering on the team in purple and black against the likes of the Pittsburgh Steelers, Cincinnati Bengals, Cleveland Browns, or whatever team comes to town on any given Sunday (or Monday or Thursday as is sometimes the case). Ravens football is engrained in the community, and those who are college seniors and younger have no memories of life without NFL football in Baltimore. From taking in training camp at the Under Armour Performance Center (the Ravens' training facility nicknamed "the Castle" for its royal appearance) to "Purple Fridays," where Ravens fans are decked out in purple in support of the team, to tailgating in the hours before kickoff, backing the Ravens has become a way of life in Baltimore.

Rallying around the Ravens for today's youth is similar to the attitude of my parents, who considered NFL football, specifically the Baltimore Colts, a religion. To that older generation, there is no quarterback greater than Johnny Unitas, the greatest game ever played was, is, and always will be the 1958 NFL Championship Game, when the Colts defeated the New York Giants in overtime, and New York Jets Hall of Fame quarterback Joe Namath is persona non grata for leading his team to a "guaranteed" upset of the Colts in Super Bowl III.

My generation is quite different. I was not even six years old and was still in kindergarten when the Colts sneaked out of town on March 29, 1984. I have no memories of the Colts in Baltimore other than those Mayflower trucks rolling out and grown men and women visibly weeping over the loss of their beloved team. I never got to experience a game with my dad or take my kids to old Memorial Stadium on 33rd Street, a place once dubbed "The World's Largest Outdoor Insane Asylum." For the longest time, I had no idea what it meant to have civic pride in my city's successful sports franchises. I ended up gravitating to Dan Marino and the Miami Dolphins because we tended to get their games each week as part of NBC's AFC package at the time.

Most of my childhood represents a particularly dark time in Baltimore sports. The Orioles, who won the World Series in 1983, would hit bottom by 1988, opening the season with a Major League Baseball–record 21 straight defeats. There was even concern that the Orioles would follow the Colts' lead and then-owner Edward Bennett Williams would pack up the team and move to Washington, D.C., if a new stadium was not built. As the Orioles floundered, Baltimore would be used multiple times by existing NFL teams, only to leverage a better deal elsewhere. I would then cry with others and later get angry when the NFL spurned Baltimore in favor of Charlotte, North Carolina, and Jacksonville, Florida, for expansion teams.

However, things began to turn around after 1988, when the state of Maryland announced that there would be a new downtown ballpark built (Oriole Park at Camden Yards) that would be open in time for the 1992 season. That stadium was, and is still, considered one of the most beautiful ballparks in the country, and the sports complex led to a renaissance of classically-built, baseball-only ballparks throughout Major League Baseball.

As for the NFL, all hope seemed to be lost for a team in Baltimore after the city was shut out in the expansion process in 1993. While the NFL seemed unlikely, professional football would soon return to Baltimore, albeit not what most fans ever expected. In 1994, Virginia businessman Jim Speros brought the Canadian Football League to town in what would eventually become the Baltimore Stallions. The Stallions were not an NFL team, but that didn't necessarily matter for many Baltimore football fans. They were just excited to see true professional football back in town. Besides, the Stallions were their kind of football team, a group of blue-collar players who didn't have multi-million-dollar contracts but were simply playing to continue their dreams. They also represented the antithesis of the NFL, a league many in Baltimore grew to despise for its perceived poor treatment of the city.

For two seasons, the Stallions were the most dominant team in the CFL, and in 1995 they became the only United States–based team in league history to win the Grey Cup, the CFL's version of the Super Bowl.

Then, just like that, the Stallions were gone and forgotten. The Stallions' fate in Baltimore was sealed the moment long-time and iconic NFL owner Art Modell announced that the Cleveland Browns were moving to town. So, after all of the heartbreak, anger, and disappointment the NFL showed Baltimore over the previous decade, the city was willing to forgive and forget simply with the promise of a team to call their own.

Don't get me wrong; I am a diehard Ravens fan. I was excited when they announced they were coming. I'm sure I even have a "Baltimore Browns" sweatshirt in a box somewhere, packed away in my parents' house. I cheered until I lost my voice with the rest of my family, friends, neighbors, and even strangers when the Ravens won the Super Bowl after the 2000 and 2012 seasons. I was even blessed to be a beat reporter for my hometown team for several years and covered every aspect of the Ravens, from training camp and the draft, to off-season acquisitions, coaching changes, and multiple playoff runs.

Still, there has always been a special place in my heart for the Baltimore Stallions. They were the first professional football team I could call my own. They taught me how to support a football team, gave the city hope, and proved to the NFL that Baltimore belonged back in the league. I never felt it was fair how players like Mike Pringle, Tracy Ham, Elfrid Payton, O. J. Brigance, Josh Miller, Chris Armstrong, and others were just forgotten in an instant as soon as the NFL came calling. In the end, the NFL was like the girlfriend who cheated on you and treated you like dirt, only to ask later for forgiveness. Then, just like that, you dumped the new girlfriend who had remained true to you with no strings attached.

Baltimore is the only city in professional football history that can lay claim to an NFL championship, a Super Bowl championship (with two franchises), a USFL title, and a CFL Grey Cup. The book on Baltimore football cannot be written without highlighting the contributions of the Baltimore Stallions. As I tell people who were not around, or not even alive, during the Stallions era, you would have a hard time truly understanding what that time was like for sports fans in town. But ask any Baltimore football fan who was 10 to 20 years old back then, and they can tell you just how important the Stallions were to them. This was my motivation for writing this book. I just hope that you enjoy reading it as much as I enjoyed writing it.

Introduction

Baltimore is a town rich in sports history.

It is the town credited with helping make the NFL the sports juggernaut it is today. The league's place as the center of the U.S.'s sports universe was solidified when quarterback Johnny Unitas handed the ball off to running back Alan Ameche for the game-winning touchdown in the Baltimore Colts' 23–17 overtime victory over the New York Giants in the 1958 NFL Championship game, dubbed "The Greatest Game Ever Played."

Baltimore is where players like Brooks Robinson, Jim Palmer, and Cal Ripken, Jr., helped lead the Orioles to three World Series titles and three additional World Series appearances between 1966 and 1983; they were considered the best team in all of baseball during that run. Charm City is the town where Ray Lewis and a dominant defense captured the hearts of the city and brought home Super Bowl wins following the 2000 and 2012 seasons. Baltimore is also the birthplace of such great athletes as Babe Ruth, Olympic champion swimmer Michael Phelps, former heavyweight boxing champion Hasim Rahman, NBA stars Carmelo Anthony and Rudy Gay, and Hall of Fame pro bowler Danny Wiseman.

But in between the golden age of Baltimore sports of the Colts and Orioles and the rise of the Ravens, there was a dark period of sports for the city. The Colts skipped town and moved to Indianapolis on a snowy March night in 1984. The Orioles went from being the model franchise in all of baseball to, in 1988, posting the longest losing streak to start a season in MLB history. In fact, there was no Major League Baseball at all in Baltimore, or anywhere else for that matter, by mid–August in 1994, thanks to the players' strike that caused the owners to cancel the rest of the season, including the World Series that year.

Without an NFL team and the baseball team on strike, Baltimore was a major league sports city without a team. This left a huge void for sports fans for a city with a tradition as strong as any town in the United States. Enter the Baltimore Stallions. In the larger book of Baltimore sports history, the Stallions are but a small chapter at best. The Canadian Football

League team lasted just two seasons in town before growing debt, the arrival of the NFL's Cleveland Browns (now the Ravens), and the overall failure of the CFL's U.S. expansion for a variety of reasons, including financial, political, and business issues, forced the franchise to close shop and eventually become the Montreal Alouettes in 1996. While the Stallions played just 42 games in their brief history, they still hold a special place in the hearts of Baltimore sports fans from that time. To many, the Stallions were their first experience in supporting a professional football team.

To longtime Baltimore football fans, the CFL franchise filled the 12-year professional football void that existed between the Colts' departure in 1984 and the Ravens' arrival in 1996. In between, the short-lived United States Football League tried to supply that hometown team when the Stars moved from Philadelphia in 1985. However, the team did not practice in Baltimore and was forced to play in College Park due to the city's lease with the Orioles that barred any professional football team from playing at Memorial Stadium until 1986. The USFL folded before that could happen, leading to a lot of what-might-have-been question marks about potential alternatives to the NFL in the United States.

As for the Stallions, the team advanced to the CFL's title game, the Grey Cup, in both of their seasons in Baltimore and won the championship in 1995. Sixteen players from that title team earned NFL tryouts in 1996, while head coach Don Matthews won the second-most games (231) and running back Mike Pringle rushed for more yards (16,425) than any player in CFL history. The Stallions' arrival in Baltimore came at an opportune time, at arguably the sole moment in sports history where such a CFL team in the city could have been plausible. Baltimore had just been rejected by the NFL for an expansion team, with the league turning to Charlotte, North Carolina, and Jacksonville, Florida, in hopes of breaking into new markets. At the same time, many in Baltimore had grown tired of being a pawn in a bid by current NFL owners to secure better deals from other cities. At the same time, the CFL began its push toward expanding into the United States. Between 1993 and 1995, seven CFL franchises attempted to gain a foothold in U.S. cities, including Baltimore.

With the dreams of an NFL team all but dashed, Baltimoreans quickly embraced this different brand of football. The Canadian version of the sport includes 110-yard fields, 12 men on the field, and three downs to gain ten yards. This compares to the U.S. brand of the sport with its traditional rules and guidelines that include a 100-yard field, 11 players on the field, and four downs to gain ten yards. As soon as Baltimore was pitched as a CFL site for a franchise, area businessman and team owner Jim Speros did everything he could to get the city excited about the Canadian brand of football. Speros even attempted to revive the Colts' name before getting thwarted in court by the NFL. "There was a great effort from a lot of people to get Memorial Stadium in shape and get the team off the ground," said former Baltimore Colts running back Tom Matte, who owned 10 percent of the team. "These guys played with heart. These were just young kids that just wanted to play football. They reminded people of the old Colts."

The Stallions refused to approach their inaugural season like a typical expansion team. From the outset, the team targeted CFL veterans with a long track record of success. This started with the hiring of coach Don Matthews and general manager/director of player development Jim Popp and the signing of quarterback Tracy Ham. Those signings, along with scouting a deep roster of talented, hungry football players, made the Stallions instant Grey Cup contenders heading into the 1994 season. That year, Baltimore, which played that season without a team name due to a court challenge of the Colts name, posted a 14–7 record (including the playoffs) with the last loss coming in a 26–23, upset defeat by the B. C. Lions in the Grey Cup.

The 1994 team was so talented that wide receiver Joe Horn, a four-time Pro Bowl selection who spent 12 seasons in the NFL with the Kansas City Chiefs, New Orleans Saints, and Atlanta Falcons, never made it off the practice squad. Another player, one-time New York Jets wide receiver Wayne Chrebet, who played 11 seasons in the NFL, didn't make it past the first day of a tryout with the Stallions. "There are only so many jobs for players in the NFL," said Ham, who retired in 1999. "Playing in Baltimore was a great experience, and it gave a lot of us the chance to play professional football in the U.S."

By all accounts, the Stallions were well-received in Baltimore. Over two seasons, an average of more than 30,000 fans packed old Memorial Stadium to support their new team. However, despite an even more successful regular season in 1995, attendance for the Stallions dropped off, especially after the NFL's Cleveland Browns announced that the team was relocating to Baltimore. The players knew, despite the love the city of Baltimore had for the Stallions, they just could not compete with the NFL. There was no room for two professional football teams in Baltimore.

"We knew something was up months before the announcement came down," said Popp, who last served as general manager with the Toronto Argonauts before being fired in 2019. "We saw that the locker rooms got totally redone and mimicked what the Cleveland Browns' lockers looked like, which was something I knew because my dad [Joe] used to be an assistant with the team."

Still, the Stallions finished the 1995 season with an 18–3 record (including the playoffs) and became the only U.S. team ever to win the Grey

Cup, when they defeated the Calgary Stampeders, 37–20. Through 2018, the Stallions still hold the CFL record for most wins in a season.

"Once the Browns said they were coming, the writing was on the wall," said former Stallions public relations director Mike Gathagan. "Once the Grey Cup was over, the CFL was done in this city. A lot of good people lost their jobs when the NFL came back to Baltimore. Those were crazy times, and we are really proud of everything we accomplished in those two years."

This book will look back at the tradition of professional football in Baltimore, how the Stallions came to capture the hearts and imagination of the city, and the team's legacy in the scope of sports in Baltimore.

1

A Tradition Is Born

Professional football in Baltimore dates back to 1947, when the original incarnation of the Colts was born as a member of the old All-America Football Conference. This team's origins trace back to 1946, when they were known as the Miami Seahawks. The Seahawks, the first major sports team in Miami, Florida, and the state's first professional football team, posted a miserable 3–11 record in their lone season in the Sunshine State. Soon thereafter, the Seahawks were taken over by the AAFC before being purchased by an ownership group that rebranded the team the Baltimore Colts.

Those Colts played three seasons in the AAFC. In their inaugural season, the Colts posted a record of 2–11–1, which was good enough for a fourth-place finish in the AAFC East division. The team improved to post a non-losing record of 7–7 and finished second in the AAFC East division before losing in the Eastern Division Championship in 1948. The team won just one of 12 games in 1949 before joining the NFL in 1950.

The transition to the NFL did not go well for the first version of the Colts, who again posted a record of just 1–11 before folding after their inaugural season in the league. Despite little success on the field, this Colts franchise did provide the starting points for the Hall of Fame careers of quarterback Y. A. Tittle and defensive tackle Art Donovan, the latter of whom would be part of the foundation for the early success of the modern-day Colts franchise.

Those Colts returned to Baltimore in 1953 after the city, in 1952, sold 15,000 season tickets and principal owner Carroll Rosenbloom purchased the former Dallas Texans from the NFL.[1] The Colts were a mediocre franchise in their first five seasons of existence before a team led by seven future Hall of Famers, coach Weeb Ewbank, quarterback Johnny Unitas, wide receiver Raymond Berry, guard/tackle Jim Parker, running back Lenny Moore, defensive end Gino Marchetti, and Donovan, took the Colts to back-to-back NFL titles in 1958 and 1959. That started more than a decade of success for the franchise which included an appearance in the NFL

Championship Game in 1964, advancing to Super Bowl III following the 1968 season (an infamous loss to the New York Jets), and a win in Super Bowl V against the Dallas Cowboys following the 1970 season.

"I went to my first Baltimore Colts game in 1957," Mike Gibbons, a Baltimore sports historian and director emeritus of the Babe Ruth Birthplace and Museum, said. "I was about 11 years old and sat in the right field bleachers of Memorial Stadium with my father. The game was the Colts' home opener and Johnny Unitas' first home opener as a starting quarterback. Before then, the Colts were not on most fans' radar screen. The Colts won that game against the Lions, who would win the NFL Championship that season, and it began the city's push toward being a football town."

The future of the Colts and of Baltimore sports took a sharp turn on July 13, 1972, when Rosenbloom and then-Los Angeles Rams owner Robert Irsay traded franchises. Irsay, a long-time alcoholic, was erratic to say the least and did little to ingratiate himself in Baltimore. This started right from the beginning, when the Colts traded Unitas to the San Diego Chargers after the 1972 season. That move represented the first of many that laid the foundation for the team's demise in Baltimore. The Colts would experience some relative success in the mid– to late 1970s, making the playoffs in three straight seasons from 1975 to 1977. However, they lost in the divisional round each time. The team's 1977 double-overtime loss to the Oakland Raiders in the divisional round would be the Colts' last playoff appearance while in Baltimore.

A downward spiral would send the Colts from one of the model NFL franchises to among the laughingstocks not just in professional football, but in all of sports. By 1982, the Colts were the worst team in the NFL, going 0–8–1 in a strike-shortened season. Many teams would have been able to parlay such a dismal performance into the start of a rebuilding effort, but not the Colts. The team had a chance to select Stanford quarterback John Elway with the top overall pick in the 1983 NFL draft. However, Elway said he had no desire to play for Irsay or the Colts and threatened to play professional baseball for the New York Yankees. Irsay, who had hinted for years that the Colts' days in Baltimore were numbered, called Elway's bluff and traded the future Hall of Famer to the Denver Broncos for offensive lineman Chris Hinton, backup quarterback Mark Herrmann, and a first-round pick in the 1984 NFL draft. The trade would go down as one of the worst one-sided trades in sports history as Elway led the Broncos to five Super Bowl appearances, winning it all in back-to-back seasons in 1997 and 1998, before walking off into the sunset as a champion after 16 seasons under center.

2

The Colts Leave Town

The prospects of the Colts leaving town grew by the day throughout 1983. Attendance at Colts games that season was abysmal, reaching turnstile numbers virtually unheard-of in today's multi-billion-dollar NFL climate. An announced crowd of just 20,148 fans were in the stands on December 18, 1983, at Memorial Stadium in Baltimore to watch the Colts close out the 1983 campaign with a 20–10 victory over the old Houston Oilers. The win meant that the Colts finished with a mediocre record of 7–9, which tied them for fourth place in the AFC East.

"There had been talk of the Colts possibly leaving for a while, but there wasn't a sense in the locker room that day after the Oilers game that we had just witnessed the last Colts game ever to be played in Baltimore," said longtime Baltimore sportscaster Scott Garceau, who was sports director at WMAR-TV, the NBC affiliate at the time.

Most fans never thought that their once-beloved Colts would abandon the city of Baltimore. But with the city of Indianapolis making an offer to lure the Colts away and Irsay unwilling to commit to stay, the city of Baltimore made a last-ditch effort to thwart a move. City leaders tried to get the state legislature to condemn the Colts and force the team to be sold to an ownership group that would keep the team in town.

With the threat of eminent domain in place, the Colts did something that at one point was unthinkable: they left town. In one of the most infamous nights in Baltimore sports history, the Colts packed their belongings into a series of Mayflower moving trucks and tried to sneak out of town and head to Indianapolis on the snowy night of March 29, 1984. Garceau said it was a surreal night as word started to get out that the Colts were heading out of town.

> While there wasn't much belief at the end of the season of the Colts leaving, things started to move very quickly once the 1983 season ended. Word started to break around 9:30 p.m. that night and we were working to get something on the air for the 11 p.m. news. We then stayed on the air for at least an hour longer than usual as Irsay finally followed through on his threat to move the team to Indianapolis. I

don't think anyone actually thought it was going to happen until those Mayflower moving vans started heading out of Owings Mills."

The sight of those moving trucks pulling out of the Colts' training complex in Owings Mills, Maryland, and heading down the highway was too much for many Baltimore sports fans to fathom and accept on any level. Many stood out in the cold and watched in disbelief. Others just cried and held each other, much as they would following the death of a loved one. The fabric of the community was literally being taken away in moving vans.

"I wasn't a huge Colts fan growing up, but I went to games at Memorial Stadium and I understood the team's importance to the city," said Pete Kerzel, a Baltimore native and a long-time sports reporter in the area. "When the Colts left, it was just devastating for the fans and for the city of Baltimore. It left a huge void that would remain for years."

Mike Gibbons called the day the Colts left town the darkest day in Baltimore sports history. Gibbons added that despite all of the rumors and even the trips Irsay took to other cities seeking offers to move the Colts, most people never thought he would actually move the team. "This town had a love affair with the Colts—almost like a religion—and it was destroyed by a devil of a man in Bob Irsay," Gibbons, 71, a lifelong Baltimore resident, said in regard to Irsay, who died in 1997 at the age of 73. "He broke down that franchise for the pure purpose of moving the team almost from the time he took over ownership in 1972."

Leonard "Big Wheel" Burrier said it was tough to see the Colts spiral downward over their final years in Baltimore. Even still, to see the team leave town was as miserable an experience as he can remember. Burrier, who turned 73 in 2018, was a huge Colts fan growing up. But it was not until 1975 when Baltimore really first took notice of him. The Colts were a mediocre 2–4 heading into a home game against the Cleveland Browns on November 2, 1975. Looking to get the crowd excited, Burrier (who admittedly had a few beers in him at that point) stood up in section 32 at Memorial Stadium and began spelling out C-O-L-T-S. Whatever Burrier did to excite the crowd that day worked, as the Colts went on to defeat the Browns, 21–7. The team would not lose another game in the regular season that year.

"I was with the Colts until the bitter end," said Burrier, who was nicknamed "Big Wheel" by *Baltimore News-American* sports editor John Steadman because he owned Leonard Tire and Wheel Co. at the time. "It got tough toward the end. It was obvious Irsay wanted to move the team and Baltimore did not do enough to keep them here. Whether anything would have made a difference, I'm not sure."

Rob Betz is a Baltimore native who was 17 years old when the Colts

2. The Colts Leave Town

left town. He and his family were season ticket holders to the Colts right up to the end. He just remembers feeling sad, angry, and frustrated all at once when Baltimore was left without an NFL team for the first time in more than 30 years. He added that fans across the city were left feeling similar to him.

> I was a diehard Colts fan my whole life to that point. Bert Jones was my Johnny Unitas and I cheered for the Colts for as long as I could remember. Everyone was aware of the Colts exploring other cities to move to, there was no secret about that. I just don't think anyone thought Irsay would actually follow through with his threats. Everyone thought something was going to be worked out in the end. That obviously never happened. It was just devastating to myself and the whole city. It just did not seem real when we saw those Mayflower moving trucks heading down to Indianapolis.

Paul Mittermeier is another Baltimore native and a longtime sports broadcaster in the area. He recalls how painful it was to see how far the Colts had fallen in their last years in Baltimore. At the same time, Mittermeier added that the Colts leaving had left Baltimore feeling empty for years. "I was 16 when the Colts left and I just remember how difficult those last few years were with the team in Baltimore," Mittermeier said. "Those last few home games, it was so cold in the stadium and the stands were less than half full because everyone in town was so frustrated with how the team was being run."

Mittermeier said years of mismanagement of the Colts by Irsay took their toll on the franchise and the city of Baltimore. The dying days of the Baltimore Colts would be a hard thing for today's football fans to comprehend when even the worst franchises typically sell out their games, even if not every seat is filled on game days. "You're spoiled today because every game is sold out and every game is on TV or you can stream the game or at least the highlights on your phone," Mittermeier said. "But back then, because the Colts couldn't sell out the game, there was a local blackout of the broadcast.

"That made [Baltimore radio legend] Chuck Thompson that much more important because the only way you could tune in the game in those years was on the radio," Mittermeier continued. "Then just like that, the Colts were gone and we were learning how to live a life without an NFL team in our city. Who do you root for at that point? My family was from Pittsburgh, so we became Steelers fans as hard as that is to understand today."

John Ziemann shared a sentiment on the Colts similar to Gibbons, Betz and Mittermeier. Ziemann, the long-time president of the Baltimore Colts Marching Band, said he felt like he was punched between the eyes that night. He said the Colts and Baltimore were synonymous with each other, adding that while there was support for the Orioles during their glory years in the 1960s and 1970s, Baltimore was a football town first. "The Colts were Baltimore for decades," Ziemann said. "Irsay took that away in one night, although he had been slowly destroying the team for years. People in Baltimore connected with the old Colts. Once guys like Unitas and Moore and Barry retired, it was hard to maintain that connection with the exception of those few years in the 1970s."

Ziemann knew he could not stop Irsay from taking the Colts. However, Ziemann pledged to do whatever he could to make sure Baltimore did not lose the history and heritage surrounding the Colts' 31-year stay in the city. The most notable step Ziemann took back then was going to great—and now considered legendary and infamous—lengths to ensure Irsay did not make off with the team's band uniforms. By a stroke of good timing, the Colts band's uniforms happened to be at the cleaners on the day of the franchise's move. The owner of the cleaners let the marching band take his company's van "for a ride."

Ziemann said band members kept the uniforms hidden for at least two months. This included hiding the uniforms at a cemetery at one point until the Colts finally said the band could keep them. The victory was small to say the least, but it was significant for longtime Colts supporters like Ziemann, who were looking for anything to hold on to in the wake of the team leaving. "That jerk Irsay already took the team," Ziemann said. "We were not going to let him take our uniforms."

Tom Guy was a member of the band and remembers being devastated over the Colts leaving. "It was such a dark day in Baltimore sports history," Guy said. "No one believed the team was actually gone."

The Colts leaving Baltimore was just as tough for many of the former players of the once-proud franchise. In a time before multi-million-dollar contracts, players worked in the off-season. It was not unusual for a player to work at the local steel mill, beer distributor, or factory when the Colts were not in season. Those players lived where the fans lived, dined where the fans dined, and their children went to school where the fans' children went to school.

Once they retired, many former Colts opted to stay in Baltimore, where they settled down, raised their families, and started mostly successful businesses. For example, Johnny Unitas ran a restaurant called "The Golden Arm" in North Baltimore, while Art Donovan took over the Valley Country Club in Towson, where for decades it was not unusual for him to mingle with fans and drink beers with those guests who booked weddings or other affairs at the club. Unitas died in 2002, and Donovan died in 2013. Both of their funerals were attended by thousands of people, and their services were aired live on local television.

2. The Colts Leave Town

Tom Matte, a former running back with the Colts from 1961 to 1972, said the heart of Baltimore was pulled out and stomped on the ground the day the team left town. "I just remember watching grown men and women crying that day," said Matte, who broadcast football games in Baltimore for decades after he retired as a player. "That jerk Irsay ripped the hearts out of the fans. He had no decency with how he handled that situation."

3

The USFL Comes to Town ... Sort Of

In the months that followed, Baltimore made long-shot efforts in hopes of having the Colts returned to Baltimore. The federal court case was eventually thrown out in 1985. But in another small victory, Baltimore was awarded the Vince Lombardi trophy the Colts won following their victory over the Dallas Cowboys in Super Bowl V. While Baltimore was not in the NFL's plans, at least in the short-term, professional football would return to the state in 1985 ... sort of. That was the year that the Philadelphia Stars of the short-lived United States Football League announced their intentions of moving to Maryland. The Stars had played for the USFL championship in 1983 and won it all in 1984, but were soon to be a team without a home.

The USFL ownership group—which included now-President Donald Trump, who owned the New Jersey Generals—announced their intentions to move the league's schedule from the spring to the fall beginning in the 1986 season. Prior to this, the Stars had shared the old Veterans Stadium with the NFL's Philadelphia Eagles and MLB's Philadelphia Phillies. But with the team unable to find a suitable home stadium in Philadelphia for a fall schedule, Stars owner Myles Tanebaum announced that the team would move to Baltimore for the 1985 season.

The original plan was for the Stars to play at Memorial Stadium. However, due to concerns from the Baltimore Orioles, no professional football team could play at the stadium until 1986. This forced the Stars to be a nomadic team in the truest sense of the word. In what can only be described as the realm of the absurd that was the USFL, the Stars continued to practice each week in Philadelphia but played home games at the University of Maryland's Byrd Stadium in College Park. Yet at the same time, the team was officially known as the Baltimore Stars. The Stars came to town with a roster, coaching staff, and front office that included several men who would go on to have considerable success in the NFL. Head

3. The USFL Comes to Town ... Sort Of

Dear Season Ticket Holder:

Your support of the Baltimore Stars is great and I'm writing to thank you for being a "pioneer" Stars fan and season ticket holder. Our entire organization is proud to have you as a fan and I hope you've enjoyed getting involved with our football team in these initial weeks of the season. We've been working extremely hard to produce more wins for you. What we experienced in fan support the first two home games has been tremendous. Those attending the games produced enough noise to really fire up our players and coaches. With you being one of those loyal fans in the stands, we extend a special thank you for providing such great motivation to our team.

It's obvious our team responds to a stadium filled with vocal supporters and, as one of our 16,000 plus season ticket holders, I'm asking you to go one step further in helping us round up support for the team. Bring a friend to our games on April 14th and 21st ... spread the word ... let someone you know experience Baltimore's newest sports tradition ... wear Star's RED to the game and make Byrd an ocean of wild fans in crimson and gold. In fact, at each home game, we will award a game ball to the person who wears the most Stars RED and cheers the loudest. If each of you would bring a friend to our Memphis game, we would have our largest crowd ever!

It's no secret that the nation, not to mention the NFL, is looking to the City of Baltimore to see if this area <u>can</u> support a new pro football team. You and your friends could help prove to the country that Baltimore <u>is</u> still a great football town.

Again, thanks for being the best. And don't forget ... bring a friend and wear Stars RED!

Sincerely,

Carl D. Peterson
President & General Manager

CDP/

Form letter sent to season ticket holders of the USFL Baltimore Stars, who played in College Park, Maryland, in 1985, their lone season in town (photograph by Ron Snyder).

coach Jim Mora, Sr., would find success leading the New Orleans Saints and, coincidentally later, the Indianapolis Colts. Team president and general manager Carl Peterson later spent 20 seasons in the same role with the Kansas City Chiefs from 1989 to 2008.

Among the Stars players, linebacker Sam Mills played for 12 seasons in the NFL for the Saints and the Carolina Panthers, from 1986 to 1997. He then worked as a defensive assistant and later linebackers coach for the Panthers from 1998 to 2004 before dying of cancer on August 3, 2005. He was just 46 years old. Another player of note was punter Sean Landeta. Joining the Stars was a homecoming of sorts for him. He grew up in Baltimore County, Maryland, where he graduated from Loch Raven High School before playing college football at what was then known as Towson State University (now Towson University). Landeta played 21 years in the NFL, winning two Super Bowl rings with the New York Giants (in 1986 and 1990), and was a two-time Pro Bowl selection while playing for seven teams before retiring in 2006. Landeta was the last former USFL player to retire from playing.

Despite the championship-caliber team, the arrangement with the Stars left much to be desired, from the fans' perspective at least. Baltimore fans had little desire to make the 40-minute commute south down Interstate 95 to watch games in College Park, and the Stars' attendance figures reflected that. The team averaged just 14,275 fans at Byrd Stadium in 1985, compared to 28,668 the previous season in Philadelphia. Many fans claimed to be holding out for a year until they could watch games at Memorial Stadium again in 1986.

"It was a tough situation with how the team was set up," said Baltimore sportscaster Scott Garceau, who along with former Baltimore Colt Tom Matte were the radio voices of the Stars in 1985. "It was great to have football back in town, but it was not easy for the fans to embrace a team that was set up in such a unique fashion."

The unique setup appeared to have a detrimental effect on the Stars early in the season. They limped out to a mediocre 1–3–1 record after five games of the 1985 campaign. However, the Stars rallied to finish 10–7–1 in the regular season to secure a wild card berth. The team remained hot throughout the playoffs, which started on July 1, 1985, with a 20–17 win in the divisional round at the New Jersey Generals. Six days later, the Stars captured their third straight Eastern Conference championship with a 28–14 win at the Birmingham Stallions. The Stars capped their impressive run on July 14, 1985, with a 28–24 victory over the Oakland Invaders at Giants Stadium in East Rutherford, New Jersey, to capture the team's second straight and final USFL title. "We played for the Stars because we wanted to support Baltimore professional football," said John Ziemann,

3. The USFL Comes to Town ... Sort Of

the president of the Baltimore Colts (now Ravens) Marching Band. "They never really connected with the fans because they played closer to D.C. than to Baltimore."

Sports historian Mike Gibbons said that by the mid- to late–1980s, Baltimore was just looking for any professional football team to latch onto. Filling the void of the Colts would be harder, and eventually take longer, than anyone thought at the time. "It was football, and championship-level football at that, but it wasn't the NFL," said Gibbons, referring to the Baltimore Stars. "At the same time, leaders in Baltimore understood and believed that if the city was ever going to get an NFL team again, we had to show that we were a football town that could support any professional football team. The Stars presented the city that opportunity. Unfortunately, the league didn't survive long enough to see how the team would have fared had they been given the chance to actually play in Baltimore at Memorial Stadium."

Leonard "Big Wheel" Burrier said he supported the Stars and felt they were a good product on the field. At the same time, it was obvious that the league's long-term future was in doubt. He remembers flying out with the Stars for a mid-season game at the Los Angeles Express, and there were fewer than 10,000 fans in the cavernous Los Angeles Coliseum, which could hold 90,000 fans. "The Stars had some good players, and they won,

A *Baltimore Sun* preview section in 1985 for the USFL's Baltimore Stars. Despite the Baltimore name, the Stars trained in Philadelphia and played their games in College Park, Maryland (photograph by Ron Snyder).

which was fun," Burrier said. "But it was obvious it was not going to last long-term. Looking back, one of the more exciting things I can remember is being on the field prior to a game at the New Jersey Generals and Donald Trump comes out and we met. Who knew he would be president one day?"

Any chance the Stars and Baltimore fans had to connect after the back-to-back titles died on July 29, 1986, when a federal grand jury found in favor of the USFL in its antitrust suit against the NFL. Unfortunately for the league, the jury awarded them only $1 in damages, which was tripled to $3 under antitrust laws. The USFL, which rolled the dice on its future with the lawsuit, ceased operations the next day and became just another member of the professional football league graveyard, albeit a league with a legacy that was rich in individual players who went on to have Hall of Fame careers in the NFL. Most notable in this group were Houston Gamblers quarterback Jim Kelly, Chicago Blitz head coach Marv Levy, LA Express quarterback Steve Young, and Memphis Showboats defensive end Reggie White. The Stars went down as the most successful team in the USFL's brief history, having posted a record of 41 wins and 13 losses in the regular season and an impressive seven wins and one loss in the playoffs. Garceau stated:

> It was disappointing how it ended. The Stars tried to make the best of the setup that season because it was hoping to move to Memorial Stadium in 1986. They really tried to treat the players like they were in the NFL. They did everything first class and it was pretty good football. Along with the players that went on to the NFL, the Stars had several coaches and front office people that were successful in the NFL. Obviously there was Carl Peterson and Jim Mora, but assistants like Dom Capers, Vic Fangio and Vince Tobin had nice runs in the NFL, too.
>
> It was tough for Baltimore in the end to really embrace the Stars because of them playing in College Park. Even though it's just a 40-minute drive, it might as well have been in Los Angeles. I'm curious how the team would have been supported at Memorial Stadium had the team been able to play there.

4

"Give Baltimore the Ball"

With the USFL no longer in operation, Baltimore once again turned its attention to finding a way to get back in the NFL. This included getting the state to develop a financial package with funding for a new stadium in hopes of luring either an existing team or an expansion franchise back to Charm City. Among the teams that nearly came to Baltimore during the mid-to-late 1980s was the Cardinals. Owner Bill Bidwell had expressed for years his frustrations at playing in St. Louis and was openly looking for a new place to call home outside of Missouri. By 1987, Baltimore was in a bidding war with St. Louis, Jacksonville, and Phoenix for the right to be the hometown of the Cardinals.

While those cities were bidding to join the prestigious club that is the NFL, they were obviously not bidding on one of the league's elite franchises. The Cardinals roots dated back to 1898 in Chicago, but their last taste of post-season glory came when they won the 1947 NFL Championship. After years of playing second fiddle to their cross-town rival Chicago Bears, the Cardinals moved to St. Louis in 1960. Over their 28-year stay in St. Louis, the Cardinals made the playoffs only three times—1974, 1975 and 1982—and they never hosted or won a post-season game in that span. Even with a dismal track record like that, Baltimore fans and city leaders were salivating at the thought of bringing an NFL franchise—albeit a mediocre one at best—back to town.

However, the stars were not yet ready to align for Baltimore. Bidwell made his intentions known in January 1988, when he notified NFL Commissioner Pete Rozelle that he wanted to move his franchise to Arizona. Maryland Gov. William Donald Schaefer, who was mayor of Baltimore when the Colts left town, told reporters that Baltimore "couldn't have done anything more" as part of its bid, and he believed the warm Arizona climate played a major factor in Bidwell's ultimate decision. The city would also lose out in similar fashion over the next few years in attempts to lure the Rams and Buccaneers to Baltimore. In hindsight, what may have foreshadowed Baltimore's NFL future was that Cleveland Browns owner Art

Modell (the eventual owner of the Baltimore Ravens) was among those owners who defended Bidwell's decision to move his franchise out of St. Louis. Specifically, he highlighted the Cardinals' perceived lack of support from the city and its leaders. "No one wants to see a franchise move," Modell said in a January 16, 1988, article in the *Washington Post*. "But Billy Bidwill has kept the league informed for four years about the problems he's been having in St. Louis. This is no overnight move. It appears it got to the point where he couldn't operate in St. Louis anymore."

By the 1990s, Baltimore turned its focus toward bringing an NFL expansion team to town. Many in the league were impressed with Baltimore's financial package in its bid to attract the Cardinals. That gave the city and state of Maryland motivation to move forward with the expansion team process. Maryland's General Assembly passed legislation that would allow the state to finance a new stadium by utilizing lottery funds at the Camden Yards complex adjacent to the recently opened Oriole Park at Camden Yards baseball stadium. There were also multiple legitimate bidders willing to pay the hundreds of millions of dollars needed to purchase an expansion team. Those potential team owners for Baltimore included Merry-Go-Round Enterprises founder Leonard "Boogie" Weinglass, famed novelist Tom Clancy, Bob Tisch, and businessman Malcolm Glazer and his family.

As the expansion process continued, others passionate about bringing football back to Baltimore sought other ways to show the NFL, and anyone else who would listen, that the city deserved another team. John Ziemann and the old Colts Marching Band were among the loudest in this group. The band stayed together and continued to play at other NFL games, parades, and anywhere else that would hire them. The band was eventually profiled in an ESPN *30 for 30* special, entitled "The Band That Wouldn't Die," in 2009. There are many in Baltimore who cannot watch that documentary without getting choked up about that period in the city's sports history. "We tried to be the pulse of the Baltimore football community during those years," Ziemann said. "We wanted to show the world that Baltimore is an NFL community and deserves a team. We were going to say to the NFL. 'We're not giving up. We're bringing professional football back to Baltimore.'"

Baltimore's largest rallying cry directed at the NFL came on August 27, 1992, when 60,021 fans packed into a sold-out Memorial Stadium for an exhibition game between the Miami Dolphins and the New Orleans Saints.[1] The game offered some glimpses into Baltimore's football past as the city tried to develop a path into the future. Dolphins head coach Don Shula returned to the same stadium where he played as a defensive back for the Colts from 1953 to 1956 and was head coach from 1963 to 1969.

4. "Give Baltimore the Ball" 23

The Saints were led by coach Jim Mora, Sr., and linebacker Sam Mills, who would likely have played at Memorial Stadium for the Stars had the USFL remained in operation after 1985.

The Saints ended up defeating the Dolphins, 17–3. The game came at the end of the preseason and was basically a meaningless contest to the two franchises on the field. But that was far from the case for those in attendance, fans who helped make the game a sellout just hours after the tickets went on sale the previous January. The message to the NFL was clear: "Give Baltimore the ball!" The game also provided a platform for former Baltimore Colts to show that their support continued to lie with the city and the fans, not the team in Indianapolis, and definitely not the owner many blamed for the downfall of the franchise in Baltimore. Even if it was just for one night, Baltimore fans wanted to show the football world why Memorial Stadium was once known as "The World's Largest Outdoor Insane Asylum."

"The 'Give Baltimore the Ball' game was designed to show the NFL that Baltimore was a solid football town," said Mike Gibbons.

Before the Colts, Baltimore was considered by many to be nothing more than a pit stop between Washington and Philadelphia. When the Colts defeated the Giants in

Above and following two pages: **Promotional shirts, program, buttons, cups, pompoms, and keychains in support of the "Give Baltimore the Ball" push to the NFL in 1992 (photograph by Ron Snyder).**

  NEW ORLEANS SAINTS VS. MIAMI DOLPHINS
MEMORIAL STADIUM
AUGUST 27, 1992

the 1958 NFL Championship Game, it did not just put the NFL on the map, it did the same for the city of Baltimore. We now were identified as a football town, and a championship football town at that. With the Colts gone, we needed to prove ourselves to the NFL all over again.

4. "Give Baltimore the Ball"

It was a very difficult time in Baltimore sports. I remember taking my son to the Dolphins-Saints game and he could just not believe how that many fans came out to watch what was a meaningless preseason football game to just about everyone. But to those that were there that day, the game meant everything for the future of NFL football in Baltimore.

Fans in the stands chanted "Give Baltimore the Ball" throughout the game and did everything they could do to prove to the NFL that the city should be awarded an expansion team. "Give Baltimore the Ball" was the theme throughout the city that week, as there was even a pep rally held at the Baltimore Inner Harbor prior to the game. The highlight of the evening came when Colts tight end John Mackey, who died at the age of 69 in 2011, received his Hall of Fame ring with more than 70 former Baltimore Colts by his side. "Baltimore was teased so many times during that time with the hopes of getting another team," said former Colts safety Bruce Laird, who played in Baltimore from 1972 to 1981, in a 2014 interview. "We were used by other owners to get a better deal elsewhere."

Laird said the former Baltimore Colts wanted the city to get a new team as much as, if not more, than the fans. The players, he said, felt abandoned too when Irsay packed up the Colts and skipped town under the veil of snow and darkness. "From 1958 to 1972, the Colts were one of, if not the, premiere franchises in all of sports, not just the NFL," Laird said. "Then Robert Irsay ran the franchise into the ground and took everything away from Baltimore without any concern over who he hurt in the process. Us as players were left without a home."

Even with the show of support at the "Give Baltimore the Ball" game, having ownership groups in place, and with stadium funding secured, the NFL once again opted to leave Baltimore out in the cold in its expansion process. The first nail in the proverbial coffin came on October 26, 1993, when the NFL awarded a franchise to Charlotte, North Carolina, and businessman Jerry Richardson. Ironically, Richardson played his entire two-year NFL career with the Colts from 1959 to 1960 and used his bonus money from the team's 1959 NFL Championship Game to launch his restaurant empire.

"I paid for tickets with friends to go to the 'Give Baltimore the Ball' game," veteran Baltimore sports reporter Pete Kerzel said. "We all packed the stadium and cheered to show how much we appreciated football. In the end, it was nothing more than a show. The NFL knew what it wanted to do with expansion. If what Baltimore did during that game meant anything, then the city would have gotten a new team not long after it was played. Instead, it took four more years for the NFL to return to the city."

The final nail in Baltimore's expansion team coffin came about a month later, when the NFL surprised many people and awarded the second expansion franchise to Jacksonville, Florida, and businessman Wayne Weaver. Compounding the sting for the city of losing out on an expansion team, NFL Commissioner Paul Tagliabue famously suggested that Baltimore could have built a museum or plant instead of an NFL stadium. "It was really awful how the NFL used Baltimore during those years," Tom Matte said in 2014. "We put together the strongest expansion package and got turned down twice. Time has proven that was a mistake on the NFL's part."

That time was a low point for many of those who had fought for years to bring professional football back to Baltimore. "I was ready to quit the band after we lost the expansion battle but my wife wouldn't let me," Ziemann said. "She said as long as there was funding available for a stadium, there was a chance to bring football back to Baltimore."

Paul Mittermeier agreed with Ziemann's assessment. He added that to many in Baltimore, losing out on an NFL expansion team was in many ways worse than the Colts leaving. He felt that way because at least when the Colts left, there was hope that another team would soon replace them. After Jacksonville and Charlotte won out over Baltimore, that hope was lost for much of the community as it pertained to the NFL.

4. "Give Baltimore the Ball"

The city of Baltimore went all in with that "Give Baltimore the Ball" game with the Saints and the Dolphins. We sold that thing out and did everything the NFL wanted to prove we deserved a team. Then, even after all of that, the NFL goes and punches us right in the face and goes with Jacksonville and Charlotte in the end. I believe we got to the point collectively as a city that the NFL was never going to come back to Baltimore. We were OK when Charlotte got a team because we knew it was an untapped market, but Jacksonville? Jacksonville? They basically gave Jacksonville a team because we were just the city between Washington, D.C. and Philadelphia.

Longtime Fox 45 sportscaster Bruce Cunningham said he too thought Baltimore's chances of ever getting an NFL team again died with the expansion process.

> I had nightmare visions of heading down to Washington to cover the Redskins during the NFL season. The decision for the NFL team to add a team in Charlotte made sense to me because there were nine million fans in an untapped market for the league. But the decision to move to Jacksonville stung. That was the feeling of the fans and others around town. They understood Charlotte, because it was a new market, but Jacksonville. The decision to put a team in Jacksonville pissed people off.
>
> The owners in their expansion meetings in Chicago had maps with circles around 150-mile radius for each of the five finalist cities: Baltimore, Charlotte, Jacksonville, St. Louis and Memphis. What was around Baltimore? Washington and Philadelphia, and there was concern about oversaturation. Jacksonville had Orlando in its map circle. I think the league would have rather placed a team in Orlando, but the ownership group never materialized. They figured folks from Orlando would make the drive to Jacksonville to support the team. That never really happened, which is partly why they have struggled with attendance throughout much of their existence. Baltimore also had a secondary television market issue. In Washington, their secondary markets are Richmond and Norfolk, Virginia. In Baltimore, the secondary markets were Salisbury and Hagerstown [in Maryland]. That's just really small markets.

Scott Garceau said the decision to give Jacksonville a team over Baltimore was simply devastating to the city. He was one of the thousands of people in the city left wondering where the city would go from this point as it related to the NFL and professional sports overall. "People all over the city were just angry and frustrated at that point," Garceau said. "It took a while to get over that snub by the NFL."

Longtime Baltimore football fan Tom Guy said the decision by the NFL to grant Jacksonville an expansion team truly angered him. "I was ready to bust my TV that night when the announcement was made," Guy said. "I'm sitting there expecting them to say Baltimore. How could they not choose our city? It made no sense. I figured the NFL was done with us after that."

5

Southern Expansion

The NFL was not the only professional football league seeking to expand in the early 1990s. The Canadian Football League officially dates back to 1958, when it was formed by the merger between the Interprovincial Rugby Football Union (founded in 1907) and the Western Interprovincial Football Union (founded in 1936). Prior to 1993, the CFL showed little interest in expanding south of the border. There also appeared to be little interest in the Canadian brand of football in the United States. Those mainly attracted to the CFL in the U.S. were players looking to continue their football careers. Among the notable NFL alumni to establish themselves first in the CFL were Hall of Fame quarterback Warren Moon, Heisman Trophy-winning quarterback Doug Flutie, and wide receiver Raghib "Rocket" Ismail.

That did not mean that the CFL was not interested in exposing its game to American football fans, especially through television. ESPN made the CFL a fixture on its network in the early 1980s, long before it became the dominant power in sports broadcasting. NBC even briefly aired CFL games on Sunday afternoons in 1982 as replacement television when the NFL went on strike. Unfortunately, the games that aired were blowouts, and NBC opted to black out the games to stations closest to the Canadian border. The experiment was deemed a failure.

By the early 1990s, most of the teams in the CFL were facing some sort of financial hardship, for a variety of reasons. This began in 1987, when the Montreal Alouettes folded during the pre-season. The Toronto Argonauts faced serious ownership issues not long after the high-profile purchase of the team by hockey great Wayne Gretzky, actor John Candy, and businessman Bruce McNall in 1991. McNall, who also owned the NHL's Los Angeles Kings at one point, greatly inflated his wealth and spent around six years in prison after he pleaded guilty in 1993 to five counts of conspiracy and fraud, after he admitted bilking six banks out of $236 million over a ten-year period.

Other long-time CFL teams such as the Calgary Stampeders, Ottawa

5. Southern Expansion

Roughriders, and Hamilton Tiger-Cats also faced financial troubles. This led to a new generation of owners getting involved in the league with the intention of seeking out new revenue streams for the long-time, but financially struggling, football league. Enter Larry Smith. Smith first joined the CFL as a player when the Alouettes selected him with the first overall pick in the league's 1972 draft. The running back played his entire nine-year career in Montreal while also earning a law degree.

Smith was hired in 1992 as the CFL's eighth commissioner and was tasked by the league's owners to pursue expansion into the U.S. The idea was that such expansion would lead to increased television revenues, and the existing teams would be able to share funds generated from expansion fees, which many deemed a necessity to pump some immediate cash infusions into the coffers of the financially struggling franchises.

There is no doubt that trying to be a successful football alternative to the NFL in the U.S. is a risky proposition. Very few attempts at such an endeavor prove successful. The American Football League had success in its head-to-head battle with the NFL in the 1960s. But in the end, the AFL would merge with its competition, bringing the New England Patriots, Buffalo Bills, Houston Oilers, Miami Dolphins, New York Jets, Cincinnati Bengals, Kansas City Chiefs, Denver Broncos, San Diego Chargers, and Oakland Raiders into the NFL following Super Bowl III.

The World Football League followed, but lasted only one full season in 1974 before folding during the 1975 campaign. Then, of course, came the USFL, which latest from 1983 to 1985 before its failed battle with the NFL. But a confluence of events appeared to open a window for the CFL to take its shot where others had failed.

First, an announced crowd of more than 15,000 attended a June 1992 exhibition game in Portland, Oregon, between the Calgary Stampeders and the Toronto Argonauts. This came as the CFL received more than 20 applications from potential owners interested in the U.S. expansion plans. The CFL's plans also coincided with the folding of the World League of American Football, which had been formed by the NFL in 1991. The hope behind the league, which had teams in North America and Europe, was to provide the NFL with a spring developmental league. However, that league—which would later be reborn as NFL Europe—folded after the 1992 season. But two of those teams now without a league of their own—the Sacramento Surge and the San Antonio Riders—applied to join the CFL.

While both teams gained approval from seven of the eight CFL owners at the time, only the Sacramento team—now rebranded as the Gold Miners—entered play in the league in time for the 1993 season. In a sign of future troubles, the San Antonio franchise was forced to fold before entering the league after an ownership dispute forced owner Larry Benson, brother of the late New Orleans Saints owner Tom Benson, to pull out of the league. While the Gold Miners posted a record of just 6–12 in their initial season, they did average around 17,000 fans per home game and sold 9,000 season tickets while playing at the less-than-desirable Hornet Stadium on the campus of Sacramento State University.

Over the next two years, the CFL would welcome a bevy of U.S. teams into the fold, including the Las Vegas Posse, the Shreveport Pirates, the Birmingham Barracudas, the Memphis Mad Dogs, and the San Antonio Texans (formally the Gold Miners). However, when it was all said and done, no U.S. team would have a greater impact on Canadian football than the expansion team that would arrive in Baltimore in 1994. "The CFL was really struggling north of the border at that time," longtime Baltimore sports reporter Pete Kerzel said. "The idea of expanding into the United States was the league's way of simply trying to survive."

6

Baltimore Got the Ball

Baltimore and the CFL found each other at just the right time. The city offered many qualities that other potential expansion team sites did not have at the time. Baltimore was the only CFL expansion site to have had an NFL team prior to the CFL's arrival. The city also had a professional-level stadium that could be converted to just about meet the CFL's playing field measurements. Most importantly, Baltimore had a rabid football fan base with a proud tradition. Baltimore's fan base was also angry at the NFL after the league let the Colts leave, and they felt abused by other league owners who used the city as leverage to get better deals elsewhere. After being snubbed once again in the expansion process in favor of smaller-market cities like Charlotte and Jacksonville, Baltimore was ready to figuratively and literally tell the NFL to stick it. The fans wanted nothing more than a platform to vent their anger, rage and resentment toward the NFL and to show the entire world that Baltimore was still a major professional sports town.

Businessman Jim Speros was ready to be the person to bring Baltimore and the CFL together in a marriage that appeared to be mutually beneficial to all parties involved. Speros was just 35 years old when he decided to pursue an expansion team. The Potomac, Maryland, native came to Baltimore full of enthusiasm and optimism, something he displayed early and often throughout his career. Speros, a three-sport athlete at St. John High School in Washington, D.C., played college football at Clemson University. He tried to continue his football playing career in the CFL, but he was cut at the end of the 1981 pre-season by the original Montreal Alouettes.[1]

Speros then spent four years as a strength coach for the Washington Redskins (where he won a Super Bowl ring in 1982), followed by a stint with the Buffalo Bills. He took his career on a different path, making millions in the restaurant and real estate industries before opting to take his shot at owning a professional sports franchise. "I was young and had a bull in the China shop mentality back then," Speros said. "I knew I wanted to bring a CFL team to the U.S. and couldn't think of a better city for that to happen than in Baltimore. Growing up in the Washington, D.C. area, I knew the history of the Colts and I just could not believe the NFL opted not to put an expansion team in Baltimore."

The process of bringing a CFL team to Baltimore began for Speros in June of 1993. He initially had a tough sell to Baltimore Mayor Kurt Schmoke, who was still looking to place an NFL expansion team at Memorial Stadium for a few years until a new stadium could be built near Camden Yards. It was also a tough sell for Maryland Governor William Donald Schaefer, who commended his desire to bring football back to Baltimore but was not ready to support him as long as he felt the NFL was a real possibility. For Schaefer, ensuring the NFL returned to Baltimore was something he felt he needed to solidify his legacy after the Colts left under his watch as mayor of the city.

"Gov. Schaefer teared up when telling me how much it hurt to lose the Colts under his watch," Speros said.

> At the time, he was completely committed to an NFL expansion team. However, he then told me if we don't get one, Maryland will then aggressively pursue an existing franchise and relocate them to Baltimore just like the Colts left us. This was in August 1993, more than two years before anyone thought the Browns would move here. I was committed to this endeavor. I wrote a $100,000 non-refundable check to the CFL as I made my pitch for a team in Baltimore. The CFL wasn't committed to Baltimore yet, believing that there was no way Baltimore was not going to get an expansion team. The CFL also had a backup plan that if Baltimore did get an NFL team that they wanted me to put a team in Orlando, Florida. At that point, the league just needed to get into markets if the CFL was ever going to work in the U.S. But Orlando was never really an option for me. Sports teams in that market, with the exception of the [NBA's] Orlando Magic, have never worked because there is so much to do there with Disney World and Universal Studios and all the other amusement parks in the area.

Speros was basically in a waiting game until the NFL finalized its expansion plans. In the interim, Speros was busy putting a plan in place to get his CFL franchise off the ground. This included staying in contact with politicians, businessmen, and former Colts players among others. For his plan to be successful at any level, Speros knew he needed a large network of support from the grassroots level to the political arena to the boardroom.

> I knew Mark Richardson, whose father is Jerry Richardson, from our time at Clemson together. He kept me in the loop on the NFL's plans and he seemed confident Carolina was getting a team. Of course that's what happened, but what we didn't know at the time was that the NFL would wait before announcing Jacksonville.
>
> While Governor Schaefer was waiting for the NFL, Mayor Schmoke saw an opportunity. He reiterated that he wanted an NFL team first, but stressed that

6. Baltimore Got the Ball

once that wasn't an option he was ready to back our CFL team. His priority was Baltimore City. He had an obligation to those who lived around 33rd Street in Baltimore where Memorial Stadium was. The Orioles were gone, and the Baysox, who just finished up playing their minor league baseball season, had moved to Bowie.

Mayor Schmoke wanted to find a tenant for Memorial Stadium. There would be amusement taxes for each tickets sold and other economic opportunities for so many in the city. He also knew Memorial Stadium was in bad shape and they needed someone to be able to use it so upgrades could be made. Once the NFL announced Jacksonville was getting a team, I don't think I waited two days before getting things moving forward to get the franchise approved.

Once Baltimore was eliminated from the NFL picture (for the time, anyway), both sides came together and on February 15, 1994, Speros and Schmoke finalized a five-year lease for his yet-to-be-named CFL team to play at Memorial Stadium on 33rd Street in Baltimore.[2] Two days later, the CFL officially awarded an expansion franchise to Speros and the city to begin play in the 1994 season. Pete Kerzel, who would cover the new team for the Associated Press, said the CFL came along at the perfect time for Baltimore.

> People in Baltimore were really football starved after the Colts left town. Then after the NFL jerked the city around with expansion, the fans grew frustrated. They

Kurt Schmoke, center, was Baltimore's mayor in 1994, when he helped negotiate a lease that brought a CFL team to Baltimore (photograph by John Patrick Kelly, from the archives of John W. Ziemann).

needed something to latch on to. They wanted a football team to call their own. You've got to remember that by this point, Baltimore had been without an NFL team for a decade. We were at the point of almost an entire generation in Baltimore had no idea what it was like to support a hometown football team. The older fans could still look back and remember Baltimore and Memorial Stadium when it was the "World's Largest Outdoor Insane Asylum." But to the younger fans, they had no concept of that. Then all of the sudden you have this brash owner come into town willing to bring a team to Baltimore.

According to Speros, the terms of the lease called for the Stallions to pay $1 a year to Baltimore, with the city getting an additional $7,500 bonus whenever the team had a crowd of at least 30,000 fans. Speros thought he had gotten a favorable deal, especially getting to play at a stadium with a tradition as rich as Memorial Stadium had. It was an advantage none of the other CFL expansion teams had. "After Jacksonville got the expansion team, Mayor Schmoke came up to me and asked me if it was time to give the CFL a chance," Scott Garceau said. "All the emotions were so raw at that point and I wasn't sure that was the time to think about it, but the interest was there and it was time to explore all options."

With that official, Speros now had less than five months to get his team ready for the 1994 season. First came fixing the 40-year-old stadium. The Memorial Stadium of 1994 was much different from the stadium that the Colts and the Orioles called home for more than 30 years. Memorial Stadium had been basically vacant for the past three years after the Orioles moved to Camden Yards following the 1991 season. The only tenant during that time was the Bowie Baysox, the Orioles' Double-A minor league affiliate, who played in Memorial Stadium for their inaugural season in 1992 while their stadium was being constructed in Prince George's County, Maryland. To get Memorial Stadium ready for football game action once again would require a lot more than replacing a few boards and applying a few coats of paint, like Speros initially thought.[3]

"Memorial Stadium was in bad shape by that point," said Tom Matte, a minority owner and part of the broadcast crew of the Stallions, in a 2014 interview. "Rows of seats needed to be fixed. There were busted pipes and rotten floor boards. We managed to put in the work necessary to get the stadium ready for the season. But it took a lot of trading and bartering to make it happen."

Roch Kubatko was a sports reporter for the *Baltimore Sun* and helped cover the CFL team for the newspaper in 1994. He agreed with Matte that Memorial Stadium was in a state of disrepair, as the city of Baltimore did little to assist with its upkeep after the Orioles left for Camden Yards. "Memorial Stadium was on its last leg," said Kubatko, who is now the lead Orioles reporter for MASN. "It was still able to host football games, but

6. Baltimore Got the Ball

Memorial Stadium was the home for the Baltimore Colts and Orioles before later being home to the CFL's Baltimore Stallions and the NFL's Baltimore Ravens. It last hosted a game in 1997, played by the Ravens (photograph by John Patrick Kelly, from the archives of John W. Ziemann).

there was a feeling that it could crumble at any minute. People were advised not to drink from the water fountains. Flushing too many toilets simultaneously could have burst the pipes. But that water would have been safer to drink. Thank goodness for fans creating an electricity in the air. It probably kept the lights on."

Speros stressed that the city and state, along with many businesses in the area, came together to help make the upgrades and repairs to Memorial Stadium possible. The physical signs of professional football coming back to Baltimore were quickly taking shape. They did not have a choice in that, as the CFL season was literally right around the corner.

> Memorial Stadium was a mess. The elevators didn't work, the escalators didn't work, the pipes were messed up, and we needed a lot of repairs to make the stadium presentable. The community just rallied behind us. Just a few months before, no one knew who I was in Baltimore. Next thing I know, I'm being introduced to people like John Paterakis and William Jews. Then Brunning Paint Company donated $400,000 worth of paint, and then we had City Parks and Recs coming out to paint the stadium. Everything was just lining up perfectly. Having Tom Matte involved with the team opened up so many doors early in the process. He had connections all over town and really helped garner support right from the start from people who wanted to see football back in Baltimore.

Before the team ever took the field, or even had a name to call their own, Speros had already invested $10 million in the endeavor, which included about $5 million of his own money. Whatever the cost, legitimate professional football was finally coming back to Baltimore, an accomplishment not lost on Speros and his team. "We really believed this was going to work for us and the city would support what we were trying to do," Speros said. "I legitimately put everything I had into making this team as successful as possible as quickly as possible."

7

The CFL Colts Are Born

The new Baltimore CFL franchise had an owner in Jim Speros, a home in Memorial Stadium, and a start date in the 1994 season. Speros worked to help garner public support and build a fan base for his new team. This even included bringing in the Colts Marching Band to be a part of the team. Those with the band were more than happy to work with Speros and to be associated with a new Baltimore-based football team. "I met with Jim at the Ed Block Courage Awards that year and I liked what I heard," John Ziemann said. "This was a chance to promote professional football in Maryland, which was part of our mission. The prospects of getting the NFL back at that point appeared dim at best, so we were willing to give the CFL a chance."

The next step in the process was to come up with a name for the new team. Speros believed that was easy. There was only one name a team from Baltimore could have: Colts. When Speros announced that a CFL team was coming to Baltimore, he wanted to write a new chapter in the city's football history while also embracing its impressive and successful past. The team's color scheme included the traditional blue and white utilized by the Colts, while adding silver to the uniforms. Instead of a horseshoe on the helmet, the new team would feature a stylized blue horse's head logo. Speros said he could tell that he and his team were starting to build some momentum toward community support early in the process. "Going around town to Dundalk and Towson and Perry Hall and meeting with the old Colt Corrals, they all wanted the name to be the Colts," Speros said. "The Colts Marching Band wanted to march with us. Still, I wasn't sure whether the Colts would be the right name."

All of that changed, Speros said, when he met with legendary Baltimore sports reporter John Steadman. Speros still gets chills when he reflects on that meeting with the veteran reporter, who was working at the *Baltimore Sun* at the time. Steadman, who attended Baltimore City College for high school, was the last of a dying breed. At a time when reporters were told there was no cheering in the press box and they had to

The Baltimore Colts Marching Band has supported every outdoor professional football team since 1947 (photograph by John Patrick Kelly, from the archives of John W. Ziemann).

remain neutral, Steadman was an unabashed Baltimore cheerleader, not necessarily for the teams, but for the city itself.

Steadman's journalism career dated back to 1945, when he was hired by the old *Baltimore News-Post*. Steadman covered all types of sports in town, but it was football where he truly made his mark in the city, starting in 1952, when he was the first to report that Baltimore was getting an NFL team. Steadman attended every professional football game from the Colts through the Ravens—a streak of 719 games in a row, which ended right before his death of cancer on January 1, 2001, at the age of 73. Steadman also attended the first 34 Super Bowls, and unfortunately died just weeks before the Ravens played in and won Super Bowl XXXV, 34–7, over the New York Giants in Tampa, Florida.

After leaving the *News-Post*, Steadman became the Colts' assistant general manager and publicity director. However, he left that job in 1958 to become sports editor of the old *Baltimore News-American*, a position he held until the newspaper folded in 1986. Steadman then joined the staff at the *Evening Sun* before that paper's demise in 1995, moving over to the *Baltimore Sun* for the rest of his career. Steadman's hallmark during his

7. The CFL Colts Are Born

career was his love of the underdog, a role many in Baltimore embraced as the city took on the NFL in the years after the Colts left town. Steadman saw another underdog in Speros and Baltimore's new CFL team and offered the team some of his wisdom. "John Steadman tells me he knows all about me and my family and admires what I'm trying to do in bringing football back to Baltimore," Speros said. "But, you will not last a day in this town with this team if you don't name them the Colts. Once he said that, I knew there was no other name we could use."

On March 1, 1994, Speros announced his new team would be named the Baltimore CFL Colts. The team name struck the right chord with fans in the city, and the team sold more than 22,000 season tickets in the days after they announced they were going to be named the Colts.

Tom Guy was a Baltimore CFL supporter from the start. He was among a group of people who assisted early on in regard to ticket sales, community relations, and fan clubs. He was ready to go all-in to support a team that he felt wanted to be here more than the NFL.

Businessman Jim Speros (second from left) announced at a press conference in 1994 that he was bringing a CFL team to Baltimore and naming it the CFL Colts. With him, from left, are Dr. Jack Vaeth, Ken Stastny and John Ziemann, Colts Marching Band drum major, vice president and president respectively (photograph by John Patrick Kelly, from the archives of John W. Ziemann).

I had already bought my season tickets when I was approached about helping get the word out. This was football back in Baltimore. Yes, the game was different, but there was something exciting about the whole game experience that was different than the NFL. It was the perfect storm to bring a CFL football team to Baltimore. It would not have worked in any other era. Then when they announced that Colts was going to be the name, I was hooked. We were all at the point where we said, "Screw the NFL. Screw Bob Irsay. We have the CFL."

Speros thought that between calling the new team the CFL Colts and using a horse's head instead of a horseshoe logo, the team could get around any copyright infringement concerns. After all, the NFL's Detroit Lions and the CFL's BC Lions have co-existed for decades. The NFL did not feel the same way and sued Speros and the team, arguing that between the similar names and color schemes, fans could be confused over the brands. A judge agreed with the NFL and blocked the team from using the Colts name right before the team's first exhibition game in June 1994. "I told [Speros] don't name the team the Colts, the NFL is going to come after you and you'll lose," Ziemann said. "I was right about the lawsuit, but he won the battle of public opinion in Baltimore, and it was a great marketing idea."

"In his heart of hearts, I'm not sure Speros believed the NFL would

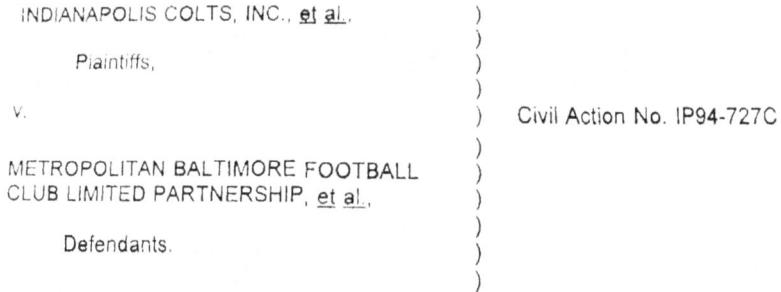

Copy of part of the deposition in the lawsuit between the Indianapolis Colts and the owners of the Baltimore CFL Football Club (photograph by Ron Snyder).

7. The CFL Colts Are Born

Jim Speros, who brought a CFL team to Baltimore, discusses the franchise during an April 1994 news conference. His initial plan was to name the team the Baltimore CFL Colts (photograph by John Patrick Kelly, from the archives of John W. Ziemann).

ever let him use the Colts name," Fox 45 sportscaster Bruce Cunningham said. "But the move built excitement for the team and helped them gain momentum."

The NFL going after Baltimore's new CFL team only galvanized the city even more and led to one of the most unusual stories in sports history. Fans continued to lash out against the mighty NFL, the entity that took away their team, blocked them from getting another, and then wouldn't allow them to name the team what they wanted when they finally did get a team. "It had to be named the Colts," Matte said in 2014. "That was one of the best ways [Speros] could get the Baltimore fans to buy into what we were trying to do with the CFL in town."

Bonnie Downing was the director of community and public affairs for the Baltimore CFL team. She left a job with what was then the NBA's Washington Bullets (now Washington Wizards) to take a chance on the new football squad. Like many of the others who took a leap of faith with Speros and the CFL team, she has never regretted the decision. To her, helping bring football back to Baltimore was as much a civic duty as it was a job.

> Like everyone else from Baltimore, I was traumatized when the Colts left. It was my dream to one day work for the Baltimore Colts. Then this exciting new owner comes to town and promised to bring football back to Baltimore. We were just so glad to have professional football back in town.
> At that point it didn't matter that it wasn't the NFL. Many people were so upset with the NFL at that point. It was a much different time. Then when they said they were going to call them the Colts, that was what put many over the edge and willing to give the team a shot.

Paul Mittermeier was 26 when the CFL arrived in Baltimore. Not long out of broadcasting school, Mittermeier was producing radio programs and taking on other freelance opportunities in the Baltimore sports media market when he was hired as the assistant director of public relations for the team. He believes the CFL's arrival was just what Baltimore needed after years of being hurt and disappointed by the NFL.

> I think it was that mindset and frustration of the city that only added to the allure of the CFL in Baltimore. We just believed that our time in the NFL was over, and then this Jim Speros guy rides into town and sells us on the CFL. We bought in because it was professional football in Baltimore again. Sure, the rules were different and the fields were different, but it was professional football and it was finally back in Baltimore. There was a lot of excitement back in town once again.

Leonard "Big Wheel" Burrier was also ready to revive his superfan routine for a third team in Baltimore. He, along with a few others, would work in the ticket sales and form the "Special Teamers," a group designed to garner fan support in the city. "They wanted to come into town and show the fans they were willing to set up shop like an NFL team would," Burrier said. "They really wanted to make it a family-friendly event, and they were able to do just that."

With the court injunction in place so close to the start of the season, Baltimore's CFL team was placed in a difficult position. The end zones already had "COLTS" painted on them. Making matters worse for the team, hundreds of thousands of dollars' worth of merchandise, tickets, programs, advertisements, TV commercials, and signage was out there with CFL Colts on it. In one memorable commercial on WMAR-TV, the word "Colts" was bleeped out before new commercials could be produced. "We literally had people blacking out shirts, programs, and anything else with the Colts logo on it," said Mike Gathagan, a former sports producer at WMAR-TV and the team's public relations director for its entire time in Baltimore.

With no time to come up with a new name before the start of the 1994 season, the CFL Colts became the team with no name. Officially, the franchise was referred to as the Baltimore Football Club, although most in the media and many fans called them the Baltimore CFLers, which made

7. The CFL Colts Are Born

The original name for the Baltimore Stallions was the Baltimore CFL Colts. A court injunction during a legal battle with the NFL over the Colts name led the CFL team to play without a formal name in 1994 (photograph by Ron Snyder).

for interesting newspaper headlines at the time. "The legal battle over the name gave fans one more reason to detest the NFL, and it created some awkward sentences in game stories for the *Baltimore Sun*," former *Sun* reporter Roch Kubatko said. "The beat crew and columnists had to refer to the team as the CFLers, which read every bit as ridiculous as it sounded. Of course, they became the Stallions the following—and final—season after I left the beat. But it was like the NFL took every opportunity to stick it to Baltimore."

From the players and coaches to the media and fans, the name issue was something they never dealt with before or since that time. "The fans were already upset at the NFL over the Colts leaving and being left out during expansion," former Stallions slotback Chris Armstrong said. "We came at just the right time. They were looking for a team to call their own, and they embraced us completely from the moment we came to town."

Former Stallions quarterback Tracy Ham agreed. He said that whatever happened in court, Speros and the team had already won the battle of public opinion over the Colts name. The fans were not going to let the courts or the NFL stop them from calling their new team the Colts. What

Baltimore's CFL team officially played without a name during its inaugural season (photograph by John Patrick Kelly, from the archives of John W. Ziemann).

mattered to the fans was that football had finally returned to Baltimore, and no judge, jury or attorney could take that away from them.

> Mr. Speros did a great job marketing the Colts name controversy. He knew what he was doing. Trying to bring the Colts name back got the fans excited, and the legal action by the NFL kept the team in the news for months, bringing attention to what we were trying to do in Baltimore.
>
> The fans in Baltimore were already upset with the NFL over losing the Colts and not getting an expansion team, and the legal action only galvanized them that much more in supporting the CFL team. Those visions of the Mayflower trucks pulling out of town will be visions fans from that time will never get over.

Baltimore running back Mike Pringle said trying to use the Colts name was the perfect way to connect with fans who were still skeptical of the CFL brand of football. Pringle said he has never experienced anything as unique as this name battle at any point of his career. The battle really solidified the team and the city of Baltimore as underdogs ready to take on any and all comers, including the mighty NFL and even a leery CFL audience who were not necessarily ready to share their sports league with U.S. fans. "Everything with the name battle worked out to our advantage," Pringle said. "I'm not sure if they actually thought they would be able to

7. The CFL Colts Are Born

use the name in the end, but it got us more and more support from those upset over their treatment by the NFL."

Speros said that even knowing today the legal battle that would ensue over the Colts name, he agrees with Steadman's assessment of the situation. The media attention and sympathy from the fans in Baltimore, and even around the country to a lesser degree, was invaluable to the team as they prepared for their first season. There was no way to place a value on that type of media coverage, and the legal battle only added to the team's legend in future years.

"I was literally threatened with jail time if we used the Colts name after the injunction was issued," Speros said. "But what that lawsuit did was make us a national story. It got us on ESPN and *Sports Illustrated*. I had Venable LLP offer $500,000 of pro bono legal help to fight this case. Everyone in Baltimore wanted us to be able to use the Colts name again. You could not have written a better script to start our franchise."

8

Building a Team

The next step for Speros was to put a team together to compete on the field. Many of the other U.S. expansion teams did not appear to fully grasp the differences between the American and Canadian styles of football. Speros understood that and knew that if Baltimore was going to buck the trend, they had to bring in the right personnel from the beginning. Speros had an organized plan centered on bringing in coaches, personnel executives, and players who were familiar with the CFL brand of football instead of seeking out a name with NFL experience. By the time Speros announced his intentions, the core of that approach was in place. This started at the top with the hiring of head coach Don Matthews and general manager Jim Popp.

Known to those within the CFL as simply "The Don," Matthews had a resume that was second to none in the league. The Beaverton, Oregon, native's coaching career spanned 44 years, which included 31 seasons in the CFL. Matthews was 54 years old when Speros tabbed him as Baltimore's head coach. At that time, Matthews had been a head coach in the CFL for nine seasons, including from 1983 to 1987 with the BC Lions, taking the team to two Grey Cups, winning it all for the first time as a coach in 1985.

Matthews had spent the past three seasons prior to coming to Baltimore as the head coach of the Saskatchewan Rough Riders, during which time his team posted a 25–22 record and advanced to the division semifinals in back-to-back seasons in 1992 and 1993. "The Don" also interviewed with the Las Vegas Posse for their head coaching opening before being hired by Speros in Baltimore.

"There has never been a better coach in the CFL than Don Matthews," Gathagan said. "He was the perfect person for [Speros] to hire. He was the foundation of the team and what we were trying to accomplish."

If Matthews was the ultimate CFL lifer, then Popp was the up-and-coming player executive prodigy and the perfect complement to the grizzled head coach. Popp, an Elkin, North Carolina, native, was just 29 years old when he came to Baltimore. Out of high school, Popp was recruited

8. Building a Team

to play defensive back at Michigan State before a knee injury derailed his playing career and set him on path as a coach and general manager that continues to this day.

After college, Popp became an assistant coach at Michigan State in 1986 before taking on similar roles at North Carolina (1987) and The Citadel (1988–1990). His career path altered forever in 1992 when he joined the Roughriders, where he spent two seasons as the wide receivers coach and the director of player personnel before being hired in Baltimore. It was Matthews who initially hired Popp in Saskatchewan and later recommended him for the job in Baltimore.

> Everything came together fast. I started talking with the U.S. teams when expansion began. I met with Las Vegas first before getting the call from Baltimore. I had been involved in start-ups in the past with the World League of Professional Football—which would go on to become NFL Europe—and later doing consulting with player personnel for the Professional Spring Football League, which was slated to begin play in 1992 but folded before playing a game.
>
> During that time Dan Rambo, who was with the Saskatchewan Roughriders at the time, liked the work I was doing with the PSFL, and told me to give him a call if this didn't work out. That helped set me on my CFL journey. Don Matthews was there at the same time and when he came to Baltimore, he wanted me there with him. It was definitely a huge break in my career.

With the leadership team in place, Popp and Matthews were now tasked with putting together a roster in time for the upcoming season. The U.S. teams had an advantage in that they were not limited in how many American-born players they could have on their roster, unlike their Canadian counterparts, who were required to have a set number of native-born players on their team. U.S. labor laws forbid the teams from discriminating against players based on nationality, and Baltimore took full advantage of that in setting their roster. "I had Don Matthews signed to a guaranteed contract before we even got the rights to the franchise and the stadium lease finalized," Baltimore owner Jim Speros said. "We were blessed to have all of the best people in place."

Baltimore's approach was simple: bring in the best players who were the right fit for their roster, not simply the best players available. While other U.S. expansion teams in the CFL concentrated on NFL castoffs, former college players, and those known locally, Popp and Matthews took a systematic approach toward building their roster, targeting players familiar with the CFL style of football while also scouting current college players and others who they believed would make a smooth transition to the Canadian game.

"One of the things we were able to do compared to the other U.S. teams in the CFL was find experienced coaches and players who could grasp the Canadian game," Popp said. "Once we had Don and me in place, we built the shell of our team around players like Tracy Ham, Mike Pringle, Chris Armstrong, and O. J. Brigance. Those players then helped mold the rest of the roster around what we were trying to accomplish. We just had leadership on both sides of the ball."

The first signing was arguably their most important: quarterback Tracy Ham. Ham's career as a dual-threat quarterback began in college at what was then I-AA Georgia Southern, where he led the Eagles to back-to-back national titles in 1985 and 1986. Ham also became the first college quarterback to rush for 3,000 yards and pass for 5,000 more in his career. Despite being drafted by the Los Angeles Rams in the ninth round of the 1987 NFL Draft, Ham opted to sign a three-year contract with the Edmonton Eskimos because he wanted to continue to play quarterback and not be forced to switch positions. Ham's career got off to a winning start as he won a Grey Cup championship as a rookie backup signal-caller in 1987.

Ham was entrenched as the Eskimos' starting quarterback by 1989, when he led the team to a 16–2 record, passed for 4,366 yards and 30 touchdowns, and rushed for 1,005 yards and ten more scores. That season, Ham was named the CFL's Most Valuable Player despite his team being upset by the eventual Grey Cup champion Roughriders in the West Division finals.

The Eskimos got back to the Grey Cup in 1990, with Ham again leading the charge under center. That year, Ham threw for a nearly as impressive 4,286 yards and rushed for 1,096 more before Edmonton was routed by the Winnipeg Blue Bombers, 55–10, in the championship game. Ham played two more seasons with the Eskimos before spending a disappointing 1993 season with the Toronto Argonauts, when he threw for just 2,147 yards and rushed for only 605 more yards as the team went just 3–15 while having difficulty adapting to the run-and-shoot offense employed by head coach Dennis Meyer. Meyer was fired after the team won just once in its first ten games that season. The Stallions signed the 30-year-old Ham to a three-year contract in February 1994, in a deal that reportedly made him one of the highest-paid players in the CFL. The signing reunited Ham with Matthews, who was the defensive coordinator with the Eskimos in 1989. Both were eager to get to work with this new endeavor in a new city for both men.

"The great thing with Tracy Ham is that in a new franchise, there may be new people around," Matthews told the *Baltimore Sun* in a February 20, 1994, article. "When things break down, Tracy can do it alone. That type guy, the ad-lib guy, is of tremendous importance to the franchise. This gives us credibility when it comes to signing other free agents. It tells them we're serious. It was a big step toward being competitive."

8. Building a Team

Stallions quarterback Tracy Ham was inducted into the CFL Hall of Fame in 2010. He was the first player signed by the franchise (photograph by John Patrick Kelly, from the archives of John W. Ziemann).

Ham provided the Baltimore team with instant credibility in the league, especially among players who were intrigued with the idea of bringing the CFL to a football-rich-tradition city like Baltimore. Ham said U.S. players, including himself, loved the idea of playing in America, helping expand the CFL brand, give more players the chance to continue their careers, and give them an opportunity to play in cities where their families had a better chance to watch them play in person. It was especially the last reason that became a selling point for many players who signed with Baltimore.

> It was an interesting time for sure. The other U.S. teams did not fare so well and Sacramento was still trying to get settled. I was a free agent at the time, and I was looking for the best situation possible. Baltimore appeared to have a plan on how to succeed in the CFL. The CFL football brand has a lot of similarities to the American game, but there are also a lot of differences that can take time to adjust to as well.
>
> I felt that being in my eighth and ninth year in the league I was more of an elder statesman, and it was my job to teach the younger players how to be successful in the CFL. I felt my experience both in the CFL and working with Don made the transition easier for being an expansion team. Canadian football is still football.

You still have to run, pass, catch, and tackle. It was just important to understand the differences.

Jim Speros understood football, but knew he did not necessarily know all of the intricacies of the CFL game. That's why he was so smart to bring in Don Matthews as the coach and Jim Popp as the general manager. "The Don" was there to coach the players and Popp was there to pick the players, and [Speros] could take care of the rest.

Other players would soon follow Ham, including running back Mike Pringle, slotback Chris Armstrong, defensive back Irvin Smith, defensive end Elfrid "SWAC" Payton, linebacker O. J. Brigance, defensive lineman Jearld Baylis, punter Josh Miller, and offensive tackle Shar Pourdanesh. Most credited the hiring of Matthews and the signing of Ham as key reasons why they wanted to come play in Baltimore. To a person, former Baltimore players said the pair of Matthews and Ham gave Baltimore an instant sense of credibility compared to the other U.S. expansion teams and even to the existing Canadian squads.

"You could not have put together a better roster," Armstrong said. "There were so many great CFL players on that roster, but that's not what made the team great. What made it work was everyone's ability to get on the same page, check their egos at the door, and work toward the common goal of trying to win a championship. All the credit goes to Popp and Coach Matthews and Mr. Speros for making that happen."

Pringle was another multi-dimensional offensive threat who, like Ham, garnered interest from the NFL, but whose greatest success would come in the league based north of the U.S. border. Pringle, a Los Angeles, California, native, began his college football career at the University of Washington. He transferred to California State-Fullerton, for his final two seasons and that is where he really started to blossom as a dynamic offensive player. His breakout season came as a senior in 1989, when he rushed for 1,727 yards and 16 touchdowns, with 28 receptions for 249 yards and three scores.

The Atlanta Falcons were impressed enough with Pringle to draft him in the sixth round (139th overall selection) of the 1990 NFL Draft. Unfortunately for Pringle, he would never play a down for the Falcons. Initially, he spent most of the 1990 season on the Falcons' practice squad before being cut at the end of training camp in 1991. The NFL's loss would turn out to be the CFL's gain as Pringle would join Ham and Armstrong as members of the Eskimos in time for the 1992 season. However, much like in college, it would take time for Pringle to show everyone what he was truly capable of on the field. Pringle appeared in just three games and rushed for 129 yards on 22 carries in 1992 before he was released by Edmonton. He finished out the season with the Sacramento Surge of the World League of American Football.

8. Building a Team

Stallions running back Mike Pringle is arguably the greatest player in CFL history. He is the league's all-time leader in rushing yards and was inducted into the CFL Hall of Fame in 2008 (photograph by John Patrick Kelly, from the archives of John W. Ziemann).

Pringle remained in Sacramento, where he became a member of the CFL expansion team, the Gold Miners, in 1993. That season, he rushed for 366 yards and four touchdowns in limited playing time in his only season with the team. Baltimore eventually acquired Pringle in a trade heading into the 1994 season. Pringle admitted that as a West Coast native, he was not initially happy with being dealt to an expansion team based on the other side of the country. But he was willing to give Baltimore a chance as he continued to seek a permanent home for his talents. Going to Baltimore would arguably turn out to be the best decision of Pringle's career.

"That year started out under not the best of circumstances for me as I was traded from Sacramento," Pringle said. "It was tough because I'm from California and I wasn't sure what to expect in Baltimore. But having a quarterback like Tracy Ham in my corner, a player who believed in me and my abilities, meant a lot. He saw something in me and knew I could play at a certain level."

Shar Pourdanesh's journey to Baltimore began much farther away than simply traveling from the West Coast to the East Coast like Pringle did. The offensive lineman grew up in Tehran, Iran, before his family escaped the country after the overthrow of the Shah. Pourdanesh's family moved to Irvine, California, in 1982 when he was just 12 years old. Pourdanesh discovered football relatively late and did not even play the sport until he got to high school. In fact, Pourdanesh was arguably a better prep wrestler than a standout on the gridiron in high school. But Pourdanesh developed his football talents enough to be recruited by the University of Nevada. The team posted a record of 32-7 in Pourdanesh's three seasons at the school. During that time, Nevada lost to Georgia Southern in the 1991 NCAA I-AA championship game and played in the Las Vegas Bowl in 1992, the school's first season as a Division I-A (now Football Championship Subdivision) program.

Pourdanesh tried to make it in the NFL as the Cleveland Browns signed him as an undrafted free agent. The NFL was not in the cards at that time for Pourdanesh, who was cut by the Browns not long into the 1993 pre-season. He weighed his options, both in and out of football, before deciding to take a shot at the CFL and Baltimore. Pourdanesh said taking the CFL route was the perfect option for him as he came to a crossroads in his football career.

> I wasn't sure what I wanted to do. I was really tired of football when I went to training camp with the Browns and it showed, which is why I was cut so early. Steve Buratto then contacted me and couldn't believe I wasn't in the NFL, and asked me about coming to Baltimore. He told me I'd be there two years and would then be back in the NFL, and that's exactly what happened.
>
> If you look at our line, it was as big as many in the NFL. All of the guys we brought in were 6–2 to 6–5 and weighed over 300 pounds each. The offensive line played a big role in establishing our style of play.

Building a quality offensive line was key for Matthews, who brought in plenty of players who had passed through NFL camps.[1] Along with Pourdanesh, Baltimore signed another NFL castoff in Neal Fort. The 6-foot-7, 340-pound Fort starred at Brigham Young University in the late 1980s and early 1990s, where he protected quarterback Ty Detmer, one of the most prolific passers in college football history. Fort was selected in the sixth round of the 1991 NFL Draft by the Los Angeles Rams. He spent the 1991 season on the developmental roster before being assigned to the Orlando Thunder of the World League of American Football in 1992, but he never played for them. Like many others shut out by the NFL, he opted to sign with Baltimore in the CFL. The offensive line truly provided Baltimore with the foundation necessary to accomplish what they hoped to on that side of the ball.

> I had a friend who played safety in the CFL, Brad Clark, who had signed on with Baltimore. He was excited with what they were building there and suggested I give Jim Popp a call. I decided to give it a shot and called the team. Jim Popp told me he

8. Building a Team

knew exactly who I was, offered me a contract, and that was that. I was playing in the CFL. The ironic thing is that Brad was traded to the Toronto Argonauts before I ever arrived in Baltimore, so we never got to experience the ride together.

Fort was aware of the CFL, having watched some games on TV through the years, but did not have a deep understanding of the league. That did not change his excitement about testing himself in the Canadian league. "I had caught some games on ESPN on some nights at 11 o'clock at night or 12 and 1 o'clock in the morning when they had filler games on. I felt I was built to play in the league. The offense we ran at BYU involved a lot of no-huddle and hurry-ups, and the pace was very similar to what the CFL ran. I didn't think the adjustment would be too hard at all."

Other vital members of Baltimore's offensive line would be acquired shortly after the season started. This included the signings of identical twins Guy and John Earle. The Red Bank, New Jersey, natives signed with Baltimore in August 1994 after they were cut from NFL camps: Guy Earle by the Washington Redskins and John by the Atlanta Falcons. Guy Earle, who was 6-foot-4 and 290 pounds, played collegiately at Chadron State, a Division II team in Chadron, Nebraska. John Earle, who was 6-foot-5 and 300 pounds, played his college football at Western Illinois.

> I had just been cut by the Redskins and I was weighing my options. I had not even thought about the CFL at that point. My agent gave me a few options, including waiting to see what NFL teams might be interested. Or I could go right up the road and play for this new CFL team in Baltimore. I was young, not married at the time, and already loved spending time in Baltimore. I then told my agent let's go play some football in Baltimore.
>
> Then, coincidentally, my brother was cut by the Atlanta Falcons. The team had brought in a bunch of offensive linemen to fill a particular need. Coach Matthews liked what he saw in us and signed us both. Then two days later, we're playing in games. Think about it, even signing five games into the season we still had 13 games to play because of the 18-game CFL season.

John Earle shared a similar mindset as his brother about his decision to sign with Baltimore. He was initially content with sitting at home and waiting for another NFL team to call. But in the end, there was something intriguing to Earle about playing for a CFL team in a U.S. city. Getting the chance to play professional football alongside his twin brother was also too good an opportunity to pass up and one he was not sure if he would ever get again. Both brothers said there was little hesitation in taking a leap of faith with Baltimore. They agreed that it was a no-lose proposition for them.

> I was used to sitting by the phone in hopes of catching on with another NFL team. Then my agent called and told me about this CFL expansion team in Baltimore and that my brother was signing with them. The only thing was that if I signed, it

would be for at least a year, with an option for a second year, meaning there would be no shot at the NFL at that time.

I thought about it. I could take another shot at the NFL and be a second- or third-teamer where I might get a shot on special teams before possibly getting cut again, or I could go to Baltimore and just play football. The chance to play right away and to play with my brother was a great opportunity, so I told my agent, "Let's do it. Let's go to Baltimore."

Like Pourdanesh, Fort, the Earle brothers, and others, Armstrong was looking for a football team to call home. Prior to arriving in Baltimore, Armstrong was a football nomad in the purest sense of the word. He would partake in a football odyssey that took five years, with stops at eight teams in three leagues before signing with Baltimore. For the Fayetteville, North Carolina, native, his professional football journey began in 1989 after he did not play his senior season at Fayetteville State due to academic reasons. In 1990, Armstrong signed with the now-defunct Washington Commandos of the Arena Football League, where he finished with 37 catches for 592 yards and nine touchdowns. His play there led to the chance for Armstrong to attend the NFL's Washington Redskins training camp in 1991.

After being cut by the Redskins, Armstrong spent two seasons with the Eskimos, the first chance he had to team with Ham. Armstrong had a combined 54 catches for 1,104 yards and 11 touchdowns in Edmonton over the next two seasons. Armstrong parlayed his performance there into a tryout with the NFL's New England Patriots during their training camp in 1993.[2] Despite Armstrong believing he had played well enough to make the team, Patriots coach Bill Parcells opted to cut him, which opened the door for him to explore career options in the CFL. The next trip on Armstrong's journey was Las Vegas, when he went to try out for Posse in the CFL in 1994. Armstrong spent three weeks with the team and attended its rookie camp before leaving after the CFL Players' Association filed a grievance with the league.

During this time, Posse coach Ron Meyer, who had previously served as head coach of the New England Patriots and Indianapolis Colts and later coached the XFL's Chicago Enforcers, decided to cut Armstrong, leaving him available for Baltimore to sign. "Tracy and I played together in Edmonton, so when he got to Baltimore, I reached out to him, Armstrong said. "He had nothing but good things to say about the situation and put in a word for me with the team."

Armstrong recalled a unique story of how he initially came to sign with Baltimore. "Coach Matthews knew how to get the most out of players," Armstrong said. "After my initial workout on my first day here in Baltimore, Coach Matthews told me that if I could run a 4.5 40-yard dash, that he would sign me on the spot that day. I then go out there after it had rained and the field was muddy and ran like a 4.4 40. They asked me if I wanted to do it again and I said, 'No, I'm not good.'"

Another key receiver signed by Baltimore provided the new team in town with a hometown hero of sorts. Walter Wilson was a native of Baltimore who starred at Southern High School before he moved on to play college football at East Carolina University. Wilson improved each year at the Greenville, North Carolina, school. As a freshman in 1986, Wilson finished with 11 catches for 220 yards and two touchdowns. By his senior year at East Carolina, Wilson improved to 43 catches for 771 yards and nine touchdowns in 1989. He was selected in the third round of the 1990 NFL Draft by the San Diego Chargers. In his lone season with the team, Wilson had ten receptions for 87 yards. He next played for the Ohio Glory of the World League of American Football in 1992 recording 65 catches for 776 yards and two touchdowns. Wilson received another shot at the NFL the next year, but was soon cut by the Miami Dolphins. At that point, Wilson began to weigh his options, which included the possibility of playing in the CFL, although he initially was unsure about that idea as well.

> I flew up to Canada after I got released by the Dolphins, but realized pretty quickly I didn't like it up there. Then as soon as I got off the plane in Baltimore, I heard about a CFL team coming to the city. I got in contact with them, worked out for the team, and they decided to sign me. The rest was history. Getting to play in my home town was a dream come true, although it came about in a different way than I ever expected.

Like most punters, it took Josh Miller some time to convince a team to sign him. Prior to signing with Baltimore, Miller went undrafted out of the University of Arizona and was cut during training camp by the Green Bay Packers in 1993. A native of East Brunswick, New Jersey, Miller was a first-team, all-Pac-10 pick and a first-team All-America selection by *The Sporting News* and the Football Writers Association of America after averaging 42.7 yards per punt as a senior in 1992. Miller averaged 40.6 yards per punt during his two-year career at Arizona.

"Those years gave me a life jacket," Miller said of playing in Baltimore. "It allowed me the good fortune to continue to play the game that I love and figure out what I want to do with the rest of my life. It was a fun, special group of guys who came from all walks of life that came together with an expansion team of all things, with a common purpose and goal in life: one more chance to play professional football."

Veteran CFL players were also present on the defensive side of the ball. Brigance arrived in Baltimore after three stellar seasons with the BC Lions. During that time, Brigance, who starred collegiately at Rice

University, played in 54 games with the Lions and was a two-time CFL West All-Star selection. His best season came in 1993, when he had 20 sacks.

For defensive back Irv Smith, the Baltimore CFL team, much as it did for Wilson, allowed him to come home to his family. Smith grew up in Montgomery County, Maryland, a suburb just outside Washington, D.C. He played for Poolesville High School before going on to play college football for the University of Maryland from 1985 to 1988.[3]

Smith played for six teams in three leagues and three countries over the next five years. He first attended training camp with the NFL's New York Jets (1989–1990) before playing for the London Monarchs of the World League of American Football (1991–1992). Smith was also signed by the CFL's Hamilton Tiger-Cats in 1991, but was released before the season. In 1992, he made the practice squad of the Saskatchewan Roughriders, but never made it on the field for an actual game. Smith also received tryouts with the NFL's Washington Redskins and Minnesota Vikings, but failed to get a deal in either case. Like many of his future teammates, Smith was wondering if he had any future left as a professional football player. He finally received his big break in 1994 when he signed on with the new CFL team in Baltimore. "This was a big deal to me because I grew up a Baltimore Colts fan, even though I grew up in Redskins country," Smith said. "The first NFL game I went to was at Memorial Stadium. I was devastated when the Colts left Baltimore. To get a chance to play in that stadium was a dream come true."

Baylis was among the most experienced CFL players to sign with Baltimore. The former Southern Mississippi standout was 32 years old and a veteran of eight CFL seasons before coming to Baltimore. Baylis had played for the Toronto Argonauts (1986–1989), the BC Lions (1991), and the Roughriders (1992–93). He won the CFL's Most Outstanding Defensive Player Award in 1993 and had already been named a CFL All-Star from 1987 to 1993.

Payton also had a firm grasp of the CFL game when he arrived in Baltimore, which really lucked into signing the defensive standout. The one-time Grambling State standout was 27 when he signed with Baltimore. He began his career by spending 1991 to 1993 with the Winnipeg Blue Bombers. In his last season there, Payton was an All-Star after recording 22 sacks and earned the James P. McCaffrey Trophy, awarded annually to the outstanding defensive player in the CFL's East Division. Payton started the 1994 season with the expansion Shreveport Pirates before signing with Baltimore five games into the campaign.

Payton, a Gretna, Louisiana native, signed with the Pirates to be closer to home. Unfortunately for him, his brief time in Shreveport proved to

8. Building a Team

Defensive lineman Jearld Baylis (No. 98) played 10 years in the CFL and was a key member of Baltimore's defense in 1994 and 1995 (photograph by John Patrick Kelly, from the archives of John W. Ziemann).

be a less-than-desirable time in his career. He never really got along well with Pirates coach Forrest Gregg, a Hall of Fame offensive lineman with the Green Bay Packers. Gregg was part of six NFL championship teams as a player, coached the Cincinnati Bengals to the Super Bowl in 1981, and helped revive Southern Methodist University's football program after it had received the "death penalty" in the late 1980s. But his record in the CFL was a mediocre 8–28 in 1994 and 1995. At one point, Gregg threw Payton out of practice after an altercation with a teammate. The Pirates released Payton not long after that. Payton said that release was one the best things that could have happened to him, and it paved his way to come to Baltimore. "I was cut by Shreveport, but it didn't have anything to do with my play," Payton said of his release by the Pirates. "It just wasn't a good fit personality-wise between Forrest Gregg and myself."

With Payton an unexpected free agent, there were plenty of teams willing to bring in a player that talented. Payton's final choice came down to Baltimore or the Las Vegas Posse. Payton said his choice was a relatively easy one to make. "I was leaning toward heading out to Las Vegas to play for the Posse because they played a 3–4 defense and that's what they ran in Winnipeg when I had 22 sacks," Payton said. "Baltimore ran a 4–3 defense, but when I got a call from Tracy Ham about coming to Baltimore, I knew where I wanted to play. It was the best decision I could have ever made."

Linebacker Tracy Gravely was another veteran CFL player who signed with Baltimore in 1994. However, unlike Baylis and Payton, he was more of a marginal player looking for the right fit in the CFL before arriving in Baltimore. A native of Kimball, West Virginia, Gravely was the West Virginia Intercollegiate Athletic Conference player of the year out of Division II Concord University. He attended training camp with the NFL's New York Giants, but was cut. He signed in 1991 as a free agent with the Ottawa Rough Riders. He played in just five games for Ottawa before being released in July 1992. He then signed on with the BC Lions and appeared in eight games that season.

Gravely appeared in five games with the Lions in 1993 before once again being released. He saw Baltimore as a way to revitalize his career and knew Matthews was a coach who could get the most out of him. He was correct about that assessment.

> [Baltimore defensive coordinator] Bob Price knew of me from our time in Ottawa. When he got to Baltimore, he told me of the opportunity there. Signing with Baltimore changed my career. There's so much motion and movement in the CFL game. Coach Matthews was great at taking oversized defensive backs and converting them into linebackers.
>
> The funny thing is despite all the talk of the talent we had, looking back, Baltimore was home to a lot of outcasts who were cut by other teams. Baltimore gave a lot of guys a chance and it changed the course of their careers. Playing in Baltimore also gave me a great opportunity to have my family watch me play. Every week, I had family members make the four- to five-hour drive to watch me play in Baltimore. That wasn't possible in Canada.

Defensive back Ken Watson came to Baltimore with a larger track record in the CFL than Gravely. Watson was a four-time All-Gulf South Conference selection at Division II Livingston University (now the University of West Alabama). He entered the CFL in 1989 with the BC Lions, where he played through the 1991 season. His best season was in 1990, when he had 56 tackles and three interceptions. After playing for the San Antonio Riders of the World League of American Football, Watson signed in 1992 with the Calgary Stampeders, where he appeared in 27 games over two seasons and won a Grey Cup his first season with the team before signing in Baltimore.

> I had finished my contract in Calgary when I got a call about possibly playing in Baltimore. Having the opportunity to play football in the United States was a great opportunity. It did not have the feel of a regular expansion team in Baltimore. They brought in quality CFL players and young players who fit in perfectly with what Don Matthews and Jim Popp wanted to accomplish. It was a place where a lot of players received their big break. Coach Matthews brought a focus with him that I

8. Building a Team

knew we were going to win from the first day of training camp. There were guys all over the roster who had success in the CFL and knew what it took to win in the league.

Ham said his relationship with Matthews, combined with his ability to convince fellow players to take a chance on coming to Baltimore, made for an exciting time for those associated with the newest CFL franchise. Everyone associated with the team believed they had the chance to make a difference both on the field and in the community. Just about everyone took those dual roles seriously, Ham said.

> Don and I went back all the way to 1989 when were with the Edmonton Eskimos together. I knew he was the perfect coach to lead Baltimore. Then you sprinkle in players like Chris Armstrong, Mike Pringle, Jearld Baylis, and Elfrid Payton and you have the core of who we were. We had great players, but more importantly, we had the right mix of players who had CFL experience and understood what it took to be successful as a team.

Matthews took a similar approach toward building his coaching staff as he hired a mix of those with CFL experience and those looking for a big break in the sport. The end result was a coaching staff that truly complemented one another and set in motion the careers of many coaches who continue to credit the CFL, specifically their time in Baltimore, for their later success.

Offensive coordinator and quarterbacks coach Steve Buratto had more than a decade of CFL coaching experience and 30 years of experience overall by the time he arrived in Baltimore. His experience included seven years at Boise State, where he coached the defensive line (1973–1975) before being promoted to defensive coordinator (1976–1979). Buratto actually began coaching in the CFL while still at Boise State, when he spent two seasons as a guest coach with Winnipeg (1977) and Saskatchewan (1978–1979).

Buratto joined the CFL full-time in 1980 when he was hired as the offensive line coach for Saskatchewan. Three years later, he took over as defensive coordinator for the BC Lions before the Calgary Stampeders hired him as head coach in 1984. The Stampeders went just 7–17 under Buratto before he was fired midway through the 1985 season. He returned to the Lions in 1986 as their co-offensive coordinator/offensive coordinator. Buratto would stay away from the CFL for seven years until Matthews hired him to be the offensive line coach for Saskatchewan in 1993.

Baltimore defensive coordinator and defensive backs coach Bob Price and linebackers coach/special teams coordinator Daryl Edralin also joined Matthews from Saskatchewan. Both served in similar roles for the Roughriders in 1992 and 1993 before coming to Baltimore. Price's experience before that was largely in college, where he took on assistant coaching

Linebackers and special teams coach Daryl Edralin addresses his players on the sidelines at Memorial Stadium (photograph by John Patrick Kelly, from the archives of John W. Ziemann).

jobs with Idaho State (1979–1980), Eastern Utah (1981–1983), Nevada (1984–1985), UNLV (1986–1989), and Cal-Berkeley (1990). Price entered the CFL in 1991 as the secondary coach for the Ottawa Rough Riders. Prior to joining the CFL, Edralin coached the linebackers for the Orlando Thunder of the World League of American Football in 1990. From 1978 to 1989, Edralin coached the linebackers, running backs and special teams at the University of Hawaii, his alma mater.

"I have nothing but positive memories about that time," Price said. "From the moment Mayor Schmoke gave us the keys to Memorial Stadium, we got right to work. The fans were just ready for football and we had a coach in Don Matthews that could just adapt to any situation. We had a unique group of men who really believed in what we were trying to do, and we had top-notch talent level to match."

Baltimore's defensive line coach, Marty Long, and receivers coach Donald Hill-Eley were newcomers to the CFL when they were hired by Matthews. Long, who starred at running back at The Citadel in the mid–1980s, coached the defensive ends and was the recruiting coordinator at the South Carolina military school from 1987 to 1993 before coming to Baltimore.

8. Building a Team   61

Defensive line coach Marty Long talks to linebacker Ernest Fields on the sidelines at Memorial Stadium during a game in 1994 (photograph by John Patrick Kelly, from the archives of John W. Ziemann).

Hill-Eley was just 25 when he arrived in Baltimore. His career began when he starred at quarterback at Division II Virginia Union University. He entered the coaching ranks right out of college. He coached the wide receivers at his alma mater from 1989 to 1991 before taking on a similar job at Hampton University in Virginia from 1992 to 1993. Hill-Eley said he did not initially have plans to coach in the CFL, but Matthews and Popp expressed interest in the up-and-coming assistant after he held a CFL open tryout combine at Hampton. The chance to join a professional football coaching staff, and to learn from a veteran coach like Matthews, intrigued Hill-Eley.

> We had one of the first combines when Baltimore was in the process of putting its roster together. I met Jim Popp and Don Matthews for the first time at that combine. They seemed to be impressed with the way I organized the workout and interacted with the players, and they offered me the chance to be the receivers coach. It was definitely an interesting time for me. Most of the players I worked with were older than me, and I was the one working with them to teach them about techniques and schemes.

9

Football Officially Returns to Baltimore

The Baltimore CFLers were placed in the CFL's East Division for their inaugural season. The division also included the Winnipeg Blue Bombers, Toronto Argonauts, Ottawa Rough Riders, Hamilton Tiger-Cats, and Shreveport Pirates. Baltimore would even have plenty of local broadcast exposure, with the games being broadcast on radio on WJFK-AM and select contests on television on WMAR-TV. There were also limited games broadcast nationally on ESPN 2, which was in its infancy.

The radio broadcasts in Baltimore were handled by veteran Fox 45 sportscaster Bruce Cunningham and former Baltimore Colt Joe Washington, while Scott Garceau and former Colt Tom Matte led the television broadcast for WMAR. Another former Colt, Bruce Laird, also contributed to the television and radio broadcasts. Down the road, Garceau and Matte broadcast Ravens games for their first ten seasons in Baltimore. "I had the chance to interview Jim Speros on my Sunday night show early on in the process of bringing the CFL to Baltimore," Cunningham said.

> I was impressed with his enthusiasm and felt it had a chance to succeed. Then I saw 400, 500 fans out at the team's first training camp at Towson University and was excited to see what the future held. That first season was so unique because of the name issue. Joe Washington and I broadcasted 23 games on the radio and could only refer to the team as Baltimore. That is not something that is easy to do.

Baltimore's first official regular season game took place on the road on July 7, 1994, before an announced crowd of just 13,101 against the Argonauts at SkyDome (known today as Rogers Centre). Offensive lineman Shar Pourdanesh said the team was slightly nervous, and possibly a little uptight, heading into the team's first game ever. So Pourdanesh took it upon himself to ease the tension.

> Coach Matthews used to have a rule that players had to wear a hat to practice the day before the game. Coach never said what type of hat only that it had to be a hat. So the day before our game in Toronto, I put a jockstrap on my head and waited

9. Football Officially Returns to Baltimore

The inaugural team photograph of the 1994 Baltimore CFL Football Club (photograph by Ron Snyder).

around to see what he was going to say. He then took one look at me and said, "That's a hat." It was just another way for him to keep the locker room loose. Matthews was just a unique coach in that way.

That approach seemed to work for Baltimore, which led for most of the game at Toronto. But a victory was anything but certain heading into the fourth quarter. Toronto quarterback Mike Kerrigan connected on a 10-yard touchdown pass to wide receiver Bobby Gordon to pull the Argonauts within 22–20, late into the final quarter. However, the CFLers gave themselves some breathing room when kicker Donald Igwebuike, who had spent six seasons in the NFL with the Tampa Bay Buccaneers and Minnesota Vikings, connected on field goals of 40 and 37 yards to extend the lead to 28–20.

Toronto tried to tie the score late in the game, but Baltimore's Charles Anthony stopped Gordon inside the CFLers' 5-yard line to secure the victory. Baltimore quarterback Tracy Ham threw for 260 yards and two touchdowns—both to slotback Chris Armstrong—and Igwebuike booted four field goals in the win for the visiting squad. "All of the players from one to thirty-seven on the roster just cared about wanting to win right from the beginning," defensive coordinator Bob Price said. "They practiced so well and wanted to be right in practice. We had great leadership right from the start, and it showed."

Longtime sportscaster Scott Garceau (in dark jacket) was the lead television play-by-play man for the Baltimore Stallions (photograph by John Patrick Kelly, from the archives of John W. Ziemann).

While Baltimore was excited to win its first game, the team and fans were more excited to play in the first regular season football game at Memorial Stadium since the Colts left town more than a decade ago. Expectations were high for those hungry for football. "Baltimore does not just have a great football tradition, but a great sports tradition," running back Mike Pringle said. "The fans would not accept anything less than a quality product on the field."

The teams might have been different, and they played in a different league with different rules, but the atmosphere and the emotions of those in Memorial Stadium on July 16, 1994, were familiar to those fans who cherished Baltimore's football past, with the new CFL team set to host the Calgary Stampeders. The team even arrived on the field in a moving van, symbolizing the return of football after the Colts' moving vans rolled away a decade earlier.

Baltimore receiver Walter Wilson, who was 27 years old at the time of the CFL's debut, said he could not believe that he was getting a chance to play on the same field as so many of his childhood heroes. For him, that first game at Memorial Stadium represented a promise he made to himself and others as a child.

9. Football Officially Returns to Baltimore

> Growing up, I was lucky enough to have [former Baltimore Colts wide receiver] Glenn Doughty speak at my youth football banquet. He was a player I looked up to as a child. I told him that one day I was going to play in the NFL and play professional football at Memorial Stadium. I'm proud that I was able to keep that promise.
>
> I watched the Orioles growing up. I watched the Colts growing up. I got to see legends like Johnny Unitas and Lenny Moore with the Colts and Brooks Robinson and Jim Palmer with the Orioles play on that field. Now I had the chance to do the same thing in my hometown in front of my friends and family. It was a pretty special year in my career.

Punter Josh Miller said growing up in New Jersey gave him an appreciation for getting to play at Memorial Stadium. The opportunity to play at such a venue was not lost on him, even as a player in his early 20s. "I'm a person who always takes in everything," Miller said of his appreciation of history. "Growing up in New Jersey with the Meadowlands, I was familiar with the history of Memorial Stadium. It was like playing in a sports museum to me."

Price, who like Miller was also originally from the New York area, shared a similar sentiment. "Growing up, you knew the Baltimore Colts were a special team with special players," Price said. "Baltimore is an awesome city for football, and those in the stands were passionate about football, loved cheering on their team, and were just knowledgeable about the game."

From the inclusion of the Colts Marching Band to honoring the great Colts of previous generations, to creating a Ring of Honor for Baltimore's sports heroes, the CFL team worked to bring in the city's old fans while helping the younger ones experience professional football for the first time. It was a dynamic that no other CFL expansion team could offer their fans and a dynamic that made a difference from the start. "It was exciting to have football back in Baltimore," John Ziemann said. "It wasn't the NFL, but it was quality football and a team to call our own."

Tom Guy agreed with Ziemann's assessment. Guy said that to truly understand the emotions of the time, you had to have lived through it all in Baltimore. From the Colts' glory days to the team leaving to being spurned in the NFL expansion process and by other existing teams exploring a possible relocation to the city, the previous decade was a painful one for Baltimore sports fans. "Jim Speros did a great job of putting the right people in place to generate excitement about the team," Guy said. "Who would have ever thought anyone could get 30,000 Baltimore fans to watch a CFL game?"

Baltimore native Rob Betz, a former season ticket holder with the NFL Baltimore Colts, knew from the time the announcement of a CFL team coming to town was made that he was going to support the new

Stallions owner Jim Speros (center) presents Orioles Hall of Famers Jim Palmer (left) and Earl Weaver with a plaque inducting them into the Baltimore Sports Ring of Honor in 1994 at Memorial Stadium (photograph by John Patrick Kelly, from the archives of John W. Ziemann).

squad. After a decade of frustration with the NFL, Betz was ready for an alternative professional football option and was willing to give Speros and company a chance to win him over. He and his wife, Marie, were two of the team's original season ticket holders and remained two of their most ardent fans.

9. Football Officially Returns to Baltimore

Baltimore Colts Hall of Famers Johnny Unitas, Lenny Moore and Art Donovan were among the stars inducted into the Baltimore Sports Ring of Honor in 1994 (photograph by John Patrick Kelly, from the archives of John W. Ziemann).

> When we got screwed over by the NFL not once, but twice by expansion, I was disgusted with them and was kind of done with the league for a while. Then Jim Speros came into town and was a breath of fresh air for the city. We didn't know much about the CFL, but it was professional football and it was a team that wanted to play here in Baltimore. We decided to go all in from the start. We were excited to finally be season ticket holders for a Baltimore professional football team again.

Glenn Clark offers a different perspective. A Baltimore native and a longtime radio sports talk show host in the area, Clark was just 11 years old when the CFL team arrived. He was an infant when the Colts left town and therefore had limited exposure to professional football as a child. The hardest part for Clark was trying to find a team to support that would give him a rooting interest in watching and following the sport.

> I remember when the Redskins and the Bills played in the Super Bowl in 1992 and I rooted for the Redskins because I had cousins that lived in the northern Virginia area. I wasn't a Redskins fan, but I cheered for them just so I would have a team to

The Baltimore Sports Ring of Honor at Memorial Stadium (photograph by John Patrick Kelly, from the archives of John W. Ziemann).

root for. Then when Joe Montana and Marcus Allen signed with the Kansas City Chiefs in 1993, I was all in with the Chiefs for a brief time. But I still really wasn't into football too much. Then we got a CFL team and I was obsessed. We finally had a team to call our own.

That first home game of the CFL team in Baltimore meant as much to the players as it did to those in the stands. The sense of history and the emotion of the moment were not lost on the players, Armstrong said. The team understood that the game represented much more to the fans in Baltimore compared to other expansion cities because of the frustration, turmoil, and disappointment the city dealt with over the previous decade. Everyone appeared ready to turn the page and begin writing a new chapter in the history of professional football in Baltimore. "The feelings around that first game were surreal," Armstrong said. "There were tens of thousands of fans packed into Memorial Stadium. There were old fans of the Colts and younger fans who had never had the chance to see a professional football team in Baltimore."

Dozens of former NFL Colts were recognized at halftime, with the largest standing ovation reserved for Johnny Unitas. The CFLers said that without the support of the old Colts, garnering fan support for their team

9. Football Officially Returns to Baltimore

A court injunction did little to stop Baltimore CFL fans from yelling "C-O-L-T-S" during the 1994 season (photograph by John Patrick Kelly, from the archives of John W. Ziemann).

would have been much more difficult. To the CFLer players, having the old Colts' blessing was the ultimate sign of respect, one which they greatly appreciated. "It really helped that the old Colts embraced us, too," Armstrong said. "They were left without a team, without a home really after the Colts left. They treated us with so much respect, and it was so great that Mr. Speros brought them into the fold with us."

Ham agreed with Armstrong's observations. The quarterback said the former Colts did not view him and his teammates as CFL players, but simply as football players. The retired players understood what it meant to have professional football back in Baltimore, as they always considered themselves Baltimore Colts, even if their statistics are included in the Indianapolis Colts' record books. "Having the former Baltimore Colts embrace us and what we were trying to do was huge as we tried to build a connection with the fans," Ham said of the influence of the retired Colts. "We weren't the NFL. We weren't trying to be or compete with the NFL. But we were still football, and good football at that. I think some of those older players remembered the AFL and the different brand of football they played, especially by the time of the NFL-AFL merger. They respected quality football and that meant a lot in that first season."

Defensive back Ken Watson said that the memory of seeing the old Baltimore Colts on the sideline still makes him emotional. Watson is not sure whether the fans would have supported the CFL with as much passion without the blessing of the greats of Baltimore's football past. "Those old Colts were looking for a home, too," Watson said. "Baltimore was their home, not Indianapolis. I think they saw our wide open game, that we played for the love of the game, not necessarily the money, just like they did, and they wanted us to succeed."

Adding to the emotion of the day was the controversy surrounding the Colts name. While the team was barred from using the name, it did not stop the fans from expressing their views on the issue. Throughout the game, when the public address announcer would say "Your Baltimore CFL...," he would purposely pause for a moment so the fans could scream "Colts."[1] There were also plenty of "C-O-L-T-S" chants throughout the game as fans donned replica jerseys of Unitas, Moore, Berry, Donovan, and Mackey among others that had laid dormant in closets for the previous ten years.

Leonard "Big Wheel" Burrier said he felt like he was home again, being out there at Memorial Stadium and leading the "C-O-L-T-S" chant

Baltimore football fans showed their disdain for the NFL in 1994 and 1995 after being shut out in the expansion process (photograph by John Patrick Kelly, from the archives of John W. Ziemann).

9. Football Officially Returns to Baltimore

once again. To him, it did not matter that the team was in the CFL. He was just glad to be cheering for a professional football team once again. "We saw the NFL skip over us for Charlotte and Jacksonville and couldn't figure out why," Burrier said. "Now we had a team, and an owner in Jim Speros that wanted to be here. It was easy to support. The fans just wanted football back in Baltimore. The CFL did just that."

Many even donned "Screw the NFL" and "Screw Tagliabue" T-shirts, a symbol of the vitriol many in Baltimore had for the NFL. "The rules were different, the field was different, but it was still professional football back in Baltimore," Baltimore sports reporter and former AP beat reporter Pete Kerzel said.

> The game was also fun to watch. We had a confluence of events come together to make this possible. For years we had this rabid fan base without a team to cheer for and a stadium in Memorial Stadium that represented so much NFL history that had sat empty for years. The fan base had been poked like someone would poke a bear with a stick for years and now finally, they had a chance to feel like fans again.

Former *Baltimore Sun* reporter Roch Kubatko remembers how excited the city was about having football again and how they welcomed the team with open arms. At the same time, Kubatko described the relationship as "an awkward love affair."

> Baltimore felt like it settled. This wasn't the NFL. This wasn't what it really wanted. But it was better than nothing and it sort of felt like football. The ball was the same shape, the players wore helmets and pads. But what the heck was a rouge?
>
> I'll always remember that first game and how fans used the opportunity to thumb their noses at the NFL. Many of them chose a finger. They learned the rules quickly and identified their favorite players, including Mike Pringle, who proved that running the football in the CFL wasn't against the law. And the old Baltimore Colts were there to give their approval, welcoming football back to Charm City. If it was OK with them, it should be OK for everybody else. That was huge.

Betz said the emotion and the excitement of that first game was impressive and brought back memories of sitting in Memorial Stadium cheering on the old NFL Colts. He added that people he knows who were not around Baltimore during that time have a hard time grasping how the city could fully wrap their arms around a CFL team like they did. "Naming the CFL team the Colts meant so much to the fans in Baltimore," Betz said. "It was a way of telling the NFL that we did not need them. Even after the lawsuit and the injunction, the team might not have been able to call themselves the Colts, but no one person or no lawsuit could stop us from calling the team whatever we wanted to."

Mike Gibbons recognized that the CFL team also impacted the younger generation of football fans. To them, the CFLers represented the first football team they had the chance to root for as the home team. The

Members of the Baltimore CFL team's cheerleading squad in 1994 (photograph by John Patrick Kelly, from the archives of John W. Ziemann).

CFL game was also likely the first time many of them had ever attended a professional football game in their home state.

> The CFL was not the NFL, but they still were a fun and interesting brand of football. My son in 1994 was about the same age as I was when my dad took me to my first Colts game 40 years earlier. There was 37,000 fans there for those CFL games, and we sat in the right upper deck of Memorial Stadium. It was as much a bonding experience for my son and I as it was for my dad and I back in 1957. The CFL team established their own identity in Baltimore and were fun while they were here. At the same time, there were still plenty of people who didn't believe that the CFL was the long-term replacement for the NFL in Baltimore.

Sentiment like that shared by Betz and Gibbons was not lost on the players. They understood what having a football team again meant to the fans and the city of Baltimore overall. They wanted nothing more than not to disappoint the thousands of people who looked to them to return quality professional football to the town. "Just getting to play professional football in Memorial Stadium was so special," Baltimore offensive lineman Guy Earle said. "This was the field where Johnny Unitas played. This was the field that I watched Bert Jones and so many other greats play on when I was a kid. Then to hear the C-O-L-T-S Colts chant gave me chills. It made us feel like part of that great tradition."

9. Football Officially Returns to Baltimore

Added John Earle, "Playing with the CFL team in Baltimore felt like playing with a high school team because of the great emotional attachment we shared with the city. The fans were able to come out and watch practice and get up close to us. That just doesn't happen with professional football today. The fans in Baltimore were just starving so bad for football after everything the NFL and the Colts put them through. It was like a love affair between the city and the team from the moment we announced we were coming."

Offensive lineman Neal Fort said the team was able to tap into the city's love of football and lock on to the enthusiasm the fans had for the sport. "Baltimore just appreciated us being there," Fort said. "Then to get to play on the field where teams like the Colts and Orioles, that won the Super Bowl and the World Series, made the time even more special for me."

Linebacker Tracy Gravely said the fan support so early in their existence was amazing. Even 25 years later, he hasn't experienced anything like that before or since. "There was so much history in Baltimore and the hurt was still there from how the NFL left town," Gravely said. "Then we come in and bring some excitement back to the city and 40,000 fans show up for a Canadian Football League team."

The CFLers had the home crowd advantage, the emotions of the day, and momentum on their side as an announced crowd of 39,247 made the trek to 33rd Street and packed Memorial Stadium for their home opener against the Stampeders. A storybook ending to the day appeared all but certain that evening. "That was quite an emotional day," defensive back Irv Smith said. "We brought football back to Baltimore."

Receivers coach Donald Hill-Eley said the fans took out a decade of frustration while cheering for their team on that day. "The football fans in Baltimore are just diehards about the sport," Hill-Eley said of the city's love for football. "All they wanted was to have a team to cheer for. It was just surreal to see the passion these American football fans showed to this CFL team."

All of the elements were there for the perfect ending to a decade of frustration. However, the Stampeders apparently did not receive the message on that day. Calgary quarterback Doug Flutie, the 1984 Heisman Trophy winner and the face of the CFL at the time, had other plans for the visiting team. The game actually turned into the perfect homecoming for Flutie, who was born in Manchester, Maryland, a suburban community about 35 minutes outside of Baltimore. He passed for 284 yards and two touchdowns and ran for 82 yards and another score as the Stampeders pulled away in the fourth quarter to win, 42–16.

Baltimore had actually pulled to within 22–16 following a 21-yard field goal in the third quarter by Igwebuike. However, Calgary scored the final 20 points of the game, all in the fourth quarter, to seal the win. Ham had a 20-yard touchdown pass to Armstrong, Pringle had 197 all-purpose yards, and Igwebuike kicked three field goals for Baltimore in the loss. "The league brought out Flutie—the star of the league—for a reason," Cunningham said. "They wanted to highlight the talent in the league. The crowd for that first game showed me fans were ready to see what this team had to offer."

Despite being an expansion team and going up against arguably the best team and player in the CFL, the players did not feel good about their performance in their first home game. "The first home game was tough and embarrassing to lose in front of our fans like that," Shar Pourdanesh said. "We weren't going to let something like that happen again."

Speros said that the loss notwithstanding, that home opener is a day in his life that he will never forget. Bringing professional football back to Baltimore is something he continues to take pride in, regardless of what else he may accomplish in later years. "We brought football back to Baltimore," Speros said. "People were so grateful to us for that."

Garceau said that while there may have been some old-school, die-hard Baltimore Colts fans who refused to cheer any team but their old team, many of the younger fans who had never experienced a team of their own were willing to give this new CFL team a chance.

> People in Baltimore were just fed up with the NFL by 1994. The city had gone through the "Give Baltimore the Ball" campaign, got passed over for expansion, and had danced with owners of existing teams like the Cardinals, Rams, and Buccaneers and had nothing to show for it. Now, there was a team that wanted to be in Baltimore. They went all out right from the beginning to try and connect with the fans and the city.
>
> Fans understood that this wasn't the NFL. But at that point, many fans said, "Screw the NFL." We have a team now, and it may not be the NFL, but it is football and the product on the field appears to be entertaining. Before the CFL, Baltimore had gone ten years without professional football and the city was just thrilled to finally have a team of their own again.

10

More Than an Expansion Team

Despite the loss in the home opener to the Stampeders, Baltimore was excited about their new CFL team. An average of 37,347 fans attended the CFLers' nine home games at Memorial Stadium in 1994. To put that in perspective, the average attendance for the 12-team league that season was 21,741. The next closest team to Baltimore was the Edmonton Eskimos at 29,867 fans per game, or 7,480 fewer fans per game than the CFLers. The Las Vegas Posse, another U.S. expansion team, was last in attendance at 9,527 fans per game.

"We had a very unique situation," general manager Jim Popp said. "We had a city that was hungry for football and ready to embrace us. Plus we had an iconic place like Memorial Stadium to play and we had the old Colts like Johnny Unitas, Tom Matte and Bruce Laird who all wanted us to succeed in Baltimore. It was a great formula for success."

Interest in the Baltimore team increased as the season progressed as fans—and media—soon figured out that the CFLers were far from the typical expansion team which usually struggles on the field while laying the foundation for success in the future. "The fans were really into it," Baltimore statistician Dan O'Connell said. "They were just glad to have legitimate football back in Baltimore, even if it wasn't the NFL at that point."

Punter Josh Miller said the city completely embraced the team from the beginning. That, he said, only fueled the players' desire to succeed more and not let down fans who came out to watch them play.

> We were lucky to come to a city with a football tradition and built-in fan base. Ownership treated us like an NFL team. The only difference was the paycheck. First-class city, first-class facilities, first-class nightlife, and first-class fans. The experience would have been different if we were playing as an expansion team in a Canadian city. We were playing in an NFL city where arguably football became America's game. Plus when guys like Tom Matte and John Mackey welcome you and accept you it meant so much more.

Also helping the Baltimore CFL team during its initial season was the Major League Baseball strike. With the Orioles not playing, no NFL team in town, and little interest in college football programs such as the University of Maryland and the Naval Academy, the CFL was the only sports game in town, literally. The historic and infamous moment represented the perfect time for an upstart team to capture the hearts and minds of the sports public in Baltimore. "We were it for those looking for professional sports in Baltimore that summer," Jim Speros said. "This script was perfect for us. We were blowing out sponsorship and attendance records for the CFL that year."

"We had perfect timing in that regard," defensive back Irv Smith said. "There were no Orioles or even Nationals at that point, and Baltimore wasn't going to follow the Redskins. We were it. Mr. Speros and company made the tickets affordable, the game was different and exciting, and the fans came out to watch it."

Bonnie Downing, Baltimore's director of community relations, said a perfect storm came together which put the Baltimore CFL football club in the best situation possible to succeed in the first season. The baseball strike also opened the door for additional media opportunities and sponsorship deals that would likely not have been available under most other conditions. If the team was going to succeed, this was the ideal time to try and make it happen, players and team officials agreed.

> We did everything out there to get out in the community. We were at schools, community groups, businesses, and anywhere else to try and connect with the fans. There was especially a lot of energy put in to make sure we reached out to the young fans, many of whom had no memories of football in Baltimore. We were even able to get "Homicide: Life on the Street" to film scenes for their show at Memorial Stadium and include our team in the footage. We actually had ["Homicide" actors] Ned Beatty and Richard Belzer on the field. It took a lot of work to make that happen. That was really huge for us. We even had the "Mighty Morphin Power Rangers" come out to a game one time.

Paul Mittermeier, the team's assistant director of public relations, said that the CFL was just a fun brand of football and everything about that time was fun for everyone associated with the team. What made the period even more enjoyable was how accessible the players were to the media and the community.

> It was fun because we were doing what we loved to do, everyone was excited about the team, and we were all inclusive about it. The league needed to gain exposure, so if reporters wanted credentials, we gave it to them. The players were everywhere in the community and were happy to do interviews whenever was necessary. That's just not the case today in today's multi-billion-dollar sports industry. The access to players like that isn't there. The connection is not the same.

10. More Than an Expansion Team

That was the case at the time with the Orioles, too. Camden Yards was new and there were 30,000 fans there a night, and no one could buy a ticket because it was so popular. Then you had Cal Ripken's run to 2,131 [consecutive games played streak] in 1995 and the team was good in 1996 and 1997, so the Orioles didn't necessarily need to reach out like the Stallions did. Then there was the baseball strike in 1994 and the football team in town at the opening to bring in more fans.

Brendan Marr was a CFL fan from the start. He agrees that the baseball strike led many sports fans in town to see what the new football team was all about. The CFL provided a very affordable entertainment option in town at a time where there were still plenty of people who missed Memorial Stadium. The Orioles were also one of the hottest tickets in town before the strike, and getting a decent ticket at the new Oriole Park at Camden Yards was very difficult with crowds reaching more than 30,000 fans a night.

Actor Richard Belzer films a scene for "Homicide: Life on the Street" at Memorial Stadium in 1994 (photograph by John Patrick Kelly, from the archives of John W. Ziemann).

> What helped the CFL franchise immensely in the first season was that MLB went on strike that summer and stayed on strike until the following baseball season. It was a time when Camden Yards was brand new, and it was rather difficult to get a decent Orioles ticket. Camden Yards was sold out night after night. It was *the* thing to do on summer nights in Baltimore. Then the MLB players union goes on strike in early August. No more O's games that year, no more nights at Camden yards. Many, many O's fans had a special place in their heart for Memorial Stadium. Many of them were not ready to see it go. So, with the MLB players' strike, the CFL games—professional football at Memorial Stadium—became the thing to do that summer, and for a brief time, 33rd Street came alive again. Did it sell

out? Of course not. But the crowds for those games were every bit as large as the crowds on an average Orioles game at Memorial Stadium, and fans were just happy to be back home again.

Baltimore radio talk show host Glenn Clark said he treated the CFL team like baseball fans would treat the Orioles. He considered them a major league sports franchise and considered himself one of the team's biggest fans. "I had the sweatshirts, the hats, and other memorabilia," Clark said. "They were the first team I really followed. This was like a love affair for me. I went to as many games as I could. I watched them on television and loved that there were games on nationally on ESPN2, which was still pretty new at the time. I read all I could about the team and couldn't wait to talk with my friends about the games at school even if none of them cared."

Clark said the CFL team just did a lot of things to ingratiate themselves into the community. He believes this was especially true for those fans around his age, who had no allegiance or recollections of the great Colts teams of yesteryear. Following the CFL team allowed him to create his own fond memories of cheering for his own football team. "My dad would take me—whether I needed it or not—to the barbershop each Saturday," Clark said. "The men there would socialize and reminisce about the Colts and even go over specific plays. I never understood at the time why they would get so emotional, and even weepy, over a team that no longer existed. But once the CFL team arrived, I got it."

Jim Popp said that while many doors opened that normally would have been closed to the team under normal conditions, it still required a lot of work to get as many people to buy into what the team was trying to accomplish in its inaugural season. Popp admitted it was far from an easy sell and process even as the team began to win.

> Surprisingly while we benefited from a media, advertising and marketing perspective after the baseball strike, it did not necessarily help attendance. People who were conditioned to go to baseball games during that time decided to do other things like going on vacation to the beach. I took that as a lesson wherever I worked in future years. My goal has always been to condition fans to follow and support the team.
>
> The strike also benefitted us in other ways as we got great deals to charter planes, something the CFL wasn't used to. Without baseball, the charter industry was looking to make up the business and we got great deals to charter flights.

Roch Kubatko said that the Baltimore CFL team definitely benefited some in regard to media coverage because of the baseball strike. Readers of the newspaper were also glad to see Baltimore teams prominently features in the sports section again. The newspaper had increased its coverage of Washington sports in the years after the Colts left town to help fill the void.

10. More Than an Expansion Team 79

There was going to be a ton of media coverage no matter what happened in Major League Baseball, but it didn't hurt that it was the only game in town for a while. There wasn't an NBA or NHL team. And there was such a curiosity over the CFL that even casual fans paid closer attention to it. I know a lot of people were upset that the hometown paper adopted the Redskins, putting their game stories on the front page and assigning a writer to cover them. You can't force fans to start following a different team, especially with the Baltimore-Washington rivalry.

After the home-opening loss to the Argonauts, Baltimore again alternated wins and losses. First, they scored 28 second-half points on the way to a 40–24 victory against the Shreveport Pirates on July 23, 1994, before an announced crowd of 31,172 at Memorial Stadium. In the win, Tracy Ham threw for 320 yards, connected on touchdown passes of one, two and 15 yards, and rushed for another score. Five days later, Baltimore squandered a 25–10, third quarter lead before losing to the host Winnipeg Blue Bombers, 39–32, before an announced crowd of 22,398 fans at Winnipeg Stadium in Canada. The CFLers' record was a mediocre 2–2, not bad for a first-year expansion team, but not what the Baltimore players had hoped for after they broke training camp.

The CFLers responded by winning four of their next six games. The victories during this stretch came in a variety of ways. On August 6, 1994, Baltimore held off the Las Vegas Posse, 38–33, before an announced crowd of 10,122 at Sam Boyd Stadium in Nevada. Trailing 23–22 at halftime, the CFLers rallied in the second half but needed a game-saving tackle by cornerback Irv Smith on Posse wide receiver Curtis Maryfield on the 2-yard line with less than a minute to play to secure the win.

Just four days later, Baltimore returned home and rolled up almost 600 yards of total offense in a 30–15 victory over the Hamilton Tiger-Cats at Memorial Stadium. Ham threw for a season-high 442 yards with touchdown passes of 23 and 60 yards, while slotback Chris Armstrong finished with 224 receiving yards, receiving both of Ham's touchdown passes in the win. Following a 31–24 home loss against the Argonauts on August 20, Baltimore won at the Hamilton Tiger-Cats (28–17 on August 27) and at the Shreveport Pirates (28–16 on September 3) before losing a heart-breaker, 30–29, against the Sacramento Goldminers, on September 10, 1994, before an announced crowd of 42,116 fans at Memorial Stadium.

"We felt most games we had the talent to win, and a lot of that was because of the job Don Matthews did as coach," offensive lineman Neal Fort said.

> He just had a way of instilling confidence in all of us. He wanted to get the most out of every player on the roster, and the fans appreciated that in Baltimore, and it only helped us get that much more over with the fans. We were lucky, because we

Receiver Shawn Beals had 28 catches for 488 yards and two touchdowns for Baltimore in 1994 (photograph by John Patrick Kelly, from the archives of John W. Ziemann).

were truly a triple-threat team. While we had a revolving door of players like most CFL teams, we did have some continuity on the offensive line, and that helped set the tone for Mike Pringle to be able to run like he did. Then we had Tracy Ham, who came to Baltimore with a lot to prove. His career appeared to be on the downturn after his time with the Argonauts, but he still had the ability to beat you with his arm or with his legs like he did in college at Georgia Southern. What he did was revitalize his career in Baltimore.

In the loss to the Goldminers, the CFLers rallied from an 11-point deficit to take a 28–27 lead after Ham connected on a 14-yard touchdown pass to Armstrong with less than four minutes remaining. Baltimore had a chance to win the game with 39 seconds remaining, but unfortunately for them, Donald Igwebuike slipped on a 21-yard field goal try, and the CFLers had to settle for a single. Seven plays later, the Sacramento kicker connected on a game-winning 47-yard field goal as time expired. The fans who shared that heartbreaking loss represented the largest crowd ever to witness a CFL game in Baltimore. The game also represented arguably the height of the team's popularity.

"We rallied around the CFL team in part because they were just like us, and in some respects like the old Colts," Rob Betz said.

10. More Than an Expansion Team

Keith Ballard, an offensive tackle for Baltimore, lived in our apartment building. Mike Pringle lived in our community. They made OK money at the time, but weren't anywhere near the millionaires of the NFL. They were just making an honest living doing what they loved to do.

The team was simply engrained in the community. There was this one home game at Memorial Stadium when my wife made a "Miracle on 33rd Street" sign and was showing it off in the stands. Keith Ballard was hurt for the game but was still being interviewed by the announcers from ESPN in the TV booth. At one point during the game, while Keith was being interviewed, they showed us on TV and he started to smile and laugh. The TV announcer asked him what was so funny. He said, "That's my neighbor. I saw that sign this morning."

Leonard "Big Wheel" Burrier said Baltimore's CFL team was everywhere in the community during that time in ways fans would never see from today's players from the Ravens and Orioles, respectively. He believes that only helped the team gain even more in popularity. "We worked to make sure the players were out and about, even setting up dinners at local restaurants where they could interact with the fans, who came out in droves to those events," Burrier said. "The players appreciated it, too. They didn't make much more, or even less than most of the fans. Tracy Ham was the only one who was really paid back then. That's just the way it was for the CFL, and in most cases it was the quarterback."

Pete Kerzel liked to arrive at Memorial Stadium early on game days just for the chance to watch the fans pour in to support the team. He said the emotions displayed by Baltimore's fans that season are hard to describe unless you were there to witness it and experience it first-hand.

> The stadium would just come to life during those games, especially during the first season. Part of it was the frustration with the NFL, part of it was the team winning, and part of it was simply the team's connection to the fans. The team was really smart about how they sold the team to the community. They did not try to compete with the NFL. They were simply trying to build a brand. They really tried to connect with the fans from a grass roots level. The team was everywhere. They were out signing autographs, speaking a schools and putting on clinics all of the time. Plus the players were a likable bunch who worked hard, had great personalities, and understood the importance of their presence in Baltimore at that point in time. They were an enjoyable team to watch and cover on a daily basis.

Despite the tough setback against the Goldminers, Baltimore would not regress. Instead, the CFLers got stronger as the season progressed and subsequently went on a four-game winning streak, capped by a 22–16 victory over the Posse before an announced crowd of 34,186 at Memorial Stadium. In the win over the Posse, Baltimore running back Mike Pringle ran for 133 yards—his fourth straight 100-yard rushing game—and slotback Chris Armstrong caught his 14th touchdown pass of the season to lead the CFLers, who improved to 10–4 overall with four games remaining before the playoffs. "We had a great team with a lot of NFL-caliber players on the roster," wide receiver Walter Wilson said. "There were dynamic players at every position on both offense and defense. I knew we were going to put it together eventually, even in our first season."

Receivers coach Donald Hill-Eley said it took some time for the team to gel and to get going on all cylinders, but once they did, he knew they had the talent to play with any team in the league. Expectations continued to rise with each victory and each passing week. "It was a process for much of that first season in Baltimore," Hill-Eley said. "We had a situation where we already had great players on the roster. Guy like O. J. Brigance, Jearld Baylis, and Elfrid Payton among others on defense. We had three defensive player of the year candidates right there.

> Then on offense, we had all of the key players in place. From Tracy Ham under center to receivers like Chris Armstrong to an amazing running back like Mike Pringle to a strong offensive line with guys like Neal Fort and Shar Pourdanesh leading the charge. It was so tough for any team to defend against us because we could attack you from so many angles and in so many ways. It was just as much a process for us as coaches. My third game into that season, Coach Matthews came to me and said to step up my game or he would find someone else who could. He was demanding but knew how to get the best out of all of his players and coaches.

Baltimore defensive coordinator Bob Price said there is always an adjustment for those who have only played the American style of football when they arrive in the CFL. Having so many CFL veterans on the roster shortened the learning curve for Baltimore in its first season.

> Players when they first arrive in the CFL don't realize how much bigger the field is and how fast-paced the game can be compared to football in the U.S. With just three downs, there are plenty of times when the defense just gets on to the sidelines and then have to get back out on the field before they even have a chance to get a drink of water. Conditioning is so important. Players learn to make adjustments quickly or they soon realize that the CFL game is just not for them.
>
> The players [in the CFL] would not put up with players who would not put the work in to make those adjustments. Attitudes like that made coaching easy during that time.

With the win over the Posse, Baltimore clinched a home playoff berth, which would represent the first post-season professional football game in Baltimore since the NFL Colts lost to the Oakland Raiders on December 24, 1977, in the AFC Divisional Round. The accomplishment was not lost on those associated with the team. "Having a roster and coaching staff with so much CFL experience really separated ourselves from the other US expansion teams," Pringle said. "I think when we first got to town, people came out more as a curiosity, and then when they saw how we played they continued to come out and support us. They were hungry for football, and we showed them how good football in the CFL could be played."

Shar Pourdanesh said the team's confidence grew with each win. The team also improved as the players got used to each other and the unique rules of the Canadian brand of football. "We could tell we had a good team as the season went on," Pourdanesh said. "The players had adjusted to one another and those unfamiliar with the CFL game at the beginning of the season began to have a better feel for the game and the rules."

Guy Earle said their offensive line was as good as any he has ever played on in his career, and getting to block for a running back like Pringle made playing for Baltimore so much fun. That approach on offense was something not necessarily common in the CFL, as having just three downs to get a first down can often limit a team's ability to run on a consistent basis, since a second and long situation can force teams into passing situations earlier and more often compared to the NFL. "We were so big across the line," Earle said. "We were like 6-foot-4 and 300 pounds each. We just pounded the ball and Mike showed why he was such a great running back."

Defensive back Ken Watson said there was definitely a feeling-out process among the players and coaches in 1994, but once that happened, they knew they had the potential to do something special. "It took time for the team chemistry to get there," Watson said. "Once we got to know each other on a personal basis, we got even better. We started to do everything as a team both on and off the field. We got closer and closer together, and when we did, the wins kept coming to us."

While the CFLers were excited about the chance to host a playoff game in their first season, they began to believe more was possible on October 29, 1994. On that date, Baltimore absolutely destroyed the Winnipeg Blue Bombers by a score of 57–10 before an announced crowd of 39,417 at Memorial Stadium. With the win, the CFLers avenged their loss from early in the season and took control of the East Division from the Blue Bombers, who had won the division just a year prior. The difference in this game against the Blue Bombers was easily in the first half, when Baltimore outscored Winnipeg, 37–0. The CFLers scored 24 unanswered points in the second quarter alone. Pringle rushed for 209 yards with two touchdowns, and in the process, set the CFL record for most rushing yards and most yards from scrimmage in a season. Also, Ham and Armstrong connected on touchdown passes of 14, 16, and 44 yards as the offense racked up 585 yards, while Igwebuike booted five field goals for Baltimore.

"The team had good players, good coaching, and were playing a confident brand of football," Pete Kerzel said. "Baltimore fans, like most sports fans around, latch onto a winner, and that was what this team was doing. Fans were just turning out in droves for this team. I remember going out

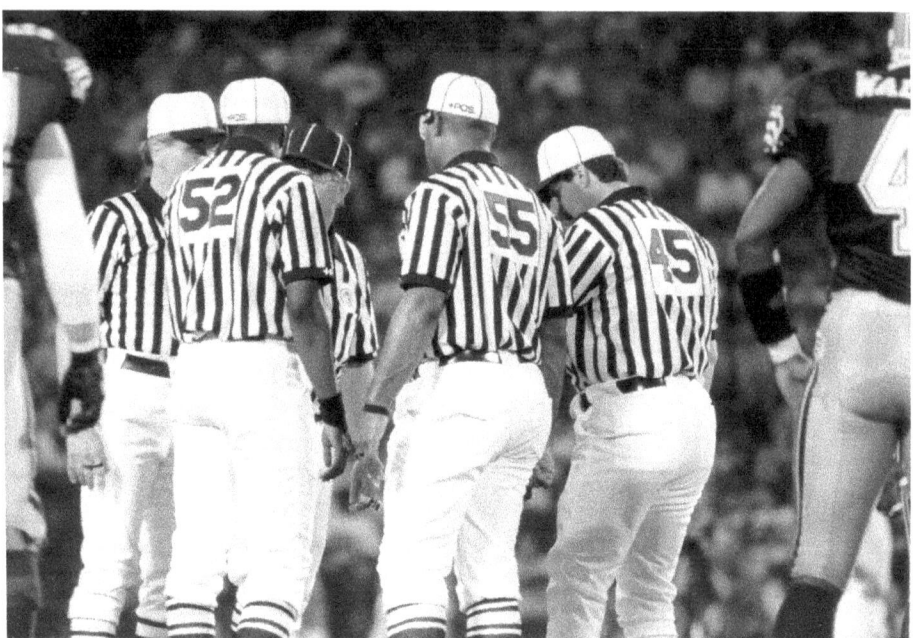

Officials gather to discuss a call during a 1994 CFL game between Baltimore and the Winnipeg Blue Bombers at Memorial Stadium (photograph by John Patrick Kelly, from the archives of John W. Ziemann).

to one of the early games on a lark with some friends. It ended up pouring down rain like crazy, but the fans stayed and cheered on the team. Most fans decided they would give the team a shot, and once they did, they realized it was an exciting brand of football."

Baltimore's defense was just as impressive against Winnipeg. The CFLers held the Blue Bombers to just 189 yards of total offense. Winnipeg's lone points came on a touchdown and a field goal in the third quarter. "We just got better that first season the more we played together," Popp said. "We had players that were still learning the rules of the CFL game. Then we got on a roll late, especially after a big win over Winnipeg, who we absolutely destroyed. Then we realized we had a chance."

Pourdanesh agreed that the Winnipeg win represented a turning point for the new franchise. It only added to the team's confidence and expectations heading into the 1994 playoffs. "We could tell we had a good team as the season went on," Pourdanesh said. "The players had adjusted to one another, and those unfamiliar with the CFL game at the beginning of the season began to have a better feel for the game and the rules. We just kicked the crap out of Winnipeg, and it just gave us the confidence we could do anything."

10. More Than an Expansion Team

Payton said the win over Winnipeg made the players on both sides of the ball for Baltimore realize there was nothing they could not accomplish if they set their minds to it. "Winnipeg should have won the Grey Cup in 1993, my last year on the team," Payton said. "We knew if we played like that the rest of the season, we were going to the Grey Cup."

Baltimore was even gaining the respect of many Canadians, who could appreciate what Baltimore was accomplishing on the field. Among those was Mike. Rogers, a Toronto resident and longtime Argonauts fan, who was 38 in 1994 when a business trip led him to Baltimore. Knowing that the CFLers were set to play that week, Rogers adjusted his schedule so that he could take in Baltimore's game against the Blue Bombers. He was impressed both by the play on the field and the fans in the stands.

> It was just amazing to see what was going on back then in Baltimore with this CFL team. The fans were knowledgeable and enthusiastic about the game. I get to old Memorial Stadium, and there was a huge tailgate going on before the game. I go inside and next thing I know, there are Baltimore fans asking me to join them. There were close to 40,000 fans there, which is a great turnout for any CFL game in Canada. It obviously wasn't a sellout, but it was such a loud crowd. Many of the connections I made on that day became friends of mine who I stay in contact with to this day.

The Baltimore CFL team went 12-6 and won the East Division title in their first year of existence (photograph by John Patrick Kelly, from the archives of John W. Ziemann).

Unfortunately for Baltimore, to make it to the Grey Cup as a first-year franchise, it would likely have to play at least one game on the road. That was because after such an impressive win, the CFLers played their worst game of the season, an 18–0 road loss against the Sacramento Gold Miners in their regular-season finale. An announced crowd of just 14,056 fans at Hornet Field witnessed the CFLers shut out for the only time that season. Sacramento limited Baltimore to just 107 yards in total offense. Making matters worse, Pringle was held to 71 yards rushing after needing 99 to rush for 2,000 yards in a season. Pringle also finished the game with just 104 yards in total offense when he needed 177 yards to break the single-season record. Pringle finished the regular season rushing for 1,972 yards, with 2,414 yards from scrimmage and 3,228 all-purpose yards.

With the loss, Baltimore finished the regular season with a 12–6 record, in second place in the East Division, one game behind the Blue Bombers. Baltimore season ticket holder Rob Betz said the success the team experienced in their inaugural season kept interest in them high in the city long after the initial excitement wore off from the season opener.

> Just as important as the team's name and their marketing throughout the season that first year was the fact that the team was really good and kept winning on the field, too. Jim Speros and Don Matthews just got it. They knew they had to mainly bring on CFL players to the roster. Most of the other coaches of the U.S. expansion teams were former NFL coaches or college football retreads who tried to play the NFL style of football in the CFL. You just can't do that and expect to win on a consistent basis. That played out over the course of the season.

11

Run to the Grey Cup

For those who waited 17 years for another home playoff football game in town, the Baltimore CFLers did not disappoint them. Playing before an announced crowd of 35,223 fans, the team with no name topped the Toronto Argonauts, a team with roots that date back to 1873, 34–15 on November 12, 1994, at Memorial Stadium. The East Division semifinal game represented the rubber match between the new rivals. The Argonauts had won the last game, 31–24, on August 20, before an announced crowd of 41,155, the second-largest attendance of the season in Baltimore.

In the playoff game, the second quarter was the difference as Baltimore scored 17 unanswered points to take a 20–10 lead at halftime. They never looked back. Running back Robert Drummond, filling in for an injured Mike Pringle, rushed for 111 yards and two touchdowns, while Tracy Ham connected on touchdown passes of 20 and 16 yards to slotback Chris Armstrong to lead the way for Baltimore. Defensively, the CFLers centered their attention on legendary CFL running back Mike "Pinball" Clemmons. Clemmons, a future CFL Hall of Famer who finished with 12,356 yards from scrimmage and 85 touchdowns in his 12-year career, was held to 64 all-purpose yards on that night. Toronto scored just five points in the second half, the last two when Ham ran out of the end zone for a safety.

Next for Baltimore came a third battle with the Winnipeg Blue Bombers. This game was the East Division finals, with a trip to the Grey Cup on the line. This game, which was played on November 20, 1994, at Winnipeg Stadium, included many more peripheral issues that would factor into the game and bring other smoldering issues within the CFL to the surface. The first issue was the weather, with freezing temperatures and blistering wind expected for kickoff. The next issue was the political ramifications of the game, as the mostly pro–Canadian crowd of 25,067 fans wanted nothing more than to ensure that a U.S. team did not play for their championship. While U.S. sports leagues had expanded into Canada in Major League Baseball, and the National Basketball Association was set to add two new Canadian teams (the Toronto Raptors and the Vancouver

Grizzlies) in 1995, many Canadians were not keen of the idea of U.S. teams encroaching on their league. "That first Grey Cup run was us against everyone," Baltimore general manager Jim Popp said. "For many people, it was Canada against the U.S., and there were a lot of people who did not want to see the Grey Cup in Baltimore."

Unlike the last meeting between the two teams, the game was anything but a blowout for Baltimore, which trailed Winnipeg, 12–8, heading into the fourth quarter. Offense was at a premium for both teams. The only touchdown came in the first quarter, when Baltimore cornerback Karl Anthony scored on a 10-yard fumble recovery. After being held scoreless for the next two quarters, Baltimore rallied in the fourth quarter with kicker Donald Igwebuike connecting on field goals of 36 and 54 yards. The latter of which came with 3:20 left and proved to be the game-winner in a 14–12 victory that vaulted Baltimore into the Grey Cup in its inaugural CFL season. Defense was key for Baltimore, which held Winnipeg to 171 yards of total offense. This included the play of Anthony, who also had an interception and two pass knockdowns.

"That game highlighted just how much Coach Matthews understood the CFL game and how the elements could play a factor in it," coach Donald Hill-Eley said. "Coach Matthews knew the wind would be in our favor when he sent out Donald Igwebuike to make that 54-yard field goal that won us the game and sent us into the Grey Cup. That kick would have been good from 60 or 65 yards the way the wind was blowing that day. A decision like that only comes from experience."

Now all that stood between Baltimore and the 82nd Grey Cup was the BC Lions. The game was set for November 27 at BC Place in Vancouver, British Columbia. It marked the first-ever professional football championship to feature a team from the U.S. against a team from Canada. The Lions finished the regular season with a record of 11–6–1 and placed third in the West Division. Heading into the playoffs, the Lions had little momentum and were a long shot to compete for the Grey Cup, having lost three of their final four regular season games. This included a 48–31 setback at Baltimore on October 22.

But little of that seemed to matter for the Lions, who appeared to be a team of destiny in their own right. In the West Division semifinals, the Lions jumped out to a 20–12 halftime lead against the Edmonton Eskimos and held on for a 24–23 victory. In the West Division finals, the Lions rallied from a 34–26 deficit heading into the fourth quarter to defeat the favored Calgary Stampeders, 37–36. Calgary had won both regular season meetings against BC, which included a 62–21 rout at home on July 29.

Much like the Winnipeg game, Canadian fans were united against Baltimore as the game represented national pride as much as a football

11. Run to the Grey Cup

The patch Baltimore and the BC Lions wore in the 1994 Grey Cup (photograph by Ron Snyder).

championship. Many Baltimore players admitted that they did not comprehend the political and cultural ramifications of that Grey Cup when they initially took the field. "It was loud as hell during that game," Baltimore punter Josh Miller said. "No one in that stadium, except the fans that made the trip from Baltimore, wanted that Grey Cup to leave Canada."

Guy Earle said they were supposed to be considered the home team in the Grey Cup, but how Baltimore was treated on that night was far from what the team expected. "We were supposed to be the home team and the U.S. national anthem was supposed to be played second," Earle said. "None of that happened for obvious political reasons. There was so much going on before that game. That game was as loud as any game I can ever remember."

Baltimore did all it could in the first half to ensure that the 55,097 fans in attendance were witness to history. Trailing 3–0 after the first quarter, the CFLers stormed back in the second quarter. Baltimore responded with 14 unanswered points thanks to a 1-yard touchdown run by Ham and a 46-yard interception return for a score after Anthony took a lateral from linebacker Alvin Walton and scampered into the end zone.

That touchdown would be the last one Baltimore scored in the game. The Lions scratched and clawed their way back into the contest in the second half. BC backup quarterback Danny McManus, who replaced injured starter Kent Austin late in the second quarter, pulled the Lions to within 20–17 with a 1-yard touchdown run with 5:21 left in the third quarter. The score came three plays after the Lions faked a 34-yard field goal attempt and holder Darren Flutie ran to the 10-yard line.

The Lions eventually took a 23–20 lead following a 27-yard field goal by kicker Lui Passaglia with 11:51 remaining in regulation. Igwebuike tied the game at 23–23 after he booted a 29-yard touchdown with 6:34 remaining in the game.

Things got even more interesting after that. With less than two minutes remaining, McManus fired a deep ball to wide receiver Ray Alexander. Alexander and Baltimore defensive back Irv Smith went up for the ball. It appeared that the ball came out when Alexander hit the ground, but officials ruled the Lions' wide receiver had possession and the ground made him lose the ball.[1] That play is considered one of the most controversial in Grey Cup history. "I was never part of a more emotional game than that Grey Cup," Smith said. "That play still hurts me. To be a part of what I thought was a big stop only for it to be ruled a catch was difficult. Thinking of that play upsets me to this day."

That controversial reception by Alexander eventually set up a failed 37-yard field goal attempt by Passaglia with 1:02 left in regulation. However, Baltimore was barely able to advance the ball out to the two-yard line. Pringle got nothing on the ground on first down, and Ham threw an incompletion on second down, forcing the CFLers to punt the ball away. "To this day I don't believe that Ray Alexander made that catch," Ham said.

Miller, who led the league in both punting average (42.9 yards) and punting net (36.9) as a rookie, was forced to punt the ball from ten yards back in his own end zone and managed just a 38-yard punt. The Lions' Darren Flutie returned the punt to the Baltimore 34 with less than 30 seconds remaining. The Lions ran two more plays before Passaglia—who would play his entire 25-year career with BC before retiring in 2000—connected with a 38-yard field goal with no time remaining to give the Lions a 26–23 upset victory and the Grey Cup championship. "There's no reason we should have lost that Grey Cup," Baltimore wide receiver Walter Wilson said.

Most of Wilson's teammates agreed with his assessment. Although the game is considered one of the greatest Grey Cups in CFL history, that provides little solace to those who played for Baltimore that night. To a man, each player on the Baltimore roster who walked onto the field that night expected to leave as Grey Cup champions. To many, the loss to the Lions represents the worst defeat of their careers at any level. "I've had thousands of kicks in my career and I remember literally none of them,

11. Run to the Grey Cup

but I remember everything about that game," Miller said. "To this day I'm still burned about my punt late in that game to Flutie that gave them the short field and set up the game winning field goal. I still wish I had that kick back."

Ham said the Alexander catch late in the game made all the difference for the Lions that night. Barring that controversial catch, Ham full-heartedly believes that Baltimore would have left the field champions in 1994. "That play flipped the field and set up the eventual win by the Lions," Ham said.

Guy Earle said no loss in his career hurt more than the loss to the Lions in the Grey Cup that season. Baltimore was the favorite, but the Lions just found a way to win the game in the end. Simply put, Earle said that sometimes it is better to be lucky than good. "No loss in my career hurt worse than when we lost to the BC Lions in that Grey Cup," Earle said. "We were supposed to win that game. But BC got some breaks along the way, and that kick was up and good. Next thing I know, there's balloons everywhere and BC is wearing the championship hats while we're walking off the field."

John Earle said that even 25 years later, he refuses to wear the ring the team received as Eastern Division winners from that season. He thinks, even if subconsciously, Baltimore underestimated the Lions and the momentum BC had through the playoffs.

> We all thought we were going to get another shot at Doug Flutie and the Calgary Stampeders. Then after the plane ride after beating Winnipeg in the Eastern Division finals and find out we're playing BC instead. We owned them the last time we played them. We just trounced them and thought we were going to do it again. I think our mental focus was built around playing Calgary. Still we had our chances and it came down to the end. It was a tough game.

Ken Watson said that defeat to the Lions in the Grey Cup is a loss he thinks about to this day. In the end, those on Baltimore's roster were able to take that defeat and turn it into a positive. "We were the favorites and worked so hard to reach that point," Watson said. "We wanted to be the first expansion team ever to win the championship in their first season. It was disappointing, but the loss gave us focus and motivation going into that offseason."

Elfrid Payton said he was more angry than disappointed as he walked off the field after that loss. He does not believe the better team won that night. "There is no way we should have ever lost that game," Payton said. "To call that a catch was a terrible call. We were the better team and had kicked the crap out of BC during the season. We felt we were the team to beat in 1994 and knew we were the team to beat heading into 1995."

Shar Pourdanesh said the way the team lost put a damper on all they had accomplished, accomplishments that set the standard for future expansion teams not just in the CFL, but in any professional sports league. "If we had lost by a lot, I think it may have felt different," Pourdanesh said. "But we were right there and we knew we had the better team. It just didn't come together for us against the Lions. Still, they gave us plenty of motivation heading into the next season."

Ham shared a similar sentiment. He walked off the field not only feeling like he let his teammates down, but that he disappointed the fans and the city of Baltimore, who stood by the team from the start and deserved more. "The loss hurt, but it kept us focused heading into 1995 and reminded us that we had unfinished business to take care of," Ham said. "We wanted to bring a Grey Cup home to Baltimore."

Pringle said that to come that close to winning the Grey Cup as an expansion team was as heart-breaking as any moment of his career. At the same time, he cannot remember another loss that motivated him more heading into an off-season than that one. "Losing any game that close is tough, but to lose a Grey Cup like we did was even tougher," Pringle said. "It left such a sour taste in our mouth. It was all about unfinished business in 1995. We were completely focused on winning a Grey Cup."

Donald Hill-Eley said that Grey Cup was played under conditions he will never forget. Baltimore had plenty of opportunities, but the Lions just found a way to hang in the game long enough before pulling off the upset in the end. Sometimes, Hill-Eley said, that game was a prime example of how anything can happen in sports, especially when the elements come into play. "That was a tough loss to handle because we felt we had the better team," Hill-Eley said. "Even with the elements and the crowd against us, we were still in it until the end. The feeling we had after that loss definitely carried over to the following season."

Defensive coordinator Bob Price thought just after the loss that his players might be dejected and down on themselves. However, that belief changed quickly once he returned to the locker room and saw the expressions on their faces. Those expressions, Price said, were not looks of dejection, but looks of determination. "When I walked in that locker room after we lost the Grey Cup, you could see the resolve in each player's eyes," Price said. "You could tell they wanted to get back there next year and win it all. There were no excuses and no one feeling sorry for themselves. They knew they just had to work harder in the off-season, and they would have another chance to win a championship."

Baltimore radio broadcaster Bruce Cunningham said the CFLers were playing with a stacked deck against them and still nearly came away with the title. That, Cunningham said, highlighted how talented the team was and just how many things needed to break the Lions' way for them to leave that game with the Grey Cup. Cunningham added that if the same teams played ten other times, he is not sure the Lions would have won any of them. "That was as hostile a crowd as you could have," Cunningham said. "The Lions had the chance to play a championship game in their home stadium filled with fans who wanted the Grey Cup to stay in Canada. It was a tough loss to swallow, but to their credit, the players came back better and more motivated than ever for the 1995 season."

Mike Gibbons said that while it was not the Super Bowl or the Stanley Cup, there was a large amount of excitement among Baltimore fans for the team's first trip to the Grey Cup. The game was the first professional sports championship game for a team that actually played in the city since the Orioles won the World Series in 1983. The excitement became evident to Gibbons as he was helping host a large fundraiser for the Babe Ruth Museum at the Fifth Regiment Armory in Baltimore.

> We had this huge bull and oyster roast planned for the same day as the Grey Cup between Baltimore and BC. There was no Internet or smartphones back then, and we had a lot of people tell us they would love to come to the event but it was at the same time as the Grey Cup. So we ended up wheeling a small TV into the banquet area, and people huddled around it to watch the game. The team had really captured the hearts and imagination of much of the city at that time.

Leonard "Big Wheel" Burrier said the team's fans were just as disappointed as the players. He expected the team to come home with the Grey Cup. Despite that, he admits that the team defied all of his initial expectations heading into the season, and he believed better things were coming the following year. "We helped organize a big pep rally after the first Grey Cup appearance," Burrier said. "We wanted to show the team how thankful we were for an amazing season. It was a tough loss to deal with, but it also provided the team a goal the next year."

Baltimore radio talk show host Glenn Clark said that the loss in the Grey Cup was the first time he remembers being upset over one of his sports teams not winning. "That loss in the Grey Cup was just devastating to me," Clark said. "I was just heartbroken over it and it ripped me up inside. I had a bunch of friends over to my house that day, and by the second quarter I realized just about all of my friends were in my room playing video games. I didn't care. This was my team. When they lost on that last-second field goal, it was tough to handle at the time."

12

Unfinished Business

Baltimore entered the 1995 season with a single-focused mantra: unfinished business. No longer just an expansion team, Baltimore knew they had the players and ability to win a Grey Cup. Everything from the time they walked off the field in Vancouver was focused toward accomplishing that goal. There would be no disappointment on the field in the team's second season. The year 1995 was going to be their time to shine and be champions. The players believed winning the Grey Cup was nothing less than their destiny, and nothing was going to stop them from reaching that milestone. "That loss left such a bitter taste in our mouths," Jim Popp said. "It was definitely about unfinished business in 1995."

Linebacker Tracy Gravely could not have agreed with Popp more, adding that there was a single focus among all of those associated with the Stallions that season. "The core of guys was there and the work everyone put in was impressive," Gravely said. "We knew how close we were in 1994 and what we had to do to get back in 1995."

The team had also given up the fight with the NFL over the Colts name and was officially rebranded the Baltimore Stallions. The Stallions name was chosen after the team held a poll for fans after the 1994 season. "We came so close to winning that Grey Cup in our first season," Stallions slotback Chris Armstrong said. "That would have been an amazing ending for an expansion team. But that loss only motivated us more. We came back in 1995 with pretty much the same team with one goal in mind, and that was to finish the job we started."

The core of the team remained in place, but Popp and company sought to upgrade the roster with players like offensive lineman Mike Withycombe, wide receiver Shannon Culver, rush end Grant Carter, and kicker Carlos Huerta. There would be no resting on their laurels and accomplishments from the previous season, Popp said. "In 1994, we knocked on the door. In 1995, our goal was simple: knock the door down and win the Grey Cup," John Earle said.

Culver, a rookie that season, beat out Walter Wilson for one of the

12. Unfinished Business

receiving spots on the Stallions roster. Wilson departed after finishing with 50 receptions for 900 yards and four touchdowns in 1994. Culver came to Baltimore out of Oklahoma State, where he had 64 catches for 975 yards and five touchdowns combined in 1992 and 1993. He also averaged 18.4 yards a return for the Cowboys in 1993. "I got hurt and separated my shoulder during training camp in 1995," Wilson said. "I was talented enough to make that roster. I just needed another two or three weeks to get healthy again, but the Stallions coaching staff and front office decided to go in another direction, so they placed me on injury waivers so they could release me."

"Unfinished business" was the Baltimore Stallions' mantra heading into the 1995 playoffs (photograph by Ron Snyder).

The Stallions name was not the only thing new to the CFL heading into the 1995 season. The league continued with its U.S. expansion attempt as the Birmingham Barracudas and the Memphis Mad Dogs were brought in as new teams. The Barracudas were coached by veteran NFL coach Jack Pardee, who brought his high-octane run-and-offense with him to the CFL after a five-year stint as the head coach of the Houston Oilers, which ended the year before after the team lost nine of their first ten games. Birmingham also signed veteran CFL quarterback Matt Dunigan, who had led the Edmonton Eskimos to the Grey Cup in 1986 and 1987, winning it all in the latter year. Dunigan advanced to the Grey Cup with the BC Lions in 1988, the Toronto Argonauts in 1991, and the Winnipeg Blue Bombers in 1992 and 1993, winning it all in 1991. Dunigan was elected to the Canadian Football Hall of Fame in 2006.

The Mad Dogs were owned by FedEx founder Fred Smith, who turned to the CFL after he failed to get an NFL expansion team for Memphis in 1993. He hired Pepper Rodgers to be the team's head coach. Rodgers was a veteran college football coach who had success at Kansas, UCLA, and Georgia Tech before eventually becoming the head coach of the USFL's Memphis Showboats in 1984 and 1985. However, this would be his first and only run in the CFL. The Mad Dogs tried to replicate the Stallions' formula for success by bringing in veteran CFL players and assistants, most notably future CFL Hall of Fame quarterback Damon Allen, the brother of Pro Football Hall of Fame running back Marcus Allen.

At the same time, the Sacramento Gold Miners moved to San Antonio, Texas, were renamed the Texans, and would play their home games in the Alamodome. The CFL also continued to find ways to promote the Canadian game to American football fans. As part of this effort, the league produced a promotional booklet, "First and Ten from the Fifty-Five: Canadian Football Explained," which was designed to help new U.S. fans understand the differences between the two brands of football.[1]

"You could definitely tell there was a difference with the players in 1995," said Ken Watson. "The players worked harder in the offseason and there was a sense that we knew we were the team to beat in 1995."

The new expansion teams also led to a realignment for the CFL, which abandoned the traditional East and West divisions for a North-South setup. The South Division would include the five U.S.-based teams, while the eight Canadian teams would play in the North Division. The league was making every effort to make the expansion effort a success over the long term and not just a way to pump expansion fees into the existing franchises. "The CFL wanted nothing more than the U.S. expansion to be more than an experiment," said Dan O'Connell, who was the long-time sports information director at Towson University and served as the Stallions' official statistician for both seasons in Baltimore. "The problem was that other than Baltimore, all of the other teams had so many issues."

The Las Vegas Posse, who had a miserable 5–13 record in their first season in the CFL, were set to move to either Jackson, Mississippi, Los Angeles, or Miami for the 1995 season. But the franchise and the league were never able to stabilize the situation. On multiple occasions in early 1995, the league offered a tentative approval to move the Posse to Mississippi. This came after approximately a half-dozen ownership groups inquired about the franchise. Had the team moved to Miami, the ownership group would have named the team the Miami Manatees. But in the end, ownership and financial issues led the team to fold, with the league dispersing their roster instead.

It was this development which led Huerta to sign with the Stallions. Huerta was a walk-on kicker at the University of Miami and a four-year

12. Unfinished Business

A pamphlet was designed to help new CFL fans understand the unique rules of its brand of football (photograph by Ron Snyder).

starter for the Hurricanes. He left college as the Hurricanes' all-time leader in points after touchdowns, field goals, and total points while helping Miami win national titles in 1989 and 1991.

Huerta was one of the few bright spots for the Posse. In his lone season in Las Vegas, Huerta connected on 38 of 46 field goal attempts and finished with 154 points. For his efforts, Huerta was honored with the Jackie Parker Trophy, given annually to the top rookie in the West Division, and was a runner-up for the CFL's Most Outstanding Rookie Award. "When Las Vegas folded, there was no team I wanted to play on other than the Stallions," said Huerta, who connected on 57 of 72 field goal attempts for the Stallions in 1995. "I made sure my agent made that clear in the dispersal draft. The talent was evident that they had the players to win a championship."

Huerta said that along with the chance to play for a winner, the fan base and football tradition were two other things that attracted him to Baltimore. For Huerta, it was Baltimore or nothing if he was going to continue to play in the CFL. He wanted to be a part of something special, and he saw that in the Stallions. "It was definitely a unique time in football history," Huerta said. "It was such a great environment to play in. There was the tradition of the Colts, plus they had the marching band, all of the Colts clubs, the Hall of Fame players like Johnny Unitas and Lenny Moore and fans upset at the NFL. They were all in for supporting us."

The Stallions also bolstered their roster by acquiring several players with local ties to Maryland. This included the signing of long snapper Rob Davis. Davis was a 1986 graduate of Eleanor Roosevelt High School in Greenbelt, Maryland—a suburban community just outside of Washington, D.C.—before playing at Division II Shippensburg University in Pennsylvania. Davis signed with the New York Jets as an undrafted free agent in 1993 but never made the active roster before signing with the Stallions in 1995 and becoming the team's long snapper.

The Stallions also added to their depth at quarterback and receiver with two very local signees in Dan Crowley and Mark Orlando. Crowley, a quarterback, and Orlando, a receiver, signed with the Stallions after graduating from Towson State (now Towson University) after the 1994 season. At Towson, Crowley is considered one of the school's all-time great players. He completed 617 of 1,169 passes for 8,900 yards and 81 touchdowns, setting school records in each statistic. Crowley started 35 for games for Towson from 1991 to 1994, with the Tigers posting a 22–13 record over that span. He was also a key player in Towson's rebuilding effort under coach Gordy Combs, who had been a player and defensive coordinator at the school. The Tigers went from 1–10 in Crowley's freshman season to 8–2 in each of his final two years, leading the school to be nationally ranked among NCAA Division I-AA schools for the first time ever at that level. Crowley's best season came in his senior year, when the Bowie, Maryland, native earned honorable mention All-America honors for the second time after he passed for a school-record 2,913 yards while throwing a record 28 touchdown passes.

Crowley said the Stallions opened up a career path he did not think was possible while at Towson. Having the team's training camp where he and Orlando went to school gave the Stallions an up-close look at scouting the local football standouts. "I never really thought professional football after Towson was in the plans for me," Crowley said. "I just wanted to make my college experience the best I possibly could. Then during my senior year, I saw the CFL team in town, which held training camp at Towson, and an opportunity presented itself. I never thought about the CFL before the Stallions came to Baltimore."

Orlando finished his career as Towson's all-time leader in receiving yards (3,460), touchdown receptions (31), and punt return yardage (644). In 1994, Orlando led the Tigers with 55 receptions for a school-record 1,223 yards, averaging 22.2 yards per catch, and tied the school's single-season record with 12 touchdown receptions. As a senior, Orlando was named a first-team All-American selection after he recorded four 200-yard receiving games. Among his highlights that season, Orlando caught 11 passes for a school-record 266 yards and three touchdowns in Towson's 48–6 win over American International. He also caught ten passes for 244 yards and one touchdown in a 36–31 victory over Kutztown.

Orlando also caught nine passes for 238 yards and a pair of touchdowns in a 32–16 win over Buffalo. Finally, in a win over Bucknell, Orlando had ten receptions for 200 yards and two touchdowns. Orlando, an Eldersburg, Maryland native, would eventually earn a tryout with the NFL's San Francisco 49ers before signing with the Stallions. In many ways, signing with the Stallions was simply an extension of Crowley's and Orlando's college career as the team held its training camp on the Towson campus. "It was an interesting transition because I'm training on the same field I spent the last four years, plus [former Towson football coach] Gordy Combs was a volunteer coach for the Stallions in 1995," Crowley said. "Then next thing you know, my first job out of college starts each Monday with me going to Memorial Stadium to break down game film."

Defensively, the Stallions brought in rush end Grant Carter to bolster an already impressive line. Carter actually signed with Baltimore late in the 1994 season. The former University of Pacific standout had attended training camp with the NFL's San Diego Chargers before joining Baltimore. Carter played in one regular season game for Baltimore and suited up for the team's entire post-season run, including the Grey Cup in 1994.

While at Pacific, Carter was a three-time all-Big West selection, including as a senior, when he made 103 tackles, including 24 for a loss, and 11 sacks in 1993.

"I suffered a concussion while in camp with the Chargers, and it really hampered my ability to make the team," Carter said. "Then my agent called me and asked if I was interested in playing in the CFL with Baltimore. I just wanted to play football so I said, 'Let's go for it.' I'm with the team like a month, and next thing you know I go from getting cut by the Chargers to playing in a Grey Cup. It all happened so fast that I didn't really have a full appreciation of what we accomplished until the off-season."

The Stallions entered the 1995 regular season as the runaway favorite to win the South Division and among the top teams expected to compete for a Grey Cup. Interest in the Stallions remained strong among the die-hard football fans in Baltimore, but it was evident from the attendance that some of the luster was gone from the first historic season. The Stallions, who would continue to host events to honor the old Colts in their second season, average 30,113 fans for their nine home games in 1995, which was behind only the Edmonton Eskimos' averaged attendance of 31,474.

After a 37–34, season-opening loss at the BC Lions in a Grey Cup

Baltimore Colts Hall of Famer Jim Parker shows his support for the Baltimore Stallions CFL team in 1995 (photograph by John Patrick Kelly, from the archives of John W. Ziemann).

12. Unfinished Business

rematch, the Stallions won their next five games. This included the team's home opener—a 50–24 victory over the Texans—in front of an announced crowd of 31,016 fans on July 8, 1995, at Memorial Stadium. "I think heading into that season, the young players from the year before understood the quality play in the CFL and what they needed to do if they wanted to be successful," Stallions quarterback Tracy Ham said.

But success would not come without struggles and adversity for the Stallions. Between July 29 and August 12, 1995, the Stallions were forced to play four games. This included three games in nine days—all on the road—that forced the Stallions to travel more than 5,000 miles across two countries and multiple time zones.[2] The road trip started July 29, when the Stallions traveled to Alabama, where they defeated the Birmingham Barracudas, 36–8. They flew to Canada and held off the Edmonton Eskimos, 19–12, on August 2.

The Stallions then lost two games in a row, 29–15 on August 6 at the Calgary Stampeders and a 25–15 setback six days later against the visiting Mad Dogs in Baltimore. The Stallions played three games in ten days and produced just one touchdown.

Linebacker Alvin Walton makes a tackle against the Winnipeg Blue Bombers in 1995. Walton is one of the few football players lucky enough to win both a Grey Cup title and a Super Bowl ring (photograph by John Patrick Kelly, from the archives of John W. Ziemann).

The loss to the Mad Dogs provided a microcosm of the Stallions' struggles during this stretch. Huerta accounted for all of the team's offense with five field goals. Defensively, the team gave up 375 yards, recorded no sacks, and made just one tackle for a loss. The fact that the Stallions fared as well as they did over this span was a minor miracle. Consider this: The NFL, which plays 16 regular season games, rarely has its teams play games on less than a week's rest, and those teams do so with a 53-man roster. The Stallions went through this stretch—part of an 18-game regular season schedule—with just a 37-man roster. The toll of that stretch became obvious with key players such has Ham and running back Mike Pringle battling injuries. "I know I was beat up at that point," Watson said. "My shoulder was hurt and it was a tough stretch. I felt like I was a guinea pig for so many of the new treatment options coming through during that time. Coach Matthews I think did his best to keep things loose and manage the roster to get us through it."

Guy Earle said that stretch of games was as difficult as any in his career. But he added that it was just the reality of playing in the CFL, and all of the teams had to experience similar struggles based on the geography of where the teams were located and the dynamics of when their respective stadiums were available. "That stretch was a rough one for us," Earle said. "It was the only time I questioned whether we were having a good time. I even wondered if it was even legal for games to be scheduled like that. Coach Matthews did a great job getting us through that period and keeping us as fresh as possible. We knew that if we could get through that, there would be no stopping us."

Stallions defensive coordinator Bob Price said difficult travel stretches were just a part of the reality of playing in the CFL. Having a veteran CFL head coach like Don Matthews at the helm was so important during that time, as he knew how to help the players weather that difficult storm. Matthews refused to let the players use the schedule as an excuse for losing, yet at the same time, he worked to minimize the discomfort as much as possible so that the team would be playing its best heading down the stretch of the regular season. "Don Matthews was such a matter of fact person and coach," Price said. "He was so cool under pressure. He basically said, 'The schedule is the schedule and there's nothing we can do about it.' We simply had to install the game plan while we were on the plane and get ready to play quickly. It was a tough turnaround, but coach Matthews helped lead us through it."

With the Stallions now sitting with a 5–3 record and ten games to play, the Stallions were at a crossroads of their season. Shar Pourdanesh said Matthews let it be known he expected more from his team and was anything but subtle about what the consequences were if those expectations were not met. "Coach Matthews knew how to motivate a team," Pourdanesh said. "He made it clear if we weren't going to play better, he would find someone who would. It was not unusual for there to be tryouts in plain view of players already on the team."

The Stallions got the message. Baltimore won its final ten games of the regular season, easily captured the South Division regular season title by three games over the second-place Texans, and secured home field advantage in the playoffs. Players and coaches alike said getting through that hectic schedule in the middle of the season proved to them that they had what it took to dominate the rest of the way. "That was as brutal a stretch of games a team could have," Donald Hill-Eley said. "That was a lot of travel in such a short amount of time. We were fortunate to only lose two of those games during that time. It said a lot about the character of the players on the roster."

Defensive back Douglas Craft was one of those players the Stallions, who dealt with a plethora of injuries to key players during this run, brought in late in the season to help stabilize the roster for the post-season run. Craft, who played collegiately at Southern University, a Football Championship Subdivision (formally I-AA) school in Birmingham Alabama, entered the CFL in 1993 with the Calgary Stampeders. The speedy Craft, who ran a 4.3-second 40-yard dash, finished with 71 tackles and seven interceptions in 1994. That performance was good enough to earn a tryout with the NFL's Indianapolis Colts, where he was a late training camp cut, allowing him the chance to return to the CFL late in the season. The Colts' loss would be the Stallions' gain.

Craft helped fill a void left when cornerback Karl Anthony suffered a season-ending knee injury in the season opener at the BC Lions. Craft appeared in just six games for the Stallions but helped bolster the team's secondary and provided a spark in the defense down the stretch. This included his home debut, when Craft recorded five tackles, a forced fumble, and a fumble recovery in the Stallions' 43–32 victory over the Shreveport Pirates on September 23 at Memorial Stadium. He finished the season with 18 tackles, the forced fumble, and the recovery during his one season in Baltimore.

Craft wanted nothing more than to win a Grey Cup after being a part of two Stampeders teams that had great regular seasons only to come up short in the divisional finals. He believed this goal was only possible with the Stallions in Baltimore. Much like Huerta earlier in the year, Craft made his intentions known that he only wanted to be a Stallion. "When I got cut from the Colts, I had plenty of options of where to sign as a free agent in Canada," Craft said. "But I told my agent the only place I wanted to play was in Baltimore with the Stallions. You could see the talent on that team

A ticket from the Baltimore Stallions' Southern Division semifinal game in 1995. The game was held on November 4, two days before the Cleveland Browns officially announced they were moving to Baltimore (photograph by Ron Snyder).

and how they went to the Grey Cup the year before. I wanted to be a part of that playoff run."

Baltimore's playoff run began on November 4, when the Stallions cruised to a 36–21 victory over the visiting Winnipeg Blue Bombers. However, an announced crowd of just 21,040 fans—the Stallions' smallest home crowd in its entire existence—attended the game at Memorial Stadium. "I don't recall that stretch in the middle of the season being physically taxing because I was young and I just was happy to be playing football," Carter said. "Once I became established with the team and was more of a contributor, I got a sense early on that we had a roster full of players that had the ability to do something special. That loss to Memphis helped us re-focus and understand we had to regroup. That was exactly what we did and just kept winning after that straight through the playoffs."

The poor attendance figure in a home playoff game would soon be the least of the Stallions' problems as it pertained to their future in Baltimore. The Stallions soon found out that they would have little time to celebrate the fruits of their labors as they worked toward a Grey Cup victory. Very soon, their entire existence would be in doubt.

13

The Baltimore Browns?

By 1995, many people in Baltimore had given up hope that the NFL would ever return to Charm City. Between the Colts leaving, franchises like the Cardinals, Rams, and Buccaneers exploring Baltimore as an option only to go elsewhere, and the sting of losing out on expansion, many in the city were just tired of being hurt. Little did the Stallions know that another marriage between Baltimore and the NFL would soon be consummated.

Cleveland Browns owner Art Modell had been fighting with the city of Cleveland for years to help fund a new stadium to replace the outdated Cleveland Stadium, which was originally built in 1932. Modell, who partially owned the stadium, was reportedly losing millions of dollars a year by 1993 once the Cleveland Indians baseball team moved to Jacobs Field, thus eliminating one of the stadium's main tenants. While Baltimore lost out on previous NFL teams, the state kept public funding for a new stadium—to be built adjacent to Oriole Park at Camden Yards—in place just in case an existing team was interested in moving to Charm City. Negotiations had continued in secret between Modell and the state of Maryland to move his Browns to Baltimore at a time when the state had debated whether to put the stadium funding back into the state's main coffers.

News began to leak out that Modell was indeed looking to move the Browns, with Baltimore the likely destination. Mark Viviano is the sports director at WJZ-TV, the CBS affiliate in Baltimore. But in 1995, Viviano was about a year into his job as a sport reporter for WBAL-TV, the NBC affiliate in Baltimore. Prior to that, Viviano worked for a television station in Dayton, Ohio, where he reported on the Cleveland Browns.

Viviano is credited as the reporter who broke the news that the Browns were indeed moving to Baltimore. However, that scoop did not come without a lot of work, as Viviano was quite aware of the many false alarms regarding other franchises heading to Charm City in previous years. Viviano received his initial tip about the potential move on October 23, 1995, when a man called to the WBAL Sports Line radio show, where Viviano was filling in as host for that day.

"Having information like that was one thing, but trying to nail it down was nervewracking," Viviano said. "You wanted to make sure you were right with a story as big and as consequential as this. Being new to Baltimore at the time, there were plenty of people in town, including other sports reporters, who had no problem telling me that I had no idea what I was talking about. It really led to a lot of sleepless night for me, questioning whether what we had was real."

After multiple follow-up conversations with the tipster, Viviano met him at a Baltimore bar. The man told him he was a mortgage broker and one of the "money men" in Modell's plan to move to Baltimore. He showed Viviano the documents to prove his claims were legitimate. Viviano, along with WBAL-TV sports director Gerry Sandusky (currently the radio play-by-play voice of the Ravens) began working the story, even when many media members from both Baltimore and Cleveland did not believe their reporting.

> As a journalist, it's rare to have documentation like we had that offered such concrete proof that the move was happening. Usually, you have a tip and then have to try and back it up with other sources. Then, having worked in Akron and having covered the Cleveland Browns, it still shocked me that this was the team I was investigating on whether they were coming to Baltimore. This was a city whose fans backed the team, and there was such great tradition. On one hand, you're excited that Baltimore will be an NFL city again, but at the same time, your heart breaks for Cleveland and their fans.

Viviano was even chastised by both Cleveland radio hosts and the mayor of the city on one day when he called into the station to discuss the Browns' potential move to Baltimore. WBAL-TV was finally able to break the story just days before the initial announcement from the city of Baltimore and the Browns. Finally, on November 6, 1995, Modell announced his intentions to move his team to Baltimore. The team, which would soon be re-branded the Ravens, would play two years at Memorial Stadium before moving into what is now M&T Bank Stadium in downtown Baltimore. At the same time, the Browns' colors and history would remain in Cleveland, and the city would be awarded an expansion franchise—also called the Browns—in time for the 1999 season. "In reality, I think Baltimore wasn't granted an expansion team because there were owners who liked the deal so much that they wanted it for themselves," Stallions statistician Dan O'Connell said. "That's eventually what happened when the Browns announced their intentions of moving from Cleveland."

Former Maryland Stadium Authority chairman John Moag said in a 2014 interview, shortly before the 30th anniversary of the Colts leaving Baltimore, that that period in his life was as stressful as any he could remember. He understood what was at stake for all parties involved and

13. The Baltimore Browns?

wanted to make sure they could deliver in the end. "I was highly skeptical we would ever get an NFL team until I started to do my homework and learned there were a lot of owners interested in coming to Baltimore," said Moag, who served as chairman from 1995 to 1998. "We had in-depth discussions with at least four teams before honing in on the Browns. It was a very intense couple of weeks between us and Art Modell," Moag explained. "Mr. Modell was in an extremely difficult position as he had to uproot his family and leave a city he loved in order to save his team."

In a 2014 interview, longtime Ravens vice president of public and community relations Kevin Byrne said Modell's decision to move the Browns from Cleveland was not made lightly. Cleveland's decision not to fund a new football stadium—as they had for the Indians and the NBA's Cleveland Cavaliers—left Modell with few options if he wanted to keep his team.

Byrne admitted that Modell was aware of the irony that Baltimore was about to return to the NFL in the same way it was booted from it: by taking a team with a strong tradition and fan base from another city. The news of the NFL returning to Baltimore obviously generated lots of excitement and discussion. While most people were happy to be getting a new team, the feeling was not unanimous. There were still plenty of people who felt it was hypocritical to take another city's team, especially one with the popularity and history as large as the Cleveland Browns. "There were people in Baltimore who felt that we 'Irsayed' Cleveland," Byrne said in 2014. "That's why it was important for us to get out there and have Mr. Modell tell his story. That was also why we left the Browns colors and history in Cleveland and pushed to ensure they got a team again."

Viviano can attest to that. It was apparent to him that as big a story as it was for Baltimore to get an NFL team again, a segment of the population was not happy about how the city accomplished that goal. "This may have been a demographic thing at the time, but there was a segment of Baltimore that swore off the NFL after Irsay took the Colts," Viviano said. "It was quite evident, at least initially, that there were some people in town who were not happy, one that we took another city's team, and two that our CFL team was now gone because of that."

14

Left Out

The announcement of the Browns coming to Baltimore came two days after the Stallions' playoff win over the Blue Bombers and six days before the Stallions were to host the San Antonio Texans in the South Division finals, with a Grey Cup berth on the line. Chris Armstrong said he was caught off guard by the Browns coming to town. He initially did not fully grasp what that meant for the Stallions, as he hoped there would be a way for the two teams to co-exist in Baltimore, especially since there was not too much overlap in the seasons. "We never even thought about the NFL coming to town at that point," Armstrong said.

Carlos Huerta said he could not believe how Baltimore went from never getting another NFL team to returning to the league in just over a year. It was a surreal time to be a football player in the city. "Everything happened so quickly with the Browns," Huerta said. "We heard about it being a possibility, but I never imagined a team with a legacy like the Browns would move from Cleveland. I didn't believe it until it was officially announced."

Stallions general manager Jim Popp was surprised by the announcement, but not totally shocked. There had been rumblings of the possibility that Modell would move the Browns. In addition, Popp had noticed that in the run-up to the announcement, there had been unannounced improvements made to the locker room at Memorial Stadium. In hindsight, the signs were there that the Browns and the state of Maryland were laying the groundwork to move to Baltimore right in front of the Stallions' eyes.

Popp said the Stallions felt the impact from the moment the Browns made their move official. It was as if the Stallions became invisible and forgotten about from the moment the NFL announcement was made. The Browns' move left those associated with the Stallions scrambling for answers. "Unfortunately, when the Browns made the announcement official, everything dried up for us," Popp said. "The attendance dropped, the sponsorships went away, and the media attention diminished. It was all

14. Left Out

about the NFL at that point. That's where the focus was, and that of course made sense from a business decision."

Stallions running back Mike Pringle understood right away that his team's stay in Baltimore was likely over soon. Trying to reduce the tension among his teammates, Pringle took the Browns' roster, wrote their names on tape, and put them over everyone's locker nameplate except his own. The attempt at levity in the locker room helped ease the sense of confusion and uncertainty among the players. "In the end, we were a victim of our own success," Pringle said. "I think the NFL would have eventually returned to Baltimore anyway, but I'm not sure it would have been so fast if it had not been for the Stallions. I'm not sure there would have been a Ravens in 1996 had we been a mediocre team. I do believe had we been back for a third year after winning a Grey Cup, we would have had crowds of 50,000 or more."

Defensive back Irv Smith was not sure what to think. He had just saved up enough money to buy his first house when the Browns' move was announced. He was watching TV when he heard about the move on the news from the old "George Michael Sports Machine" show on WRC in Washington, D.C. Then teammates began calling him. "My phone rings, and I'm hearing about how we're likely done in Baltimore and heading back to Canada," Smith said. "I didn't want to hear that. I had no desire at that time to relocate. I mean I had just bought a house. I really thought the Stallions were there for the long haul."

Guy Earle said the news and developments were coming in so fast regarding the Browns' move to Baltimore, it was difficult to digest exactly what that would mean for his and his team's future. In a time before the Internet and cellphones, the latest on the Browns' move and the Stallions' future was slow to materialize to the players, leaving plenty of room and time for speculation and rumor-spreading. "I was just trying to make sense of everything," Earle said. "It was unfortunate that the Browns' arrival would mean there wasn't a place for us in Baltimore, but it's the NFL."

Donald Hill-Eley said there was a lot of uncertainty surrounding everyone's future in the weeks after the Browns' announcement. The coaches and players did their best not to let it be a distraction from their work on the field. "We didn't know what to expect," Hill-Eley said. "All I knew was a year earlier, it appeared Baltimore was all but out of the NFL and people in the city were ready to move on. Now a storied franchise like the Browns was relocating there, and Baltimore was ready to embrace them."

Elfrid Payton said he was not concerned about the team's future because all he could concentrate on was trying to win the Grey Cup. He also believed that regardless of what happened with the Stallions, he, along with most of the other players on the roster, would have plenty of options available to them in the off-season. Whether those options included remaining in Baltimore or in another CFL city remained to be seen. "I'm not sure I really thought the Browns were really going to move to Baltimore," Payton said. "Even if they did, I felt like there was still room in town for both teams. I also felt I had another shot at the NFL next season, so I knew whether it was there or somewhere else in the CFL, there would be options available."

Grant Carter shared a somewhat similar view. At the same time, Carter admits he may not have fully grasped the severity of the situation at the time. Carter believed that as long as the Stallions remained successful, there had to be a way to find a home for them in Baltimore, or at the very least, somewhere else in Maryland. He could not fathom a team as successful as theirs reaching an early demise. "Some of us joked about it and others really couldn't understand why both teams couldn't find a way to stay and co-exist," Carter said. "For me, I guess it was a combination of youth, ignorance at the time, and just being focused on trying to win a Grey Cup."

Bob Price said the uncertainty surrounding the team's future did not affect him much, if at all. As a veteran assistant football coach, he knew moving around a lot was a natural part of the profession. This was especially true for those who played and coached in the CFL during this era of constant franchise instability and uncertainty.

> I was oblivious to the concerns over the team's future in many ways. We were so locked into the playoff run and trying to get the team ready to play that I didn't think about it much. You also need to understand what the CFL was like at that time. I coached at Ottawa and Saskatchewan before arriving in Baltimore, and it seemed like there was always some sort of crisis surrounding some teams or the league overall. You just had to go with it and see how it would play out in the end.

Leonard "Big Wheel" Burrier said the Stallions deserved better than how they were treated after the Browns' announcement was made. He believes it was a shame how much of the media and the community turned their backs on the Stallions once the NFL was coming back to Baltimore. "The Stallions did everything that was asked of them and then some," Burrier said. "It was as if they were totally forgotten once the Browns were coming. Why did all of this have to go down while the Stallions were trying to win a Grey Cup? It wasn't right."

Bruce Cunningham, the Fox 45 sports director, disagrees about whether the NFL and CFL could have co-existed. There arguably is no greater champion of the Stallions' legacy than Cunningham. However, while he is one to wear his emotions on his sleeves, Cunningham is also a realist. As soon as it was confirmed that the Browns were coming to Baltimore, he knew that if the Stallions were going to continue to exist, it would, much to his dismay, have to be in another city. The town was just simply not big enough for two professional outdoor football leagues, and there was no doubt which team would eventually win this battle.

> There were people who wondered why there couldn't be two teams in Baltimore since they were in different leagues with different seasons. Here's the best analogy I used at the time: When there is a mom-and-pop hardware store in town and a Home Depot opens across the street, what happens to the small store? It goes away. It's the same deal with the Stallions and Ravens.

Paul Mittermeier, the Stallions' assistant director of public relations, said that when Modell and Maryland Governor Parris Glendening made the announcement that the Browns were coming to Baltimore, it was tough to digest what that meant for the CFL in Baltimore.

> It was like all of the air was let out of our balloons. The rumors about the Browns moving here were out there right in the middle of our playoff run. I knew it was over right then for the Stallions. There was no way we would be able to compete with the NFL. Understanding how the media and advertising market was for sports in Baltimore, I probably understood that better than most of those with the team.

Even given all of the confirmation of the Browns' imminent arrival in Baltimore, Mittermeier said he was not completely ready to believe that the NFL was actually coming back to town. "Given Baltimore's previous history with the NFL, I didn't believe the Browns were actually coming until I saw Art Modell on that podium with during that first press conference," Mittermeier said. "Even after that, I figured the city of Cleveland would come through with a deal for a new stadium and we would be left out yet again."

15

Final Run

For the players on the Stallions roster, their long-term future was up in the air thanks to the NFL. However, they all agreed that their short-term future was completely in their hands. That future was on the field. If the Stallions were going to be no more after the season, then at least they were going to go out as Grey Cup champions. Their goal of unfinished business continued to remain within reach, even if their future after that game was uncertain at best.

"Once word came out the NFL was coming, we kind of felt like the players in the movie 'Major League,'" Shar Pourdanesh said. "There was a part in the movie when they felt like no matter what happened, the owner was going to break up the team and move away, and they said there was only one thing left to do: 'Win the whole F----'n' thing.'"

The Stallions were ready to do just that. In their final game in Baltimore, the Stallions cruised to a 21–11 victory over the San Antonio Texans in the South Division finals before an announced crowd of 30,217 on November 12, 1995, at Memorial Stadium. The game represented the last CFL game ever played on U.S. soil.

"We couldn't control what was going on with the NFL," Tracy Ham said. "All we could control was what we did on the field. We still had that unfinished business. We were winning games every which way possible and we wanted nothing more than to erase that loss from the previous year. If we weren't going to be around next year, we wanted our last game to be a win in the Grey Cup."

Ken Watson said his only focus, at least initially, was on trying to win the Grey Cup. Everything else was out of his control at that moment. Watson and his teammates put all of their energy into ensuring the end of the 1995 season did not mimic the end of the previous season with a loss, because they likely knew they would not get a third crack at a championship together. "Right then, at that point, we had a shot at a championship," Watson said. "We just missed out the year before, and this was our opportunity to get the job done."

15. Final Run

The final CFL game played at Memorial Stadium was held on November 12, 1995 (photograph by John Patrick Kelly, from the archives of John W. Ziemann).

Josh Miller said the team entered the 1995 season with unfinished business, and nothing was going to stop them from accomplishing that goal. Miller was at peace with whatever would happen after the Grey Cup. "When the Browns announced they were coming to Baltimore, we wondered what would happen to us," Miller said. "But first we wanted to go out and win that Grey Cup."

Much like the previous season, the Stallions would face a pro–Canadian crowd as they took on the Calgary Stampeders for the Grey Cup before an announced crowd of 52,064 fans at Taylor Field in Regina, Saskatchewan. The Stampeders, like the Stallions, had rolled through the regular season with a 15–3 record. Most of Calgary's run that season came with backup quarterback Jeff Garcia under center in place of an injured Doug Flutie. A four-time CFL Most Outstanding Player, Flutie had been sidelined since August following surgery to repair a torn tendon in his throwing shoulder.

Garcia, who would go on to become a four-time Pro Bowl selection and play more than a decade in the NFL, completed 230 of 364 passes for 3,358 yards, 25 touchdowns, and seven interceptions in Flutie's absence during the 1995 season. However, Flutie returned to action five months ahead of schedule, in time to lead the Stampeders in their regular season finale and through the playoffs, a decision that set off a quarterback controversy on the team.

In the playoffs, Calgary, whose history dates back to 1935, cruised into the Grey Cup with a 30–13 victory in the North Division semifinals against the Hamilton Tiger-Cats, followed by a 37–4 rout of the Edmonton Eskimos in the North Division finals. Momentum appeared to be on the Stampeders' side heading into the Grey Cup. However, Baltimore Stallions owner Jim Speros said his team was one of destiny in that year, in that moment, and on that day. "There was so much going on and the uncertainty surrounding the future of the team, I was so proud of the way Don Matthews and the players kept their focus in their pursuit to make history and win the Grey Cup," Speros said.

Baltimore and Calgary both brought high-powered offenses to Saskatchewan for the Grey Cup. The Stallions averaged more than 30 points a game in the regular season, while the Stampeders were even more prolific at 35 points per game. However, defense and the elements would play an even greater role in the championship contest. "We weren't sure what to expect, but it was apparent the Grey Cup was going to be it for us in Baltimore," Shar Pourdanesh said. "If that was going to be our last game, than what better way to go out than to beat Doug Flutie and the Calgary Stampeders."

With temperatures well below freezing and winds stronger than 50 mph, both teams knew whoever limited their mistakes the most would come out victorious in the end. The wind that evening was so treacherous that the kickoff of the contest was delayed over concerns that some of the stands erected specifically for the Grey Cup would not be able to withstand the gusts.[1] "Many Canadians were just very bitter over the U.S. expansion and the success of the Stallions," Paul Mittermeier said.

> They did not want to see Baltimore playing for a Grey Cup title. For us, though, this game did not represent what's next for us after the season. It represented this is it. This Grey Cup was going to be our last game together, and I was going to enjoy everything about it.
>
> Regina is located in the middle of nowhere in Canada. It's just a little town with some homes here and a few more homes there. They needed to add on thousands of temporary stands to be able to accommodate the crowd, and there was concern that the winds coming through would be 80 to 100 miles per hour, which would make the conditions unsafe for the fans. In the end, they obviously went through with the game, but there was some definite concern for a few days.

Having practiced all week in Regina, the Stallions believed they were prepared to handle the elements, and their roster was constructed so that, unlike most CFL teams, they could lean on a punishing rushing attack if the winds made passing the ball too difficult on offense. They entered the game with the mindset that this could be the last game of their respective careers.

Rookie running back/return specialist Chris Wright got the Stallions on the board first with an 82-yard punt return for a touchdown just over two minutes into the game to give Baltimore a 7–0 lead.[2] Calgary responded with a pair of field goals followed by a two-yard touchdown pass from Flutie to wideout Marvin Pope to take a 13–7 lead less than a minute into the second quarter. Baltimore then took control of the game and never looked back. "We couldn't focus on the NFL," Mike Pringle said. "We had to focus on the game. That was all we had control over."

The difference came in the second quarter, when the Stallions scored four times, including field goals of 30, 45, and 53 yards by Huerta, who finished with five field goals in the game. The Stallions' defense would do the rest, holding the Stampeders to seven second-half points en route to a 37–20 victory and a historic Grey Cup championship for the Stallions and the city of Baltimore. Baltimore now had the distinction of being the lone city in professional football history to be home to an NFL Championship, a Super Bowl victory, a USFL championship, and a Grey Cup title.

"Everyone made so much out of the U.S. vs. Canada angle in the two Grey Cups we played in," Ken Watson said.

> I never really understood that. Our roster was made up of so many players and coaches who were CFL veterans. Those same players and coaches had been cheered for when they played for the Canadian teams. We were in a different city but were the same players from before. This win was retribution for the loss from the previous year. We made history and no one can ever take that away from us. We beat the top teams in the CFL, and we can always say that the Baltimore Stallions were Grey Cup champions.

Guy Earle said beating Calgary to win the Grey Cup made the team forget all about the loss last year, and at least for a moment, forget about what the future held for the franchise once they walked off the field. No one would ever be able to take away that moment and that victory from the Stallions. "That Grey Cup was something we all worked hard for, beginning the moment we lost to BC the year before," Earle said. "That win can never be taken from us."

Tracy Ham, who threw for 213 yards and rushed for a touchdown, was named the Grey Cup's Most Valuable Player. He called that victory one of the most important victories of his long, illustrious career in football, if not the most important.

Tracy Ham was named the Most Outstanding Player in the 1995 Grey Cup (photograph by John Patrick Kelly, from the archives of John W. Ziemann).

"We had so much momentum heading into the playoffs, nothing was going to distract us from our goal," Huerta said. "We could have been told we were going to play in Russia, and we still would have won the Grey Cup that year. We had a talented group of guys, but they were a team that didn't try to take the spotlight away from the team. Tracy Ham wasn't trying to steal the spotlight from Mike Pringle, and vice versa. Everyone worked together."

Defensive back Doug Craft said nothing was going to stop Baltimore from bringing home the Grey Cup on that night. He knew even then that that Grey Cup was a now or never moment for the team. "That game could have been played anywhere in the world, and I believe we would have won it," Craft said. "We understood that we could not mess this up. We had the attitude that we had to win no matter what. We dominated on offense, defense, and special teams."

Like Ham, defensive end Elfrid Payton called that Grey Cup victory the most illustrious, memorable moment of his career. He only wished the

Stallions were able to celebrate properly. "We were the only U.S. team ever to win a Grey Cup," said Payton, who was memorably pictured drinking champagne out of the Grey Cup in the locker room after the game. "It was us vs. an entire country that day. Canada never wanted us to win the Grey Cup."

16

The End in Baltimore

The Stallions were finally champions of the CFL. But once the euphoria of the victory wore off, the reality of their future set in for many before they even returned to Baltimore. It is rare in professional sports that a team that many consider to be the greatest ever in their sport is left without a home after a championship run. Yet, that is exactly what was about to happen to the Stallions. "We had one of, if not the most talented teams, in CFL history," Jim Popp said.

> We won the most games in league history and were solid on offense, defense, and special teams. However, none of that changed our focus on the field and the goal of winning a Grey Cup. We played great in every facet of the game. Then we win and come home and that was it. There were a few fans at the airport and a hastily planned event at the Inner Harbor, and we went away. There was no parade or send-off or even a goodbye.

Donald Hill-Eley felt that the way the Stallions were treated in the end was like a slap in the face from the city, the fans, and the media, given their success and outreach in the community. However, as the years and decades have passed, he knows it was nothing personal, and Baltimore had to embrace the NFL again fully. Despite its long lineage, even the most ardent CFL fan and supporter admits that their league can't compete head-to-head with the billion-dollar juggernaut that is the NFL.

> "It was a tough pill to swallow at the time," Hill-Eley said of the Stallions' end in Baltimore. Here we were, a team that always wanted to be in Baltimore, was active in the community, and won on the field. We did everything that could have been expected of us. Then the NFL comes calling again after all they put the city of Baltimore through, and the city just forgave and forgot everything from the Colts leaving to the expansion snub just like that.
>
> However, being older and wiser now, it really was an easy decision to make. We could never fully compete with the NFL. The tens of thousands of fans they could pack the stadium with each week and the millions and millions of dollars they could generate annually for the city was far more than we ever could have generated. Still, it was tough to win a championship like we did and have no one there to really celebrate with us.

16. The End in Baltimore

Bruce Cunningham, who was the public address announcer of the Ravens for two decades, was disappointed that the team never had the chance to celebrate their historic accomplishment properly. "The Stallions win the Grey Cup in dominating fashion, become the only American team to win the title, and fly home only for no one to care," Cunningham said. "Once the NFL came, it was like the Stallions didn't exist. Everyone just closed their eyes and the team went away. That is the shame of it all."

Paul Mittermeier said that as quickly as the CFL arrived in Baltimore, the team was no more just as quickly.

> It is crazy how popular the team was for two years, and within a span of just two weeks the team was gone. Once that announcement was made about the Browns moving, it was like we didn't even exist in Baltimore as far as the media and most of the fans were concerned. Everyone just got swallowed up by the Browns' move and everything that came with the NFL. It was pretty obvious that if the Stallions were going to continue, it definitely would not be able to stay in Baltimore.

Veteran sports broadcaster Mark Viviano said the media ignoring the Stallions was not as simple as the local stations and newspapers not wanting to cover the team. Instead, the NFL coming to town simply became an all-encompassing story that required much more resources than a typical sports story. Unfortunately, there was just not the time, space, or resources available to cover a CFL team that was on its way out of town.

> The media climate was a little more complicated than reporters just not covering the Stallions once the Browns announcement was made. I know I was tied up covering a lot of the legal battles and meetings that took place all over the country due to the fallout of the Browns' move. Unfortunately for the Stallions, that story just paled in comparison to them. It was not meant to be a slight against the Stallions, it was just the reality of the time. I feel bad how it was all pulled away so quickly.

Viviano said that he could relate with the emotions felt by fans in both Baltimore and Cleveland as the move took shape. Viviano was born is St. Louis and worked in Ohio and Baltimore, all areas that understand the joys of getting an NFL team and the heartache that comes with losing one. "Having grown up in St. Louis and worked in Ohio and Baltimore, my perspective on the NFL may be different than most," Viviano said. "St. Louis has lost two NFL teams in my lifetime in the Cardinals and later the Rams. Then you see how Cleveland and Baltimore both lost and gained teams again. To me it seems like moves like this are just part of doing business with the NFL."

Jim Speros initially said he would have liked to find a way for his team to co-exist in Baltimore with the NFL. But it quickly became apparent that such an arrangement would be impossible. He explored options such as moving the team to Norfolk, Virginia, and Houston, Texas, a city which was about to lose the NFL's Oilers to Tennessee. However, such an arrangement never materialized. The CFL came to the realization that expansion into the U.S. would not be viable, as the teams lost a reported $20 million combined in the 1995 season alone.[1]

The Canadian teams, most of whom had never truly been comfortable with U.S. expansion to begin with, were ready to close the book on this chapter in their league's history. The Canadian teams always had issues with the U.S. teams not being required to include a certain number of Canadian players on their roster. There were talks of eliminating the Canadian player mandate, but that never came to fruition.

Even before the Browns' move, the future of the CFL in America was tenuous at best. For one, the July to November schedule works fine in Canada, but in the U.S., teams played the first half of the season in extreme summer heat, while competing with high school, college, and NFL football down the stretch. Also, it was difficult for the American teams to configure their stadium fields to the CFL dimensions. Attendance figures reflected the struggles, as other than the Stallions, no U.S.-based CFL team averaged even 20,000 fans per game during the 1995 season.

After the Stallions (30,111 fans per game), the Birmingham Barracudas were next among U.S.-based teams in attendance at 17,625 per game, followed by the San Antonio Texans (15,855), the Shreveport Pirates (14,359) and the Memphis Mad Dogs (13,691). Basically, the CFL's U.S. experiment was over. The Canadian teams' average attendance was 24,406 fans per game that season.

"It all changed so fast," Speros said. "We became the posterchild for how to set up a CFL team in the United States. [FexEx founder] Fred Smith, who 'owned' [the city of] Memphis, thought he could mimic what we did in Baltimore. The league was using us to try and attract new owners. But once the Browns decided to move here, there just wasn't room for both of us."

Douglas Craft said he could not believe the team would not be in Baltimore to defend their newly-won championship. "I didn't think the move was going to happen," Craft said.

> How can a team win the Grey Cup and then be forced to leave their city? It's just not supposed to happen like that. Having been in business for many years now, I understand the realities of the economics now, but I was naïve to that back when I was just a player. The idea of us moving did not sink in even as we returned to Baltimore with the Grey Cup. I figured that somehow, someway, a deal was going to be reached to keep us from moving.

Grant Carter said the future of the team in Baltimore did not even enter his mind after he cleared out his locker and headed home to Oregon.

16. The End in Baltimore

He was still excited about the championship win and was ready to think ahead to next season and trying to repeat as champions. "At that point, I still thought I might be able to play my way back into the NFL or at the very least build on the success I had in the CFL that season," Carter said. "Myself and [Stallions long snapper] Rob Harris drove home from Baltimore to Oregon and just talked about the season the whole way home."

In the end, the decision of the CFL to retract back into just Canada was an easy one to make. Most of the U.S. teams were set to fold or had no place to play by 1996.[2] The Shreveport Pirates were among the least successful U.S. teams in the CFL, as they posted an 8–28 record in their existence, including 5–13 and a last-place finish in the South Division in 1995. However, the Pirates had a surprisingly fairly loyal fan base as they averaged more than 16,000 fans a game over two seasons. Still, team owner Bernard Glieberman and his son, Lonnie, had hoped to move the team to Norfolk, Virginia, after the 1995 season. But that deal fell through due to lawsuits between the Glieberman family and the city of Shreveport over debts. The team folded soon after that.

The Memphis Mad Dogs went 9–9 in their lone season and just missed out on the playoffs in 1995. Compounding their struggles was the team's inability to build a fan base, as they were competing with high school football games and University of Tennessee games in the fall, leading attendance for one late-season game to dip to 7,830. Even if the Mad Dogs had not folded after the 1995 season, they likely would not have lasted much longer, as the Houston Oilers relocated to Tennessee in 1997 and played their initial season in Memphis before moving to Nashville.

The Birmingham Barracudas faced similar issues. The Barracudas were a respectable 10–8 in the regular season and placed third in the South Division. However, the team experienced extensive drops in attendance once the college and high school football seasons began. Team owner Art Williams wanted several changes to be made if he was going to continue for another season. This included reducing the size of the field to U.S. football standards, changing the name of the league to reflect the addition of the U.S. teams, and moving the season to the spring. When none of those ideas came to fruition, Williams opted to get out of the league after the Barracudas lost in the South Division semifinals to the San Antonio Texans, 52–9. The Barracudas were to be sold with the intention of replacing the Pirates in Louisiana and with hopes of establishing a U.S.-based division centered in the southwest. However, the league rejected the sale and ordered the franchise to fold.

The San Antonio Texans suffered a similar fate despite having stable ownership in place. The Texans were successful on the field in 1995, as they went 12–6 and placed second in the South Division after moving from Sacramento. Team owner Fred Anderson believed there could be a future of the CFL in the U.S. Specifically, he was hoping to see the Stallions move to Houston and play at the Astrodome with a built-in in-state rivalry with the Texans. However, with that not a possibility and no other viable U.S. teams in place, the Texans had no choice but to fold.

"It was frustrating to see the other U.S. teams not able to gain the momentum that the Stallions had," Pete Kerzel said.

> They just could never garner the same traction or level of interest as in Baltimore. Baltimore was unique because of its football, lineage, and history, and because of the expansion fight and the fight over the Colts' name with the NFL. It would have been interesting to see what would have happened had the Stallions and other U.S. teams been able to stick around longer. I'm not sure it would have worked, but they at least deserved a shot to make it happen.

Stallions offensive lineman Neal Fort said even to this day, he believes that the CFL made the right decision in trying to expand into the U.S. While the experiment only lasted a few years, the positives from the experience outweighed the negatives. "The CFL was in trouble back then," Fort said. "There wasn't a shoe contract or an apparel deal and limited TV money. The league needed to do something to breathe new life into it. It was necessary for the CFL to try and tap into the U.S. market like the USFL or the World League tried to do, to shock the sport."

Fort said there were obvious mistakes made along the way, but the CFL also did something right that, if given some additional time, may have led to the U.S. teams surviving to this day. "Unfortunately there were some cities like Memphis and Birmingham that only had one year to build an audience," Fort said. "The facilities were there, such as the Alomodome in San Antonio and the Liberty Bowl in Memphis, the infrastructure was there. They obviously could have done a better job vetting owners, and those teams could have done a better job of trying to sell the league to those towns."

The Stallions appeared to be the only team that had the possibility to continue in some form heading into 1996. But their success on the field did not mean the Stallions did not have financial troubles of their own. According to various media reports at the time, the city of Baltimore sued Speros for $73,000 in back rent and more than $1 million for a loan and for security and traffic control services during Stallions games.[3] In the end, the city settled for just $50,000 of the $500,000 it claimed the team owed them.[4] On February 2, 1996, the CFL officially folded the U.S. franchises, including the Stallions, as the league retrenched back into Canada. However, Speros was able to remain in the league as the CFL reactivated the Montreal Alouettes, a franchise which originally played from 1946 to 1981 before being revived in 1986, only to fold a year later.

16. The End in Baltimore

"We controlled the lease to Memorial Stadium and could have contested the Ravens' ability to play there on Saturdays and Sundays for the next three years," said Speros, who did pursue legal options regarding the lease before giving up the battle. "But that was never a realistic option. We were in a no-win situation in Baltimore. If we fought the lease, we would in an instant go from being the underdog heroes to the villains who were fighting to keep the NFL out of Baltimore. We needed to negotiate an end game that was beneficial to all parties involved."

Under an agreement with the league, Speros was able to connect the new Alouettes franchise with its previous incarnations' history and records. However, the Stallions' history would not be included (although it does receive a mention in its media guides). Speros would sell the team a year later to developer and investor Robert Wetenhall, who owned the team through 2019. The team was purchased by Crawford Steel executives Sid Spiegel and Gary Stern in 2020.

> We made the CFL stronger in Canada by bringing a team back to Montreal. The Stallions' footprint on that team remains there to this day. I put everything I had into this franchise, but it was time to move on. Selling the team was part of an exit strategy for me after the move. I didn't get involved in the CFL team to own a team in Canada. I just wanted to make sure the team would have a long-term commitment from the city before I sold it.

As a result of the merger and the transition to the Alouettes, all of the Stallions' contracts were cancelled. However, Speros did convince Popp to remain as general manager, and the team was able to bring in several key players from Baltimore, including quarterback Tracy Ham, running back Mike Pringle, slotback Chris Armstrong, defensive back Irvin Smith, and defensive end Elfrid Payton.

"Heading to Montreal the next season was just the next part of a common theme in my career," Ham said. "I started at Georgia Southern in college, a school that had just brought back football after being gone for 40 years, and we' won. Then I go to Baltimore and help return a championship to a town that lost their team. Then we go to Montreal, which had a team before it folded about ten years before we got there. We tried to give Montreal the same run of success that we had in Baltimore."

The Stallions players understood the business decisions that led to their demise in Baltimore. None held any animosity toward the city of Baltimore. Still, that doesn't mean seeing the Stallions come to an end was easy for them to witness. All believed that what they accomplished on the field would help eventually sustain them in the long run. "I just missed that we never got to have a parade in downtown Baltimore," Ham said. "The fans that stuck with us deserved that."

"We couldn't survive the NFL coming to Baltimore," kicker Carlos Huerta said. "There just wasn't enough room for both teams."

Payton believed the Stallions—and CFL expansion into the U.S. in general—could have worked if given a little more time. "We had a lease in Baltimore and a great fan base," Payton said. "If we would've stayed, San Antonio would have stayed and the same for Shreveport."

Linebacker Tracy Gravely said at the end of the day, the NFL was coming back to Baltimore, and the Stallions, no matter how successful they were on the field, could not compete with that. "We might have been able to stick it out one more year in Baltimore because of our fan base, but the CFL was ready to move out of the U.S. market," Gravely said. "It was tough to leave, especially having played so close to my family in West Virginia. But the move had to be made for the good of the league and the franchise."

Tom Guy, who had spent the past two years supporting the Stallions on so many levels, was initially disappointed over the Browns' announcement. For a while, he even held out hope that the NFL and CFL could co-exist in Baltimore, even though he knew that was not going to happen.

> I was drinking the Stallions Kool-Aid for a while when Jim Speros initially said he wanted to find a way to stay. We even launched an S.O.S., or Save Our Stallions, initiative.[5] We went all in to sell season tickets for the 1996 season. Then one day not long after the Stallions won the Grey Cup, myself and others involved in the initiative stopped at the lobby and [were] told we couldn't go any further as Jim was having a press conference. We would find out shortly thereafter it was to announce the move to Montreal. In the end, that move made the decision to support the Ravens easy. Jim Speros made the decision for us.

Bonnie Downing, the community relations director for the Stallions, said that she and others on the staff figured out not long after the Browns' announcement that their days in Baltimore were numbered. This time in her life was filled with mixed emotions. "We put so much work into making the team a success, and it was tough to see everything go away so quickly," Downing said. "There was some hope that the teams could co-exist, but it was apparent Jim Speros knew it just wasn't going to work. In the end, he really had no choice but to move the team."

Talk show host Glenn Clark remembered being angry at Modell and the Browns because their arrival meant the departure of his beloved Stallions. He even took a few opportunities to make his opinions known, even if it did nothing but make him feel a little better about the situation.

> The church I went to with my parents hosted a Super Bowl party every year, and they let us come to it in costumes. I was really mad with the NFL with the Stallions leaving, and I wanted to make a statement at this party. So I took my Stallions sweatshirt and put two large pieces of duct tape on it so I could write "Save Our

16. The End in Baltimore

Many of those associated with the Baltimore Stallions took turns watching over and transporting the Grey Cup prior to the team's move to Montreal (photograph by John Patrick Kelly, from the archives of John W. Ziemann).

Stallions" on it. It was a dorky 12-year-old thing to do, but I didn't care. The Stallions were my team, and because of the NFL they were now going away.

Speros said his biggest regret in regard to the Baltimore Stallions was how quickly the team went away. Just as the perfect storm came together to make the Stallions possible, another perfect storm formed to take the team away, from the Browns' relocation to the folding of other U.S.-based CFL teams to the league's desire to retrench back to Canada. "I didn't want to pack up and relocate," Speros said. "I wanted to stay in Baltimore. Unfortunately, we just couldn't make it happen."

John Ziemann, whose Colts Marching Band would go on to become the Ravens Marching Band, was conflicted when the Browns announced they were coming to town. On the one hand, a decade of work to bring the NFL was complete, and that mission was accomplished. At the same time, the Stallions would be the ones left out in the cold through no fault of their own.

When the Browns announced they were coming to Baltimore, I was torn. I was excited that the NFL was coming back to the city, but I also understood what that meant for the Stallions. We decided as a band to wait and see how things played out, and when the Stallions opted to move to Montreal, it made things easier for us.

The Stallions were the linchpin that kept the CFL's "Great American Experiment" together. Once Baltimore folded and moved to Montreal, the U.S. expansion was not going to work. If it couldn't work in Baltimore, it was not going to work anywhere. The shame of it is the 1997 Grey Cup would likely have been played in Baltimore.

Dan O'Connell, the Stallions' statistician who was also a longtime sports information director at Towson University, said that while bringing the NFL back to Baltimore was obviously the right move for the city, he hated to see how things ended for the Stallions.

> I think what bothered me the most about the whole situation is that the Stallions were in the middle of trying to win a Grey Cup and they were completely ignored once the Browns' move was announced. It would have been nice to have let the Stallions get through their season before making the announcement.... This is a story that really needs to be told completely. It was such a unique time in Baltimore sports history.

O'Connell said that the CFL game provided a great atmosphere and really helped get the NFL back in town. "The NFL and CFL had an unwritten agreement: The NFL stays down here and the CFL stays up in Canada," O'Connell said. "I'm sure the NFL wasn't thrilled to see the CFL expand in America. Then I think the NFL got annoyed to see the Stallions being so successful in Baltimore and knew they needed to get a team back there."

Stallions television play-by-play voice Scott Garceau said the city became consumed with the Browns from the moment the announcement came out, and the Stallions quickly became an afterthought.

> It was a shame because the team had supported the city and the fans had supported the team before the NFL announcement. It was sad in some ways because there were still a group of diehards that only wanted to back the Stallions.
>
> This may have been especially true for people in the 50- to 55-year-old age range who didn't want to have anything to do with the Ravens. That group of fans did not want to embrace a team who left their city like the Colts left Baltimore. Even though there were a lot of differences between the two moves, including Cleveland getting to keep their colors and history and an expansion team being placed there just three years later, there were some fans that just felt taking the Browns was hypocritical. But in the end, most fans recognized what the team would mean for Baltimore, and the rest is history.

Leonard "Big Wheel" Burrier wanted nothing more than to find a way for the Stallions and Ravens to co-exist in Baltimore. He even lobbied state lawmakers to look for possible solutions. In the end, he knew the battle was futile. He also admitted it was hard for him to back the Ravens initially after giving his heart and soul to the Colts, Stars, and Stallions, only

16. The End in Baltimore

The Baltimore Stallions posted a 32–10 all-time record (regular and post-season) in their two years of existence (photograph by John Patrick Kelly, from the archives of John W. Ziemann).

to have the first team leave, the second team's league fold, the third team move, and the franchise be re-booted.

> I'm really sorry they couldn't find a way to make it work and keep both teams here in Baltimore. It was also tough to see us get a team from a city like Cleveland, where the stadium was packed each week, only for the city not to find a way to keep them there. Also, the Stallions provided a great product, and it was much more affordable than the NFL ever could be. The most expensive ticket for a Stallions game was $25, while it's a minimum of $90 just per ticket for an NFL game.
> It was a great ride while it lasted. I just wish the ride would have lasted a little longer. Jim Speros provided Baltimore with something the NFL wouldn't give to Baltimore for ten years. I think that if given the chance, the Baltimore Stallions would have continued to succeed and win more than one Grey Cup.

Stallions season ticket holder Rob Betz said that he was at the point by 1995 where he was willing to back the Stallions for the long haul no matter what. He had even sent the team a deposit on his 1996 season tickets when there was still a sliver of hope that the Stallions would remain in Baltimore. He still has that returned check as part of his collectibles from his two years supporting the team.

We were taken aback by the Browns' moving announcement. We believed that the NFL was done with Baltimore, and we were ready to move on and support the Stallions and the CFL. I just felt so bad for the Stallions players and others associated with the team. All season long they followed the mantra of unfinished business, and now this happened. Don't get me wrong, we were happy to see the NFL come back, but we would have loved for there to be a way for the Stallions to stay, too. I know there was talk of the team fighting the lease, but in the end, it was obvious it just wasn't plausible from a financial standpoint. The whole ending was a shame for everyone associated with the team.

It was just unfair how the Stallions were just ignored by the media and the fans the minute after the Browns' announcement was official. After everything the team did for the community and how the NFL used us, the city simply abandoned the Stallions the second the NFL came back.

17

Legacy

It is not often that a professional sports team that existed for only two seasons as part of a failed expansion effort would have much of a legacy, but that is definitely not the case for the Baltimore Stallions. Just what exactly the Stallions legacy is differs depending on whom you ask. For those in Montreal, the Stallions represent the return of championship football. The Stallions' records may not be associated with the Alouettes, but their formula for success followed them to the French-Canadian province. Under general manager Jim Popp's guidance, the Alouettes appeared in eight Grey Cups between 1996 and 2016, winning it all in 2002, 2009, and 2010. "In the end, the team moves to Montreal, takes that winning culture up there, and has won consistently since then," Bruce Cunningham said. "That's as much part of the Stallions legacy as anything else."

Kevin Sherping lives in the Montreal area and has followed the Alouettes since around 2000. He appreciates the legacy of the Stallions and is grateful they were able to bring their winning formula to Canada and did not suffer a fate similar to the other U.S. franchises. "I still remember that press conference where the team owners and Jim Popp came to Montreal with the Stallions' Grey Cup in 1996,"[1] Sherping said. "I said, 'What championship team is moving here?' I've been a season ticket holder for the Alouettes for eight years now. The ten years that the team was not here, football was non-existent in Montreal. Now, it's booming."

Mike Rogers is another Canadian who looks back fondly on the Stallions and the U.S. expansion by the CFL in general. He understands why some people in his country did not like the expansion experiment, but he thinks it helped the league in the long-run. "The CFL is like the little engine that could," Rogers said. "It goes through its ups and downs, but always finds a way to survive in the end.

> I think the U.S. expansion had the chance to be successful, but it wasn't handled properly, and they picked the wrong cities and owners with the exception of Baltimore. The league was in trouble back then and they needed the cash infusion from

the expansion fees, I get that, but they still needed to find the right owners. The CFL has a following, but it has to compete against so much, especially in Toronto, where there's hockey with the Maple Leafs and the Raptors in the NBA and the Blue Jays in baseball.

I am a proud Canadian, but I thought the U.S. expansion was awesome. It was impressive what Baltimore accomplished. Their accomplishments are still recognized today as they are the only CFL team to win 18 games in a season. Montreal, which has struggled recently, also had a great run for a lot of years because of the Stallions moving here.

Four of those Grey Cup appearances by Montreal came in 2002, 2003, 2005, and 2006, during a five-year run when Popp was reunited with former Stallions coach Don Matthews. "The opportunities we provided people were amazing," Jim Speros said. "What we were a part of was so special."

Matthews won 231 games as a CFL head coach, the second-highest win total in league history through the 2018 season. He was inducted into the CFL Hall of Fame in 2011 before passing away following a five-year battle with cancer on June 14, 2017, at the age of 77.[2] "Don and I had great balance," Popp said. "I understood him and he understood me. Don was always a coach who wanted experienced CFL guys and not necessarily players right out of college. He was able to change in that regard and we grew together. We trusted one another. That didn't mean that we didn't battle from time to time, but there was nothing but respect between the two of us. That was evident in Baltimore and the years we spent in Montreal together."

Paul Mittermeier said that in his nearly 30 years in the sports media industry in the Baltimore area, not too many people have impressed him more with their job performances than Matthews and Popp. Their track record both while with Baltimore and in the years since then only verifies his assessment.

> The CFL is a unique league. Say what you want about Jim Speros, good, bad or indifferent, but he absolutely picked the two most perfect people to be the head coach and general manager in Don Matthews and Jim Popp. Both of them were simply outstanding men and amazing at their jobs. Matthews was as good of a coach as I've ever seen, and Popp has an incredible eye for evaluating talent. I'm simply amazed that Jim Popp never had the opportunity to be a general manager in the NFL because his track record over decades in the CFL is as impressive as they come.

The Stallions also proved to be the launching pad for many players, coaches, and executives who went on to long and illustrious careers after leaving Baltimore. Along with Matthews, quarterback Tracy Ham, running back Mike Pringle, and defensive end Elfrid Payton were also

17. Legacy

inducted into the CFL Hall of Fame. Others had very successful—albeit not Hall of Fame—careers in the CFL and/or the Arena Football League.

"Think about how good our team was [in Baltimore]," Popp said.

> Wayne Chrebet had a great tryout for us, but was just not the type of receiver we were looking for at the time. He was too small and not fast enough for what we needed in 1994. He goes to sign with the Jets and had a great NFL career. Then we had Joe Horn, who was every bit as good of a DB as he was a receiver, and he never even got on the field for us. He was another player who would go on to have an All-Pro career in the NFL.

Ham, who played his final four seasons with the Alouettes before retiring after the 1999 season, finished his career completing 2,670 of 4,943 pass attempts for 40,534 yards (seventh all-time in CFL history through 2018) and 284 touchdowns. He also rushed for 8,043 yards (10th all-time, second among quarterbacks) and 62 touchdowns. Ham, who was inducted into the CFL Hall of Fame in 2010, is also a member of the College Football Hall of Fame, which inducted him in 2007. "I'm proud of the legacy of our team in the CFL," Ham said. "You can't write the history of Baltimore football without including a chapter on the Baltimore Stallions. It was just a special time in my career. We were there just two years, but fans still bring that up to me to this day even 25 years later. It's just amazing. It was a short ride, but it was a great ride while it lasted."

Pringle arrived in Baltimore having carried the ball just 82 times for less than 500 yards in his first two CFL seasons. He was not even initially Baltimore's starting running back before taking over that role in game three of the 1994 season. However, Pringle became arguably the greatest player in CFL history. After being cut late in training camp by the NFL's Denver Broncos in 1996, Pringle signed with the Alouettes, where he played the next seven seasons while helping lead the team to the Grey Cup title in 2002. His 1998 season is considered among the best in league history when he rushed for a record 2,065 yards and tied the CFL record with 2,414 yards from scrimmage.

Pringle played his final two seasons with the Edmonton Eskimos, with whom he won another Grey Cup in 2003. He then signed a one-day contract with Montreal in 2005 so he could retire as an Alouette. The running back entered 2018 as the CFL's all-time leader in rushing yards (16,425) and yards from scrimmage (20,254). He also is tied for most career touchdowns with 137. "Going to back-to-back Grey Cups was amazing, but the Ravens announcement definitely put a damper on that second year in Baltimore," Pringle said. "Our legacy in Baltimore and even in the CFL remains to this day. We brought that same culture and winning approach to Montreal, and they experienced the same success we had in Baltimore."

Mike Pringle rushed for 1,972 and 1,791 yards in his two seasons with the Stallions (photograph by John Patrick Kelly, from the archives of John W. Ziemann).

Slotback Chris Armstrong was part of that winning culture. Armstrong played three seasons with the Alouettes and two more with the Winnipeg Blue Bombers before retiring after the 1999 season. He finished his career with 449 receptions for 8,104 yards and 69 touchdowns. Armstrong's best season was in 1994 with Baltimore, with 72 catches good for 1,586 yards and 18 touchdowns. He eventually settled in Maryland, where he remains active in football as the head coach of Loch Raven High School, in Baltimore County.

> Even after the Browns announced they were coming, we stayed focused on the goal at hand, and that was bringing a Grey Cup home to Baltimore. To say we were able to do that was an amazing accomplishment. I really believe that we were the greatest team in CFL history.
>
> I don't bring up my playing career much with my players, but I use the lessons I learned from that time with them. It is special, though, when their parents recognize who I am and thank me for the memories created with the Stallions. Mr. Speros also did a great job making sure we were engaged in the community. We were always out at the schools, or the community centers or wherever we were needed to help make a difference.

17. Legacy

Like Pringle, Elfrid Payton received another shot at the NFL. But just like Pringle, Payton's run in the NFL would be short-lived as he was cut by the New Orleans Saints in 1996. He played four seasons with the Alouettes, where he would be named an All-Star each year from 1997 to 1999. He also played for the Winnipeg Blue Bombers (2000, 2004), Toronto Argonauts (2001), and Edmonton Eskimos (2002–2003), winning a Grey Cup there in 2003.

Payton retired following the 2004 season after playing in 189 regular season games and recording 154 sacks, which through 2018 was the second-most in CFL history. Payton was inducted with Ham in the 2010 class of the CFL Hall of Fame. Today, Payton is likely more well-known for being the father of NBA player Elfrid Payton, Jr., who played for the Orlando Magic (2014–2018) and Phoenix Suns (2018) before signing with the New Orleans Pelicans prior to the 2018–2019 season. "After winning the Grey Cup in Baltimore, I knew I'd get a shot again at the NFL," the elder Payton said. "I was disappointed when I got cut by the Saints, but knew I could go back to the CFL. I just wish it had been in Baltimore. If we had stuck around, the Grey Cup would have stayed south of the border for years. We were that good."

Defensive back Irv Smith eventually had second thoughts about playing in Canada. He played six more seasons with the Alouettes, where he was named a CFL All-Star in 1996 and 2000. He retired after the 2001 season. Smith still lives in Maryland, where through 2018 he was a lieutenant for the Montgomery County Fire and Rescue Service. "I wish we had been able to stay in Baltimore," Smith said. "But I had a great experience in Montreal. We helped rebuild a football legacy in that city too. It's like a second home to me. I try to get up there a few times each year."

Defensive backs Ken Watson and Doug Craft and linebacker Tracy Gravely also followed the former Stallions franchise to Montreal, and all three went on to play several more productive seasons in the CFL. Watson spent the 1996 and 1997 seasons in Montreal before playing the 1999 season with the Toronto Argonauts and in 2000 with the Edmonton Eskimos. He finished his career with 371 tackles and 15 interceptions. He entered 2018 as the safeties coach for Miles College, an NCAA Division II school in Alabama, a role he has held for seven seasons.

"I really thought the CFL had a chance to succeed in the U.S.," Watson said.

> I enjoyed the chance to play in my home state when the Stallions played the Birmingham Barracudas. That was such an enjoyable time in my career. It was a special team and one that will likely never come around again. At that time, we were able to bring football back to a city that desperately wanted it. Over two years, we were No. 1 in attendance, No. 1 in wins, went to two Grey Cups, and won one of

them. Despite how it all ended, Baltimore was great to us, and it is a time in my life that I will never forget.

In many ways, I believe we could have played against some NFL teams. We were an all-American team and had so many players that would go on to get a shot with the NFL. Whether it was on offense, defense or special teams, we were a team that could dominate in any facet of the game.

I ran into Joe Horn several years ago at a camp we both attended and joked with him about his time with the Stallions. The inability of players like him and Wayne Chrebet to stay with us did not have anything to do with their talent. It had everything to do with the makeup of our roster and the players that we had. The fact that NFL-caliber players could not make our team says so much of just how much talent was on that roster.

Gravely played six more seasons with the Alouettes. He had his best season in 1996, when he recorded 110 tackles and two interceptions en route to being named a CFL East All-Star and All-CFL selection that season. He retired after the 2001 season and finished his career with 591 tackles and 10 interceptions. Entering 2018, Gravely was in his eighth season as the cornerbacks coach at Concord University, an NCAA Division II school in Athens, West Virginia, his alma mater. "We set the standard for greatness in the CFL with the Stallions," Gravely said. "We may have only been around for two years, but left a mark that will be felt for a long time."

Craft split much of his career between the CFL and serving as an active duty member of the U.S. Army. He played four more seasons, including three with the Alouettes (1996–1998), before playing his final season in 1999 with the Saskatchewan Roughriders. He finished his career with 321 tackles and 21 interceptions. Entering 2018, Watson lived in New Mexico, where he is director, president, and general manager of operations for Crystal Clear Maintenance Inc.

> It wasn't until we went up to Montreal officially that it all sunk in for me. It was that time that we truly became a full Canadian Football League team. We were now required to have a certain number of Canadian-born players, which meant there was no way to keep the whole team together. A lot went to Montreal and others followed Don Matthews to Toronto. It was a tough year or two.
>
> In the end, the legacy of the Baltimore Stallions begins with the Grey Cup. They accomplished something unique being the only U.S.-based team to advance to and win the Grey Cup. The fact that so many players went on to have great careers after the Stallions is great, but none of that would have mattered in the larger scope of history had we not won the Grey Cup that year. I'm so proud to have been a member of that championship team. I still wear the ring to business meetings. It's a great conversation starter. I'm so proud to say I never lost a game as a member of the Baltimore Stallions.
>
> Had we not won the Grey Cup, we would have been just like the Sacramento Gold Miners, the Las Vegas Posse, the Memphis Mad Dogs, the Shreveport Pirates, and the San Antonio Texans. They were expansion teams that came, stayed around

for a few years, and then went away. They were nothing more than a footnote in CFL history. We will go down as one of the great teams in CFL history.

Rush end Grant Carter had his best CFL season in 1996 after following the Stallions to Montreal. That year, Carter had a career-high 15 sacks to go along with 39 tackles and two fumble recoveries for the Alouettes. Carter played in the CFL until 2000, which also included stops with the Winnipeg Blue (Bombers 1997–1998, 1999) and the Edmonton Eskimos (1999–2000).

> Leaving Baltimore was tough, but I felt like that first season in Montreal was an extension of what we did in 1995, even if the whole team wasn't with us. Once we lost in the playoffs in 1996, I felt the Stallions were officially over because so many players would go their separate ways after that. I loved Montreal and even met my future wife during that time, but I'll never forget that magical run in Baltimore. What we accomplished was historic, and that can never be taken away.

Offensive lineman Neal Fort also followed many former Stallions to play for the new Alouettes. He stayed with Montreal through 2004, where he was named a CFL East All Star in 1996, 1997, and 2003, and a CFL All-Star in 1997. Fort also won another Grey Cup when the Alouettes captured the title in 2002. "I enjoyed my time in Montreal, but a piece of my heart will always be in Baltimore," Fort said.

> Those two years with the Colts/Stallions were two years of bliss. I just wish it could have lasted longer because who knows what we may have been able to accomplish. But, you could see some of what was possible when we moved to Montreal and brought a lot of our core with us. We would average around a 12–6 record for years thanks to many of those players and the leadership that was in place from Baltimore. Those years in Baltimore were so quick, but so enjoyable and helped make so much success possible for myself and others later in life.

John and Guy Earle would be among those who took another shot at the NFL. John Earle signed with the St. Louis Rams, while Guy Earle signed with the Houston Oilers. Neither made it through the season with their respective NFL teams. However, Guy Earle returned to the CFL and played two more seasons with the Winnipeg Blue Bombers from 1996 to 1997. "The coaches in Winnipeg told me the offensive line we had in Baltimore was simply one of the greatest in CFL history, and that was one reason they wanted to sign me," Guy Earle said.

The Earle brothers were then at a crossroads in their careers and decided to follow their hearts by becoming church pastors. Guy Earle is now the executive pastor at Gracepointe Church in Corinth, Texas. John Earle is the pastor of students at First Colleyville Church in Colleyville, Texas. "Winnipeg wanted to re-sign me after the 1997 season," Guy Earle said.

> They wanted to lock me up with a five-year deal. But at that point I had a lot more to think about. If I signed a long-term deal, I knew that I would be giving up any shot I had of playing in the NFL again. However, I also wondered if I even wanted to play football anymore. I had recently gotten married and needed to think about what I wanted to do with the rest of my life. I was getting tired of football and needed a new path. This led me to the church and the ability to give back to my community on a daily basis.

Along with their individual church responsibilities, the Earle brothers also formed Think Twice Ministries.[3] Together, they make dozens of visits a year to schools, jails, and prisons with the hope of helping people make positive changes in their lives. "I had to think about what path I wanted to take," John Earle said. "We had so many players with contracts that were up and there was so much initial confusion about the team's future after the Browns' announcement. I knew I didn't want to go to Montreal and so I took another shot at the NFL with the St. Louis Rams. After that, it was time for a change."

Guy and John Earle said that even through it has been 25 years since they played for the Stallions, the effect that time had on them will remain with them for the rest of his lives. Each believes it was the purest, most enjoyable football experience they ever had. "I spent two years in the NFL and four years playing college football, and without a doubt, the most enjoyable time I ever had playing football was when I was with the Baltimore Stallions," Guy Earle said. "That was a special time with a special group of players."

> What we accomplished was unique and something that could only have happened at that particular time as a confluence of so many events came together at once. Baltimore was the perfect city for us to play in. They were cast off by the NFL and were looking for a team to call their own. Many of us were cast off as players by the NFL and were looking for the same thing as the fans. Much of what I learned from football I try to apply toward my ministry work. I even make sure to wear my Grey Cup ring to show that hard work and teamwork and a positive attitude in life can bring you success.

John Earle added: "We take so much pride in that Grey Cup ring. That cup has been around for 100 years and it's special to know that we're a part of that history. I still wear that ring and show it to young people we speak to. We also talk about the loss from the year before and how it is possible to overcome adversity no matter what is thrown in your path in life."

Stallions backup quarterback Dan Crowley lasted another eight seasons in the CFL after his run in Baltimore. He followed the Stallions to Montreal and spent the 1996 season with the Alouettes before playing with the Edmonton Eskimos (1999–2001) and the Ottawa Renegades (2002–2003). With the Renegades, Crowley received his first opportunity to be a starting quarterback, and he will go down in history as the franchise's first signal-caller. In 2002, Crowley completed 223 of 454 passes for 2,697 yards, with 16 touchdowns and 19 interceptions.

Crowley also spent two seasons with the Bergamo Lions in the Italian Football Federation. He led the Lions to back-to-back championships in 1998 and 1999 and was named the championship game's Most Valuable Player each time. For his CFL career, Crowley completed 402 of 816 passes for 4,933 yards, with 29 touchdowns and 40 interceptions. After retiring from football, Crowley returned to Towson, where he currently works as the senior associate director of athletics, development.

> I was concentrating solely on the playoff run toward the Grey Cup at the time. Then we get back home, have the celebration at the Inner Harbor, and go back to Memorial Stadium to clean out our lockers. I think that is when everything kind of hit me that we might not be back here ever. Life is often about opportunities. Playing for the Stallions opened opportunities for me and showed me and others I had the ability to play in the CFL and was blessed to play several more years. Some of my best friends today were members of that team.

The Stallions benefited not only the CFL, but the NFL as well. Several former Stallions parlayed their years in Baltimore into lucrative NFL contracts. Most notable from this group were linebacker O. J. Brigance, offensive lineman Shar Pourdanesh, and punter Josh Miller. Brigance played seven seasons in the NFL for the Miami Dolphins (1996–99), Baltimore Ravens (2000), St. Louis Rams (2001–2002), and New England Patriots (2002). In his lone year with the Ravens, Brigance finished second on the team with 25 special teams tackles and led the team with ten special teams tackles in the post-season. The Ravens routed the New York Giants, 34–7, in Super Bowl XXXV that season, making Brigance the only player in football history to win a Super Bowl and a Grey Cup with teams in the same city.

Following his playing career, Brigance became the director of player development for the Ravens. Brigance eventually was diagnosed with amyotrophic lateral sclerosis, better known as ALS, or Lou Gehrig's disease, in 2007. He continues to fight the disease and raise money for research through his Brigance Brigade Foundation. Brigance said in a 2007 interview that he was upset about the team leaving but that it ended up being a blessing in disguise. He spent seven seasons in the NFL, including winning a Super Bowl ring with the Ravens in 2001. "I'll never forget my years with the Stallions," Brigance said. "The fans were so great, and to this day, I still get birthday cards from fans who followed the team."

Grant Carter said Brigance's fondness for his CFL days was on full display even after the Ravens won the Super Bowl. Carter was in the stands at Raymond James Stadium to watch the Ravens' championship

Linebacker O. J. Brigance is the only player in football history to win a Grey Cup and a Super Bowl with a team in the same city (photograph by John Patrick Kelly, from the archives of John W. Ziemann).

victory, one of the most lopsided games in Super Bowl history. Carter was invited to a post-game party by Brigance.

"So I'm in the post-game party thanks to O. J. and he meets up with me for a few minutes," Carter said. "Remember, he just won the Super Bowl, a dream all football players have. Once he sees me, all he wants to talk about is about that 1995 Grey Cup win. For just about all of us, that season was the most enjoyable and fun time we ever had playing football. There was just something truly special about that team."

Pourdanesh did not need to move far after the Stallions left town. He was lucky enough to sign with the NFL's Washington Redskins, who play about an hour south of Baltimore. The first Iranian to play in the NFL, Pourdanesh played for the Redskins from 1996 to 1998, followed by stops with the Steelers (1999–2000) and the Oakland Raiders (2001), before a severe knee injury forced him into retirement. Pourdanesh would later find success in the business world before returning to football a few years ago to serve as an assistant coach on his sons' high school team in California.

17. Legacy

Shar Pourdanesh, far right, was among the many players who parlayed a career with the Stallions into a career in the NFL (photograph by John Patrick Kelly, from the archives of John W. Ziemann)

> We were just a group of guys who believed in each other and worked toward a common goal. It was the most enjoyable time of my football career. I cherish my time with the Stallions much like you would with your college football team. The affection I have for that team, those players and Baltimore will never be diminished. The team just knew how to put a roster together. Jim Popp had a great eye for talent, and Don Matthews was as good a coach as there was. He made sure we had faith in ourselves and each other.

Kicker Carlos Huerta would receive opportunities to play for the NFL's Chicago Bears and St. Louis Rams in 1996 before kicking for the Florida Bobcats (1998) and the San Jose SaberCats (1999–2001) in the Arena Football League and the Toronto Argonauts. He said nothing compared to his experience with the Stallions.

> That team was the most finely-tuned, well coached, well-run organization that I ever played with. It was the most enjoyable experience in my career. They just understood how to run an organization. You saw that continue when they moved to Montreal. They simply had the best players, the best coach, and the best front office.
> I had the chance to play in the NFL and AFL after the Stallions and I hated it. Not because of the leagues, but because you could see how the organizations

were run compared to how the Stallions did it, and there was no comparison. Don Matthews and Jim Popp just understood how to run a winning football team. The results speak for themselves.

Long snapper Rob Davis played in the NFL for 11 seasons. After leaving Baltimore, Davis signed with the Kansas City Chiefs, but was cut before the season started. He was picked up by the Chicago Bears and played all 16 games as the team's long snapper. The following season, he signed with the Green Bay Packers, where he spent the next ten years, playing in the Super Bowl in his first season with them. He retired after 2007 and spent the next nine years as the team's director of player engagement. In 2017, Davis left the Packers for a position with Pierce Manufacturing.

"Special teams are so important in the CFL game," Grant Carter said. "Because of the three downs and other dynamics of the game, special teams can change the complexion of the game so quickly. That's why it's easy to see how players like Rob Davis and Josh Miller would go on to have long, successful NFL careers."

Like Davis, Miller experienced a lot of success in the NFL after leaving Baltimore. He was set to join his former teammates in Montreal—and even started to learn French—in 1996 only to have his contract purchased by the NFL's Seattle Seahawks. Seattle cut him before the season, but he signed with the Pittsburgh Steelers later that year and played with the Ravens' chief rival until 2003. Miller then signed with the New England Patriots from 2004–2006, winning a Super Bowl ring in his first season with the team. Finally, he played parts of two seasons with the Tennessee Titans before retiring in 2008. After playing, Miller's endeavors included serving as a radio and TV analyst for KDKA-FM and KDKA-TV in Pittsburgh.

> "I've had to do a lot of great things in my life, including winning a Super Bowl and play 14 years in the NFL. But I can tell you without a shadow of a doubt I never enjoyed playing football more than my two years in Baltimore. It all started with Don Matthews. He treated the locker room like men," Miller continued. "He let them do whatever the hell they wanted to as long as they performed on the field. If you didn't perform, he didn't hesitate to replace you. It was crazy sometimes with linemen who would literally be laying on the sideline with their helmet as a pillow. But, when the whistle blew, they were ready to play."

Even Matthews's assistant coaches went on to have long careers after the Stallions moved. Most of those coaches are still active in the sport in some capacity today. Offensive coordinator Steve Buratto took similar roles with the BC Lions (2003–2004) and Toronto Argonauts (2007–2008). He also took over as head coach for the Lions in 2001, where he went 9–15 over 1½ seasons before being fired after a 1–5 start in 2002. He last coached as offensive coordinator/associate head coach for the University of British Columbia from 2015 to 2017.

17. Legacy 141

Price followed the Stallions to Montreal and was the first coach of the new Alouettes. The team went 12–6 and placed second in the East Division before losing in the division finals in Price's lone season at the helm. Price moved on to the University of Virginia, where he served as running backs coach (1997–1999), defensive backs coach (2000–2004), and tight ends coach/recruiting coordinator (2005–2009) before becoming the team's football administrator in 2010, a position he still had through 2018.

Edralin would continue as a linebackers coach/special teams coordinator for the next decade throughout the CFL, where he first joined Matthews with the Toronto Argonauts (1996–1999), followed by the Hamilton Tiger-Cats (2004–2005) and finally serving as assistant coach with the Alouettes from 2005 to 2006. He now teaches in Toronto.

Bob Price stated:

> We all knew we would be split up in the end. Me taking over as coach in Montreal happened really fast. Don had made the decision to go to Toronto and coach the Argonauts. I was single at the time and was excited about the opportunity to go to Montreal. It's a beautiful city, and I was glad we were able to take a core group of players to Montreal. I wasn't worried about where we were going. I just wanted to know what the plans were and wanted to find a way to be a part of them.

Price said that at the end of the day, the Stallions' legacy was simply about winning. "We had the best running back, the best quarterback, the best punter, the biggest offensive line, and a defense that would just attack teams from the opening kickoff to the final whistle. We made history in our short time together. What we accomplished was simply phenomenal."

Defensive line coach Marty Long returned to the college game after the 1995 season. He has remained in the college ranks for more than 20 years, serving as defensive line coach at the University of Arizona (1996–2003), the University of Nevada (2004–2006), and Northwestern University, where he began in 2007 and remained entering the 2020 season.

Like Long, Donald Hill-Eley returned to college football. He first worked as the offensive coordinator and pro liaison at Hampton University (1997–2000). During that time, he helped the Pirates win an HBCU National Championship, two Mid-Eastern Athletic Conference titles, and a win in the 1999 Heritage Bowl. Hill-Eley then returned to Baltimore, where he became offensive coordinator at Morgan State University. After one season in that role, he was promoted to head coach at Morgan State, a position he held for the next dozen years. Over that span, Hill-Eley was named 2002 Mid-Eastern Athletic Conference Coach of the Year and won 59 games with the Bears, which ranks third-most in school history.

Following his time at Morgan State, Hill-Eley spent one season as receivers coach and associate head coach at Norfolk State before being hired as receivers coach at Alabama State in 2015. In 2017, Alabama State named Hill-Eley its interim head coach after the team started the season 0–5. The Hornets responded by winning five of their final six games, a performance good enough for the school to remove the interim tag following the season.

Hill-Eley uses a lot of the lessons he learned from Matthews and the rest of the coaching staff during his time in the CFL with the Stallions in his coaching today.

> There are some things I saw from Coach Matthews and others on the staff that I liked, and other things that I didn't like. Coach Matthews looked for players that were not only great on the field, but engaged in the community. That is something that is important to me. I also learned a lot about how the weather can factor into decision-making. I still think back to how we took wind conditions into play when making decisions about whether to kick or receive to start the game and which end zone to defend. Those years were very valuable to me in helping me become the coach that I am today.

Popp said the success of the Stallions players tells only part of the story about how strong the organization was built. He also stressed that there were players who went on to the NFL who were not able to make Baltimore's roster, while other players found expanded roles in the NFL after seeing limited playing time with the Stallions.

> To understand how good that 1995 Stallions team was, consider this: typically a CFL team will have three or four players a year get a shot at the NFL. That team had 16 players get signed in some way by the NFL heading into 1996. Some went on to have solid careers like Shar Pourdanesh, Josh Miller, and of course, O. J. Brigance. Others didn't work out as well, and some of those were able to rejoin us in Montreal. Much of that core wanted to stay together and build what we had started in Baltimore. It wasn't the Stallions, but their impact can be felt there.

Among those players whose careers didn't pan out was wide receiver/return specialist Chris Wright. Arguably, no player on the 1995 Stallions roster had the ability to break a game open with a single play more than Wright did. Wright was a rookie in 1995 when he broke the CFL record for punt-return yardage by a rookie with 1,236. Wright, who played collegiately at Georgia Southern—much like Ham did a decade earlier—ran back 41 kickoffs for 897 yards, giving him 2,133 in total return yardage. That mark eclipsed the rookie record of 2,202 yards held by Henry "Gizmo" Williams of the Edmonton Eskimos. For his efforts, Wright that season was awarded the Frank M. Gibson Trophy, given annually to the most outstanding player in the South Division.

Wright was another of the players who moved with the Stallions to Montreal, but he never reached the same level of success he did in Baltimore. He missed the entire 1996 season after suffering a knee injury on

17. Legacy

the first day of training camp. In 1997, Wright bounced back to finish with 1,088 yards on 52 kickoff returns and 769 yards with two touchdowns on 84 punt returns for the Alouettes. Wright finished with 671 yards on 31 kickoffs and 625 yards on 67 punt returns, but no touchdowns for Montreal in 1998. The Alouettes released Wright in 1999. He resurfaced briefly in 2002, when he appeared in seven games for the BC Lions. Wright died on July 31, 2005, murdered in a shooting in Atlanta, Georgia. He was just 32 years old. "Chris Wright was a great kid," former Stallions director of public relations Mike Gathagan said. "It was so sad that he tore his ACL. He would have been in the NFL in 1997, and his life would have been so different. Maybe if that had happened, he wouldn't have been killed."

Popp stressed that even though nearly 25 years have passed since the Stallions' demise, the team's impact can be found throughout all of the major professional sports leagues in North America. There are public relations officials, team executives, and others who got their start in some capacity in this industry working for the Stallions. "The legacy of the Stallions goes beyond the players," Popp said. "Look around the PR departments and front offices of sports teams in all of the major sports league and you'll find people who started with us as interns with the Stallions. Paul DePodesta, the chief strategy officer with the Browns, was an intern for us. The legacy of the Stallions is still being felt 25 years later and will be felt for years to come after that."

Stallions statistician Dan O'Connell said the Baltimore team understood that and were just so good in every facet of the game. "The CFL game was so fast," O'Connell said. "They could just run right through teams. I loved Tracy Ham from his time at Georgia Southern. He and the other CFL veterans on the team laid the foundation for what Don Matthews wanted to accomplish."

Pete Kerzel was amazed at just how many players associated with the Stallions received a shot at the NFL even years after the team folded. For years after the Stallions' run, he continued to keep a close eye on the players from that roster as they continued to pursue their dreams.

> For the longest time after the Stallions left, I would look at the transaction wires to see if I saw names of players from the Stallions. To many, that two-year run was the highlight of their careers with everything they went through and experienced together. Still, while they enjoyed their time in the CFL, the ultimate goal for most of them was trying to make it in the NFL. It was very cool to see just how many players at least received a shot with the NFL because of what they accomplished here in Baltimore with the Stallions.

To others, the Stallions' legacy is a little more abstract. Ziemann said the Stallions filled an important void left when the Colts left Baltimore and showed the world that Baltimore was a football town. In addition, the

Stallions taught a large cross-section of local fans—many of whom had no memories of the Colts outside of faded visions of moving trucks leaving town—how to support a football team. "The CFL team showed a younger generation how to love the Colts and football again," Ziemann said.

> We lost a generation of fans after the Colts left. Those in their teens and 20s never knew what it felt like to support a football team. The CFL gave us hope. We still had the Colts Marching Band, the Colts Corals, and the Colts alumni in town. Without the support the team got from the alumni, I'm not sure it would have worked like it did. Most of us thought the NFL was never coming back to Baltimore. The Stallions' legacy in Baltimore is that they helped prepare us for the NFL. They kept the fire burning for professional football in Baltimore. The NFL saw what we accomplished in just two years and knew they would be successful here in Baltimore again.

Stallions supporter Tom Guy said that the team filled a void that had been left open far too long after the Colts left.

> The players were blue collar like us and reminded us of the Colts of old. Their post-game meals were Papa John's pizza and Popeye's chicken. There were plenty of times my wife and I would have dinner outside the stadium with the players. It's hard to have that kind of connection in today's day and age given the huge contracts the players sign. There is a disconnect with the players and fans today compared to the players back then.

Others associated with the Stallions believe the success the team had in Baltimore played a role in the NFL coming back as quickly as it did after denying the city an expansion team. "We did too good of a job here in Baltimore," Armstrong said.

> The NFL saw how Baltimore embraced us and the success we had both on and off the field, and saw that they could be successful here. There's nothing really to be upset about in that regard. We all know that sports, including football, are a business. It was a great opportunity for the Browns, the NFL, and the city. Of course we all wish we could have continued here in Baltimore, but it just wasn't in the cards once the Ravens were coming. The city just could not support two teams.

Pringle said that the Stallions were simply a victim of their own success. "The team management, especially [Speros], did a great job marketing the team," Pringle said. "In the end, they probably did too good a job, and it would be a detriment to our future. When they saw our crowds, the NFL knew this was a city that would support a team."

Ham said that when the NFL decided to come back to Baltimore, it was the right move for them. The Stallions had showed everyone how great a football town Baltimore can be. "The NFL probably should have come to Baltimore during expansion, but I guess they wanted to enter new markets," Ham said. "We were disappointed in not being able to stay

17. Legacy

in Baltimore, but we felt like winning the Grey Cup was our gift to the city for supporting us the way they did. We helped bridge the gap for the city from the Colts to the Ravens."

Pourdanesh said the Stallions' formation was the result of ideal timing at a unique point in sports history. The combination of the CFL expansion, the NFL overlooking Baltimore, the baseball strike and a fan base starving for football all played a role in the birth of the team.

> The Stallions were the product of a perfect storm and perfect timing. Had Baltimore not lost out on expansion, we never would have been there. Had the World League not folded, we likely would not have been there. Had the strike not had occurred in baseball, we likely would not have gotten as much media attention as we did. I'm not sure the Stallions would have worked in any other time but that one.

Pourdanesh said the Stallions' legacy is as much about the opportunities the team provided as anything they accomplished on the field. Much of the success those associated with the team experienced later in life can be directly linked to being a part of the Stallions.

> I love the NFL and had a good career in the NFL, but they would not have come back to Baltimore when they did without seeing what we accomplished in the CFL. The Stallions have a great legacy on the field. They were the only team to win 18 games in a season, the only US team to win the Grey Cup, and won the championship in just their second year in existence. But the Stallions' greatest legacy may be what happened after the Grey Cup.
>
> The legacy will be the opportunities so many players received because of their time in Baltimore. Just as Coach Buratto promised, I was in the NFL the next season. Players like O. J. Brigance and Josh Miller went on to the NFL and won Super Bowl rings. Mike Pringle, who was traded by Sacramento just a few years earlier, went on to become arguably the greatest player in CFL history. Tracy Ham, Don Matthews, and Elfrid Payton are also in the CFL Hall of Fame, and Jim Popp became the greatest general manager in league history. That's the legacy of the Baltimore Stallions.

Stallions season ticket holder Rob Betz said the team's legacy is one that benefited two cities, two professional football leagues, and two countries. Along with their playing a factor in helping lure the Ravens to Baltimore, Betz believes the Stallions helped stabilize the CFL during a time when the league's long-term future and viability was very much in doubt.

> Despite the teams' overall lack of success, I believe the U.S. expansion saved the CFL. Did you see the excitement and passion from the Canadian fans when they were worried that the Grey Cup was going to be in the U.S.? Those Grey Cups were packed full of fans cheering on their teams and their country and gave them a greater appreciation for the CFL.
>
> I think with the right owners in place in the right cities, the U.S. expansion would have worked. If the Stallions had had a third year in Baltimore, they would

have started to turn a profit. Look what happened when the team moved to Montreal. Their success continued for much of the next 15 years, and they were among the most successful teams in the CFL during that run. The expansion fees paid by those U.S. teams also helped keep many of the existing team afloat.

Betz said he and many other diehard Stallions fans adopted the Alouettes as their new CFL team once they moved to Montreal. Betz, his wife, and others from Baltimore have made the trek to Canada to watch the Alouettes and even attended the Grey Cup on a few occasions. At the same time, Betz' interest has waned once the final players associated with the Stallions moved on and/or retired.

> We still viewed Montreal as our team even if the history wasn't recognized. There would be no football in Montreal had the Stallions not existed and succeeded. It was great to see the success many of the old Stallions continued to have in the CFL. We went to a game one year in Montreal, and Neal Fort saw us in the stands and invited us down to the sidelines. Not long after that, Don Matthews, who was back as the coach for the Alouettes, invited us back to the locker room. Once we get back there, Matthews pulls out a Molson and we talked for 35 to 45 minutes. I can't imagine that ever happening with fans of an NFL team.

Cunningham said much more factored in the Browns' decision to move to Baltimore than the success of the Stallions. However, he believes the NFL took notice of what the Stallions accomplished in their brief history.

> In the end, the fact that Maryland had a stadium funding in place for whichever team came to town was the biggest factor for the NFL returning. At the same time, boosters for Baltimore's bid to lure a team here pointed to what the Stallions were doing. The NFL didn't want the CFL taking away shares of its markets, even if it was a very small share. Still, the Stallions will always have a unique place in Baltimore football history.

As ardent a fan of the Stallions as anyone, talk show host Glenn Clark agrees with Cunningham's assessment of the team. However, he added that that should not take away from the Stallions' contributions while they were in Baltimore.

> Look, those outside of Baltimore will look at the U.S. experiment and laugh about how it was a total failure. In many cities, that is absolutely the case. But that wasn't the case in Baltimore. Unlike the USFL, the CFL in Baltimore never tried to compete with the NFL. They weren't trying to be something they weren't. They just tried to put a good, affordable product on the field that the fans could enjoy on a weekly basis. For the time they were here, the Stallions were a highly successful team and were very popular. They helped reignite the passion for football in a city that never should have been left behind in the first place.
>
> What occurred here in Baltimore I don't see working in any other city that lost an NFL team. If the CFL were to decide to expand again and plop a team in San Diego or Oakland, I don't think anyone there would care. Baltimore had such a

fervor for football and they were just excited to have a team, any team, to call their own. It was simply an incredible two-year run for football in Baltimore.

Sportscaster Mark Viviano said the Stallions played a small, but important role in Baltimore's sports landscape during their brief existence. In many ways, they helped legitimize Baltimore as a major league sports town.

> When I got to Baltimore, my first live shot was at the CFL team's first-ever game against the Calgary Stampeders at Memorial Stadium in 1994. Initially this led me to second-guess my initial impressions of Baltimore. This was a city that had no NFL team, was about to lose baseball for the season to the strike, and the only professional team playing was with the Canadian Football League. It was definitely a transitional period in sports for Baltimore.

Viviano admits it was fun covering the Stallions, whom he called a group of players simply trying to make a decent living doing what they loved to do: play football.

> Covering the Stallions was unique. Unlike professional sports leagues today, they were open to anything from a media perspective. The players were dedicated, and in many ways outcast, who were following their football dreams of playing in the NFL one day. The practice field they worked out on across the street from Memorial Stadium was an old high school field, and it was sketchy at best. It was a far cry from the facilities you would see the Ravens or any other NFL team play on today. But they didn't care. These players were just happy to be playing football and were appreciative of the opportunity presented to them. You had nothing but respect for players working hard in pursuit of their goals.

Viviano added that as the city transitioned from the Stallions to the Ravens and moved from Memorial Stadium to what is now M&T Bank Stadium, it was enjoyable to keep track of how the former CFL players were doing, especially Miller, Brigance, and Pourdanesh, who returned as bona fide NFL players. "Once we started the covering Ravens, it was fun to see when former Stallions would come into town with their NFL team. We also tried to follow up with them to see how they were doing in the CFL. It was great to see the success many of them experienced after leaving Baltimore."

Kerzel said that the Stallions left a complicated legacy. The team helped heal both Baltimore and Montreal, which both felt the sting of losing their previous teams. The Stallions also helped make the dreams of many people associated with it become a reality.

> As soon as the Stallions started building momentum toward the future, they were gone. But they definitely left their mark. In the end, the Stallions provided the NFL with the message the "Give Baltimore the Ball" game could not, and that was [gi]ving to the powers that be sustained proof that Baltimore could support an NFL football team again.

I mean attracting 40,000 fans to a CFL game in Baltimore had to make people take notice. Of course the Stallions were not the same thing as when the old Colts were in town, but it was cool to see Memorial Stadium packed with rabid football fans again. They energized the city at a time that it was desperately needed. Even 25 years later, those fans that experienced that run are forever appreciative of what the players on those teams meant to them and the city of Baltimore. In some respect, the same is true for Montreal. Had there never been a Baltimore Stallions team, the Montreal Alouettes would never have been reborn.

Reporter Roch Kubatko said that just because the Stallions only lasted two years in town, it does not mean they did not leave a lasting impression. The success on the field the team experienced only added to the team's legacy in the decades that followed.

> There's no way that the CFL would have survived if Baltimore had an NFL team. It was a very fickle love affair [between Baltimore and the Stallions]. [It was] sort of like dating someone on the rebound. But it filled a craving for a couple of years, and it had been a long time since fans could support a winning football team. It really helped that the CFLers/Stallions went to the Grey Cup twice and won a championship. And with an owner that fans actually liked and respected instead of someone who wasn't shopping the team and giving drunken press conferences.

To understand that even 25 years later, the Baltimore Stallions may be gone, but not forgotten, one only needs to meet Zach Wolpoff. Wolpoff, who is from Potomac, Maryland, was just 23 years old in 2018 and was born the year the Stallions won the Grey Cup. Still, he has been fascinated by the story of the Baltimore Stallions and is not shy about educating others, including many of his friends who never even knew Baltimore once had a CFL team. "When I got bored at school, at a computer lab or at home, I would go down a Wikipedia wormhole about sports and more sports teams and players," Wolpoff said. "That is what brought me to the CFL USA [expansion] and the Stallions."

Wolpoff has even educated Canadians about this history of their own league. "So when I was in Montreal for the Red Sox-Blue Jays exhibition [baseball] games, we got a tour of the Big Owe as part of the Red Sox tour," said Wolpoff, referring to a tour of Olympic Stadium, the former home of the Alouettes.

> When we were on the tour, the tour guide talked about the Alouettes, and he said they were an expansion team that came in 1996. I jumped on that as fast as I could and corrected him. He tried to refute it and I said, "Then why did Jim Speros, a Maryland businessman, speak broken French at the press conference when the team moved? And why was Mike Pringle and Tracey Ham on the team?" He then corrected the story, and all the Red Sox fans on the tour looked at me puzzled, like "Why does this kid know anything about the CFL?"
>
> As a 23-year-old, I never got a chance to see the Stallions live in person. However, I am still a big fan of the story, and I have a solid collection growing of

17. Legacy 149

Stallions/Grey Cup memorabilia. I had a picture of Jim Speros riding in on the white colt into Memorial Stadium above my bed in my dorm. It gave me motivation to get things done.

Mittermeier said that the story and legacy of the Stallions is as unique as it comes in Baltimore sports. The Stallions' two-year run included everything one looks for in a powerful sports story: conflict, overcoming adversity, community engagement, athleticism, drama, the thrill of victory, the agony of defeat, and leaving the fans wanting more. It is the wanting more aspect that still upsets Mittermeier in regard to the demise of the Stallions.

> The Stallions went to the Grey Cup their first year and won it all in their second year. What more can you ask of a team than that? It was tough to see what happened to the team in the end. That is part of the team's legacy. But just as big is how many players and others with the team went on the play in the NFL or have long CFL careers. This was all made possible by the Stallions. It is amazing that we are still talking about this team 25 years after they are gone. It was a short ride, but it was an incredible ride while it lasted for the Baltimore Stallions.

18

Postscript

In the years that followed the Stallions leaving Baltimore, much would change regarding the city's sports landscape. The Ravens came to town in 1996, and while they are fully engrained in the community today, it did not come without a lot of work. The former Cleveland Browns arrived in Baltimore without a local history, a team name, or even uniforms. The team wouldn't settle on the name Ravens until later in the year and after they had drafted left tackle Jonathan Ogden and linebacker Ray Lewis in the first round, considered the greatest first-round draft of any team in NFL history. Both players went on to be first-ballot Hall of Famers: Ogden in 2013 and Lewis in 2018.

In fact, while Baltimore was excited about the Ravens from the outset, the team was not necessarily an easy sell. There were many games in their first two years at Memorial Stadium where there were just as many fans of the opposing team as fans of the Ravens. This was especially true early on, when the Ravens' chief rival, the Pittsburgh Steelers, came to town. "We had to learn how to sell our Steeler games and not to sell to ZIP codes that weren't friendly," said Ravens vice president of public and community relations Kevin Byrne in a 2014 interview, stressing that the team has sold out every game since arriving in Baltimore. "That was remarkable to us. Obviously that is not the case anymore."

Much like the Stallions had done a few years prior, the Ravens followed a similar blueprint and worked to ensure they had the blessings and support of the former Baltimore Colts in town. The Ravens also brought the old Colts Marching Band into the fold, a relationship that continues to this day. The Ravens even took the music from the original Baltimore Colts fight song and created updated lyrics to be used by the present-day marching band and fans. Soon, the Ravens would take over the city of Baltimore much like the Colts did during their heyday in town. Names like Lewis, Ogden, Ed Reed, Joe Flacco, and Terrell Suggs mean as much to Baltimore fans today as Johnny Unitas, Lenny More, Art Donovan, and John Mackey meant to the older fans.

18. Postscript

As time passed and the Ravens went on to win two Super Bowls and advance to the AFC Championship game two other times, the memory of the Stallions continued to fade. Fewer and fewer fans today remember what the Stallions did for Baltimore, and even fewer can remember what life was like without the NFL in town. Many cannot comprehend that the city once embraced a CFL team. But there are still plenty of people in town who remember the Stallions and remain appreciative of what the players did for the city during their two years of existence. After years of regret over not giving the team a proper championship celebration or goodbye, the opportunity to rectify the past finally came around on July 26, 2015. On that date, a reunion was held at the West Village Commons Building at Towson University, organized in part with the help of quarterback Dan Crowley. "Baltimore will always be a part of my life," Jim Popp said. "It is the city that gave me my big break. It is where I met my wife, who is from there. It is where I made friends that last to this day."

Community relations director Bonnie Downing was among those who helped organize the reunion. She felt it was the right way to finally celebrate the Grey Cup victory that had been ignored and forgotten for too long. "We captured lightning in a bottle back in 1994," she said. "I'm not sure what we did in that short time could have been accomplished in any other time. Especially in that first season, the fans came out and bought tickets. Then to go to the Grey Cup twice and win it all in 1995 was special."

Paul Mittermeier said that the CFL itself and the team in Baltimore were intriguing, and the players associated with the Stallions had epitomized that. "A guy like O. J. Brigance was a superstar in the CFL and went on to play great in the NFL," Mittermeier said. "Then you had players like Elfrid Payton, who played his college football in the SWAC. He couldn't quite make it in the NFL, but he was an absolute stud in the CFL. It was players like that that made the Stallions special during their time in Baltimore."

In all, 20 former Stallions players, along with team owner Jim Speros, coaches, front office personnel, and even cheerleaders were in attendance at the reunion. "We never got to say thank you," Speros said.

> We were forced to leave so abruptly. There was no closure. The team and the fans associated with the Stallions deserved that. That 1995 team will go down as one of, if not the greatest team in CFL history. They are the only team in league history to win 18 games and the only U.S.-based team to win the Grey Cup. All of this was accomplished in just two years. No matter what happens in the future, you can't look at the Grey Cup without seeing the inscription of the Baltimore Stallions' name on it. No one can ever take that away from us.

Among those in attendance at the reunion were Popp, receivers coach Donald Hill-Eley, defensive end Elfrid Payton, quarterback Tracy

Ham, slotback Chris Armstrong, running back Mike Pringle, linebacker O. J. Brigance, offensive tackle Shar Pourdanesh, punter Josh Miller, kicker Carlos Huerta, receiver Mark Orlando, defensive back Irv Smith, and Crowley. "It was a wonderful day to get together with so many friends and former teammates," Smith said. "It was a good way to close that chapter on our lives and celebrate the championship in Baltimore in ways were weren't able to do 20 years ago."

Armstrong said that the reunion represented a special day to get everyone together and let the fans thank the Stallions one more time. "We were just together as a team for two years in Baltimore, but the bonds and friendships we created in that time will last for the rest of our lives," Armstrong said. "We were able to bridge the gap in football between the Colts and the Ravens. We helped bring football back to Baltimore and the NFL, and the rest of the world took notice. This city became my home, and I will never forget what it meant to be a Baltimore Stallion."

For Ham and Pringle, the reunion was a surreal moment. It was hard to believe how much time had passed, yet there were still so many people who appreciated what the Stallions meant to Baltimore over their two-year existence. "To reconnect like that was special and to see that fans hadn't forgotten meant a lot," Ham said of the reunion. "The chapter may have ended for those in Baltimore, but it will never close for those on the team. We will be connected through that experience for the rest of our lives."

"The reunion was the coolest thing ever," Pringle said. "It brought back so many memories and helped reconnect so many bonds that had been formed during that time. I'll never forget my time in Baltimore and what it meant to be a Stallion."

Huerta said gathering with fellow members of the 1995 Grey Cup champion team again brought a smile to his face. He said that he was glad to see how well all his old teammates and coaches appeared to be doing in the years since leaving Baltimore. "The reunion was amazing," Huerta said. "We re-connected like no time had passed. It was great to see that those that were there were legitimately happy. Everyone appeared to have experienced some sort of success after the Stallions.

"I think the only miserable days I had in Baltimore was the three games we lost that season [in 1995]," Huerta said. "It was just a special season. We still have an affection for Baltimore. We thought seriously about moving back when I was setting up my business. We opted not to for business reasons, but we have nothing but great memories of our year in Baltimore."

Pourdanesh agreed. For him, the reunion was like jumping into a time machine. Yes, the players may have been a little greyer and possibly a little heavier, but it felt like 1995 all over again for him.

18. Postscript

The reunion was beautiful. I was so glad to be able to meet up again with a group of guys I loved so much. It seemed like just two days went by, not 20 years, since the Grey Cup when we met. There wasn't a single awkward moment and a chance to reflect on those years in our lives. I was also glad to see just how well everyone was doing. We all have a lot to be thankful for and much of it would not have been possible without the Stallions.

Hill-Eley said he enjoyed the opportunity to re-connect with so many of his former players. The reunion helped bring back to the forefront the contributions the Stallions made to Baltimore's football history, contributions he believes may be lost on those Ravens fans who were not around during those years. "I'm so glad I had the opportunity to go to the reunion to commemorate the 20th anniversary of our Grey Cup win," Hill-Eley said. "We were all a little greyer and move a little slower, but for the most part, everyone looked great. The Stallions were a small chapter in Baltimore's sports history, but I think we're a memorable one."

Stallions defensive coordinator Bob Price said what the Baltimore team accomplished will never be replicated, and after going to the reunion, he was glad to see the team's story and legacy has held up over time. "I want the Stallions to be remembered for the champions we were," Price said in regard to the team's legacy. "We did things the right way right from the beginning. Jim Speros was a magnetic personality who cared about the game, the team and bringing championship football back to Baltimore. We accomplished all of that and more in just two short years. That time in Baltimore remains a special time for me in my career and in my life."

Former Baltimore receiver Walter Wilson was happy to reconnect with former teammates at the reunion after being upset he never got to come back and win the Grey Cup with the Stallions. After being released by the Stallions, Wilson was signed by the Memphis Mad Dogs. He had just 14 catches for 165 yards and a touchdown in seven games with the Mad Dogs before leaving the team. Wilson soured on the CFL after playing for the Mad Dogs, whose coach, Pepper Rodgers, made his dislike of the rule differences between the Canadian and U.S games known. Rodgers was especially frustrated at having just three downs compared to four and made his disdain known right from the beginning. It was a mindset like that by people in charge that added to the troubles of making the CFL work in U.S. cities outside of Baltimore, Wilson said. "I knew Baltimore was going to win the Grey Cup in 1995," Wilson said. "The team was that good. Still it was great to remember my time with the team when they held the reunion. Once you build a bond and camaraderie like we had, it stays with you for the rest of your life."

Rob Betz and his wife, Marie, were among the select number of fans who were able to attend the reunion. For him, the event was a time to reflect on a fun, simpler period in their lives. He was also glad that many of the players were able to return to the city where all of their success began.

> The Stallions deserved more than they got in the end, but this reunion was a nice way to rectify that. It would have been nice to have had more fans able to attend and personally thank the team for all of the great memories. The Ravens have been great and the Super Bowls have been awesome, but we just wish it hadn't come at the expense of the Stallions. We'll always be thankful for how Jim Speros and the Stallions brought professional football back to Baltimore.

Miller said that while more than 20 years had passed, his memories with the Stallions remain as fresh as if they were yesterday. He remains friends with many of his former teammates. Renewed interest in the Stallions since the 20th anniversary of the Grey Cup championship, along with the growth of social media, has also helped players and coaches reconnect with one another and with those who supported them so many years ago.

> I didn't know anything about Tracy Ham before signing with Baltimore, but he became like a brother and was definitely a leader on the team. The reunion was amazing. It was great to get together under positive circumstances and celebrate that time we spent together. For all of us, there was no more enjoyable time playing football than when we were with the Stallions. Those are memories I will never forget.
>
> In the end of the day, Baltimore is an NFL city and they deserve to have an NFL team. I just hope that we were able to be that Band-Aid for a few short years that helped fill the void left when the Colts left town.

Appendix A: All-Time Results

1994[1]

Baltimore 28, Toronto Argonauts 20 (July 7): Quarterback Tracy Ham threw for 260 yards and two touchdowns to slotback Chris Armstrong while kicker Donald Igwebuike booted four field goals of 49, 41, 40, and 37 yards, as Baltimore (1–0) won its inaugural CFL game in front of 13,101 fans at SkyDome (now the Rodgers Centre). Halfback Charles Anthony stopped Toronto's Bobby Gordon inside the Baltimore 5-yard line in the final minute to secure the victory for the visiting team.

Baltimore 16, Calgary Stampeders 42 (July 16): Visiting Calgary outscored Baltimore 20–0 in the fourth quarter to break open a close game and ruin the host team's home opener before an announced crowd of 39,247 fans at Memorial Stadium. Stampeders quarterback Doug Flutie, a Manchester, Maryland native, passed for 284 yards and two touchdowns and rushed for an additional 82 yards and a score in the win. Also for Calgary, Pee Wee Smith had a 57-yard punt return for a touchdown, while Tony Smith scored on a 5-yard touchdown run. Running back Mike Pringle had 197 all-purpose yards, and kicker Donald Igwebuike booted three field goals of 13, 16, and 21 yards for Baltimore (1–1), which trailed just 22–16 after three quarters.

Baltimore 40, Shreveport Pirates 24 (July 23): Eight players caught passes and host Baltimore recovered four fumbles in a convincing rebound win in front of an announced crowd of 31,172 at Memorial Stadium. Quarterback Tracy Ham completed 22 of 35 passes for 320 yards and three touchdowns, and ran five times for an additional 47 yards and a score for Baltimore (2–1). Defensive tackle Robert Presbury contributed three sacks for Baltimore, which outscored Shreveport, 28–14, in the second half. For the Pirates, Terrence Jones had a 1-yard touchdown run and connected on a 33-yard touchdown pass to David Lucas, while Tom Muecke came through with a 35-yard scoring pass to Tony Moss.

Baltimore 32, Winnipeg Blue Bombers 39 (July 28): Winnipeg rallied from a 25–10 deficit in the third quarter to move into a first-place tie with Baltimore in the Eastern Division. Winnipeg quarterback Matt Dunigan passed for 435 yards and four touchdowns, with 312 yards and three touchdowns in the second half alone, to lead the comeback in front of 22,398 fans at Winnipeg

Stadium. Slotback Gerald Wilcox caught 11 passes for 146 yards and two scores for Winnipeg. Baltimore quarterback Tracy Ham threw for 288 yards and a pair of touchdown, and kicker Donald Igwebuike had field goals of 27, 30, and 42 yards, in defeat. Baltimore dropped to 2–2 with the loss.

Baltimore 38, Las Vegas Posse 33 (August 6): Cornerback Irvin Smith tackled wide receiver Curtis Mayfield at the 2-yard line with just more than a minute left in the game as visiting Baltimore (3–2) held off the Posse before just 10,122 at Sam Boyd Stadium. Baltimore led, 15–3, after the first quarter before Las Vegas rallied to take a 33–31 lead following a late field goal by Carlos Huerta. Baltimore answered with the game-winning, 6-yard touchdown run by quarterback Tracy Ham. Ham, who fought off food poisoning during the game, threw for 307 yards and a pair of touchdowns and rushed for a season-high 93 yards for Baltimore. Matt Goodwin scored on an 11-yard blocked punt return, and kicker Donald Igwebuike connected on field goals of 17, 11, and 33 yards in the win.

Baltimore 30, Hamilton Tiger-Cats 15 (August 10): A well-balanced Baltimore attack racked up nearly 600 yards in total offense while the defense did the rest in front of an announced crowd of 37,231 at Memorial Stadium. Tracy Ham threw for 442 yards, slotback Chris Armstrong caught seven passes for 224 yards and two scores, and running back Mike Pringle rushed for 172 yards in the win for host Baltimore (4–2). The Tiger-Cats were held to just two first-half points. The victory represented the 100th career win for Baltimore head coach Don Matthews. Tim Rosenbach had a five-yard touchdown pass to Joey Jauch, and kicker Paul Osbaldiston connected on field goals of 40, 48, and 37 yards in the loss for the Tiger-Cats.

Baltimore 24, Toronto Argonauts 31 (August 20): Baltimore fell behind 27–10 in the fourth quarter, and a late rally fell short in front of 41,155 spectators at Memorial Stadium. Toronto all-purpose back Mike "Pinball" Clemmons rushed for 120 yards and two touchdowns and threw for another score for the Argonauts. Baltimore (4–3) tried to mount a comeback in the fourth quarter as backup quarterback John Congemi, who came in for an injured Tracy Ham, connected on touchdown throws of 62 and 32 yards to Joe Washington and Chris Armstrong, respectively. However, the score by Armstrong would be the last points for Baltimore.

Baltimore 28, Hamilton Tiger-Cats 17 (August 27): Newly acquired rush end Elfrid Payton, who had been released by the Shreveport Pirates, had five tackles, a sack, a forced fumble, and a fumble recovery as visiting Baltimore rebounded in front of an announced crowd of 15,227 at Ivor Wynne Stadium. Donald Igwebuike booted field goals of 16, 21, and 27 yards, and Tracy Ham came off the bench to connect on a 20-yard touchdown pass to running back Mike Pringle for Baltimore (5–3), which outscored Hamilton, 11–0, in the fourth quarter. Sheldon Canley scored a touchdown on a seven-yard run after a blocked punt in the win for Baltimore. Timm Rosenbach scored on a nine-yard run, and Paul Osbaldiston connected on field goals of 37, 25, and 19 yards for the Tiger-Cats.

Baltimore 28, Shreveport Pirates 16 (September 3): Mike Pringle rushed for 232 yards, which included an 83-yard touchdown run, as visiting Baltimore (6–3) won its second straight game before an announced crowd of 16,332 at

Independence Stadium in Louisiana. Baltimore's defense held tough throughout, especially in the first half when they kept the Pirates off the scoreboard. The win also came with third-string quarterback Shawn Jones, who threw a five-yard touchdown pass to Mike Alexander, leading the offense. Donald Igwebuike connected on field goals of 47, 10, 9, and 18 yards for Baltimore, who at one point led, 21–0. Baltimore's victory represented their second straight win. Robert Cobb threw a 17-yard touchdown pass to Charles Thompson, and Martin Patton had a one-yard run for the Pirates.

Baltimore 29, Sacramento Gold Miners 30 (September 10): Roman Anderson connected on a 47-yard field goal as time expired to give the visiting Gold Miners the victory before a crowd of 42,116 at Memorial Stadium. Baltimore (6–4), which trailed by 11 points at one point, rallied to take a 28–27 lead after Tracy Ham connected on a 14-yard touchdown pass to Chris Armstrong with less than four minutes remaining. Baltimore had a chance to secure the win, but Donald Igwebuike slipped on a 21-yard field goal try and had to settle for a single. Seven plays later, Anderson's kick clinched the win for Sacramento. Quarterback David Archer threw touchdown passes of 24 and 10 yards to Troy Mills and a 32-yard passing score to Rod Harris in the win. The crowd represented the largest of the season, and eventually the largest in franchise history, for Baltimore.

Baltimore 35, Saskatchewan Roughriders 18 (September 18): Peter Tuipulotu caught seven passes for 124 yards and a touchdown, Mike Pringle rushed for 173 yards and two touchdowns, and Chris Armstrong had an 83-yard touchdown reception as visiting Baltimore (7–4) rebounded after a tough loss to win in front of an announced crowd of 28,035 at Taylor Field. Leading just 18–15 at halftime, Baltimore put the game out of reach in the second half as they outscored the Roughriders, 17–3, over the final 30 minutes. Baltimore finished the game with 571 yards of net offense, while its defense held the Roughriders to just 215 yards themselves. Tom Burgess had touchdown passes of 24 and 10 yards to Mike Saunders for the Roughriders.

Baltimore 42, Ottawa Rough Riders 27 (September 25): Matt Goodwin blocked two punts and returned them 39 and 30 yards for touchdowns as Baltimore (8–4) won its second straight game in front of 20,764 fans at Frank Clair Stadium. Mike Pringle rushed for 176 yards and a touchdown, Charlie Baumann connected on field goals of 45, 37, 33, and 41 yards, and Tracy Ham connected with a 12-yard touchdown pass to Chris Armstrong for Baltimore, which improved to 8–4 with the win. Michael Richardson had two 1-yard touchdown runs for Ottawa.

Baltimore 40, Ottawa Rough Riders 13 (October 1): Baltimore clinched a playoff berth, the first for the city since 1977, as it defeated Ottawa for the second straight week before 36,187 fans at Memorial Stadium. Baltimore took command of this game in the second and third quarters, when it outscored Ottawa, 26–0. Donald Igwebuike connected on field goals of 49, 41, 42, and 36 yards, while Mike Pringle rushed for 114 yards and two touchdowns in the win for Baltimore (9–4). Horace Brooks had a two-yard touchdown, run and Terry Baker had a field goal of 31 yards for Ottawa.

Baltimore 22, Las Vegas Posse 16 (October 7): Baltimore clinched a home playoff game with a hard-fought win before 34,186 fans at Memorial Stadium. Mike Pringle rushed for 133 yards, his fourth straight 100-yard rushing game, and Chris Armstrong had an 18-yard touchdown reception—his 14th of the season—to lead Baltimore. Tracy Ham added touchdown passes of 18 and 22 yards, and Donald Igwebuike booted field goals of 28 and 33 yards for Baltimore (10–4), which extended its win streak to four straight games. Carlos Huerta had field goals of 24, 42, and 52 yards, and Jon Volpe had a one-yard touchdown run for the Posse.

Baltimore 24, Edmonton Eskimos 31 (October 16): Edmonton, the defending Grey Cup champions, jumped out to an early 21–3 lead before holding off a late Baltimore (10–5) rally before 31,918 fans at Commonwealth Stadium. Eskimos wide receiver Eddie Brown scored three touchdowns—two receiving, one on a 92-yard punt return—while Edmonton's defense held Mike Pringle to 32 yards and two touchdowns on 14 carries. Chris Armstrong paced his team's offense with 151 receiving yards, while Donald Igwebuike booted field goals on 47, 35, and 41 yards in the loss.

Baltimore 48, BC Lions 31 (October 22): Tracy Ham threw four touchdown passes to four different receivers as Baltimore (11–5) bounced back in a big way in front of 35,416 fans at Memorial Stadium. Mike Pringle returned to form as he rushed for 216 yards and a touchdown. Baltimore, which rolled up nearly 500 yards of total offense, also got touchdown receptions from Pringle, Robert Drummond, Chris Armstrong, and Walter Wilson. Alvin Walton paced Baltimore's special teams with five tackles.

Baltimore 57, Winnipeg Blue Bombers 10 (October 29): In its most dominating win of the regular season, Baltimore jumped out to a 37–0 lead before cruising in its home finale over the Blue Bombers in front of 39,417 fans at Memorial Stadium.

Mike Pringle rushed for 209 yards and two touchdowns, and in the process set the CFL records for yards rushing and yards from scrimmage in a season. Tracy Ham connected on touchdown passes of 14, 16, and 44 yards to Chris Armstrong, while Donald Igwebuike booted field goals of 23, 23, 50, 50, and 8 yards for Baltimore (12–5). Baltimore racked up 585 yards of total offense while its defense allowed just 189 yards to Winnipeg.

Baltimore 0, Sacramento Gold Miners 18 (November 5): Baltimore failed to clinch the Eastern Division title and home field advantage throughout the playoffs after a tough loss before 14,056 fans at Hornet Field in Sacramento. Roman Anderson booted field goals of 38 and 35 yards, and Troy Mills scored on a 12-yard run for the Gold Miners, who held Baltimore to 107 yards of total offense. Mike Pringle, who needed 99 yards to reach the 2,000-yard mark for the season, finished with just 71 yards on the ground in the loss. Baltimore, shut out for the only time this season, finished the regular season 12–6, in second place in the Eastern Division.

Post-Season

Baltimore 34, Toronto Argonauts 15 (November 12): Baltimore jumped out to a 20–10 halftime lead and never looked back, winning the team's first-ever playoff game in the Eastern Division semifinals before 35,223 fans at Memorial Stadium. Trailing 10–3 in the second quarter, Baltimore reeled off 27 unanswered points to put the game out of reach. Robert Drummond, filling in for an injured Mike Pringle, rushed for 111 yards and two touchdowns to lead Baltimore. Tracy Ham connected with two touchdown passes to Chris Armstrong—a 20-yard strike in the second quarter and a 16-yard score in the fourth quarter. Defensively, Baltimore did the job as they held Argonauts all-purpose back Mike "Pinball" Clemmons to just 64 yards.

Baltimore 14, Winnipeg Blue Bombers 12 (November 20): Donald Igwebuike booted a 54-yard field goal under windy conditions with 3:20 remaining to help visiting Baltimore rally and win the Eastern Division finals before 25,067 fans at Winnipeg Stadium. Defense was key for Baltimore, which held the Blue Bombers' vaunted offense to just 171 yards of total offense. Cornerback Karl Anthony, who returned a fumble recovery for a touchdown in the first quarter, also had an interception and two pass knockdowns in the win as Baltimore advanced to the Grey Cup in its inaugural season.

Baltimore 23, BC Lions 26 (November 27): Lui Passaglia's 38-yard field goal as time expired was the difference as the Lions upset Baltimore to win the Grey Cup before 55,097 fans at BC Place. Baltimore led for much of the game, eventually holding a 20–10 advantage in the third quarter after a 26-yard field goal by Donald Igwebuike. However, the Lions, who lost to Baltimore 48–31 in the regular season, slowly chipped away at the lead with backup quarterback Danny McMannus scoring on a 1-yard run and Passaglia connecting on field goals of 42 and 27 yards before the championship-clinching kick. Passaglia's final field goal came after Igwebuike tied the game at 23–23 late in the fourth quarter. Cornerback Karl Anthony had an interception and scored a 36-yard touchdown when he and Alvin Walton worked a lateral in the first quarter for Baltimore.

1995

Stallions 34, BC Lions 37 (June 30): In a rematch of the previous season's Grey Cup, the host Lions once again edged Baltimore, in front of 23,999 paying customers at BC Place Stadium. The Lions took control of the game early as they jumped out to a 14–3 lead after the first quarter. The Stallions (0–1), who were playing their first game with their new nickname, eventually rallied to tie the game at 27–27 heading into the fourth quarter, only to come up short in the end.

Stallions 50, San Antonio Texans 24 (July 8): A 24-point second quarter was the difference as Baltimore rolled to an easy win in its home opener against the Texans before 31,016 fans at Memorial Stadium. Tracy Ham completed 17 of 25 passes for 233 yards and two touchdowns, Mike Pringle rushed for 99 yards, and rookie wide receiver/return specialist Chris Wright had a 69-yard punt return for a score to pace the Stallions (1–1). Defensively, the Stallions were led by linebacker O. J. Brigance, who had seven tackles, while rush end Elfrid Payton finished with three sacks and a fumble recovery in the win. San Antonio quarterback David Archer threw for 348 yards for the Texans.

Stallions 28, San Antonio Texans 23 (July 15): Playing the same team for the second time in a week, Baltimore needed to rally from behind three times to top the Texans before an announced crowd of 18,112 at the Alamodome. Carlos Huerta kicked field goals of 41, 37, 23, and 48 yards for the Stallions (2–1), who needed a strong defensive stand to hold off the Texans in the final minute. Mike Pringle rushed for 125 yards, and Reggie Perry had a touchdown reception for Baltimore.

Stallions 43, Winnipeg Blue Bombers 7 (July 22): Tracy Ham threw for 270 yards and three touchdown passes, Mike Pringle rushed for 97 yards and a touchdown, and Chris Wright finished with 284 all-purpose yards as Baltimore cruised to their third straight victory before 30,641 fans at Memorial Stadium. The Stallions (3–1) jumped out to a 15–0 first quarter lead and never trailed in the contest. Baltimore, which had won three straight games, eventually turned a relatively close game into a route by outscoring Winnipeg, 20–0, in the fourth quarter.

Stallions 36, Birmingham Barracudas 8 (July 29): The Stallions jumped out to a 13–0 first quarter lead and completely dominated the Barracudas before 30,729 fans at Legion Field in Alabama. Baltimore won its fourth straight games after leading 27–8 at halftime. The Stallions (4–1) scored just nine points in the second half on three field goals by Carlos Huerta, but the defense did the job, holding the Barracudas scoreless over the final 30 minutes.

Stallions 19, Edmonton Eskimos 12 (August 2): Defense was key for the Stallions, who became the first U.S. team to defeat the Eskimos at home, in front of 30,698 fans at Commonwealth Stadium. Charles Anthony scored Baltimore's lone touchdown when he intercepted Edmonton quarterback Kerwin Bell and returned it 52 yards for a score in the second quarter. Linebacker O. J. Brigance helped secure the win in the fourth quarter when he stripped the ball from Edmonton receiver Jim Sandusky inside the 20 to squash a potential game-tying touchdown. Free safety Lester Smith recovered the ball for Baltimore (5–1). Carlos Huerta added four field goals in the win, the fifth straight for the Stallions.

Stallions 15, Calgary Stampeders 29 (August 6): The Stallions' brutal travel schedule continued as they were held to just two singles in the second half, losing to the Stampeders before 24,463 fans at McMahon Stadium in Calgary. The Stallions (5–2) actually led, 10–7, after the first quarter, but the travel—more than 5,000 miles over nine days—along with injuries to several key players, including Tracy Ham, took its toll on Baltimore, which was outscored 12–2 in the second half.

Stallions 15, Memphis Mad Dogs 25 (August 12): Playing their third game in their third city in ten days, the Stallions struggled before losing to the visiting Mad Dogs before 31,221 fans at Memorial Stadium. In the loss, the Stallions (5–3) were held without a touchdown with Carlos Huerta accounting for all of Baltimore's scoring on five field goals. The Stallions turned the ball over five times and allowed five sacks on offense, while the defense gave up 375 yards against the expansion Mad Dogs. Backup quarterback Rickey Foggie completed 11 of 22 passes for 159 yards and led Memphis to two touchdown drives, while fullback Bruce Perkins and running back Al Shipman rushed for 58 and 59 yards in the win. Even with their offensive struggles, the Stallions trailed only 15–12 heading into the fourth quarter.

All-Time Results

Stallions 16, Memphis Mad Dogs 13 (August 19): A fourth quarter goal-line stand proved to be the difference for the visiting Stallions, who snapped a two-game losing streak in front of 18,249 fans at the Liberty Bowl in Tennessee. Carlos Huerta booted the game-winning field goal with 8:14 left in the game for the Stallions, who also avenged their defeat at the hands of the Mad Dogs from the week before. However, the Stallions' victory was not certain until late in the game as the Mad Dogs' Kendrick Jones took the ensuing kickoff 73 yards to the Baltimore 19. The Mad Dogs reached the one-yard line two plays later after the Stallions (6–3) were called for pass interference in the end zone. Baltimore's defense responded by stuffing fullback Bruce Perkins twice and running back Charles Miles once to force a turnover. Mike Pringle rushed for 122 yards, Tracy Ham completed 14 of 18 passes for 144 yards, and the Stallions' defense held the Mad Dogs to 205 yards of total offense in the win.

Stallions 41, Toronto Argonauts 14 (August 26): The Stallions scored on their first four possessions en route to their second straight victory before 27,853 fans at Memorial Stadium in Baltimore. Tracy Ham completed 13 of 19 passes for 166 yards and two touchdowns, while Chris Wright gained 159 yards on seven punt returns, including one for 57 yards, for the Stallions (7–3). Defensively, Elfrid Payton had three sacks and Matt Goodwin had an interception to pace Baltimore. Toronto quarterback Kent Austin completed 21 of 29 passes for 215 yards and two touchdowns before being taken out of the game in the fourth quarter.

Stallions 41, Hamilton Tiger-Cats 14 (September 2): Mike Pringle rushed for 200 yards and four touchdowns on 31 carries as the visiting Stallions won their third straight game before 23,120 fans at Ivor Wynne Stadium. The Stallions (8–3) did most of their damage in the second quarter, when they outscored the Tiger-Cats, 24–7. Among the other highlights for Baltimore included a sack by O. J. Brigance of Hamilton quarterback Anthony Calvillo and a blocked punt by defensive back Alvin Walton. The Stallions scored just ten points in the second half, but the Tiger-Cats could only muster a fourth quarter touchdown in the final 30 minutes.

Stallions 28, Birmingham Barracudas 20 (September 9): Tracy Ham completed 25 of 35 passes for 315 yards and two touchdowns and ran for 53 additional yards as the Stallions rallied to win their fourth straight game in front of 29,013 fans at Memorial Stadium. The Stallions (9–3) trailed, 17–11, heading into the fourth quarter but scored the game's final ten points to cap the comeback. Ham gave the Stallions the lead for good on a 69-yard drive that was capped by a four-yard touchdown pass to Chris Armstrong. Carlos Huerta, who kicked four field goals in the game, gave the Stallions some breathing room with his final field goal with 1:26 remaining. Armstrong finished with six catches for 103 yards, while Robert Drummond rushed for 67 yards on 17 carries and Chris Wright had 271 all-purpose yards for the Stallions. Barracudas quarterback Matt Dunigan threw for 384 yards and a touchdown in the loss.

Stallions 24, Shreveport Pirates 17 (September 15): Despite being outscored 14–0 in the fourth quarter, the visiting Stallions held on to win their fifth straight game before 12,455 fans at Independence Stadium in Louisiana. Linebacker Matt Goodwin had an interception, forced a fumble deep in Baltimore territory, and blocked a punt that safety Brian White recovered and took in for a touchdown for the Stallions (10–3). Tracy Ham completed 16 of 28 passes for 269 yards and rushed 11 times for 57 yards in the win. Shreveport quarterback Billy Joe Tolliver completed eight of 17 passes for 87 yards in the loss.

Stallions 42, Shreveport Pirates 32 (September 23): The Stallions topped the Pirates for the second straight week and clinched a playoff spot in the process before 27,321 fans at Memorial Stadium. Tracy Ham completed 14 of 18 passes for 229 yards, threw three touchdowns, and ran for 39 additional yards for the Stallions (11–3), now winners of six straight games. Mike Pringle racked up 135 rushing yards on 19 carries for Baltimore, which led 39–3 after three quarters. The Pirates rallied to scored 29 points in the fourth quarter to at least make the game respectable. Shreveport quarterback Billy Joe Tolliver threw for 395 yards in the loss.

Stallions 28, Saskatchewan Roughriders 24 (October 1): Tracy Ham ran for a 45-yard touchdown with less than four minutes remaining as the visiting Stallions (12–3) rallied to win before 30,758 fans at Taylor Field. Trailing at one point, 15–3, the Roughriders rallied to rake a 24–18 lead after Tom Burgess connected on a ten-yard touchdown pass to Don Narcisse with 8:39 remaining. However, the Stallions responded by scoring the game's final ten points. Ham's run gave the Stallions a 25–24 lead. Baltimore then scored two points on a safety that came one play after defensive lineman Jearld Baylis sacked Burgess at the Saskatchewan 2. Punter Josh Miller scored Baltimore's final point when his 63-yard punt went through the end zone for a single.

Stallions 29, Saskatchewan Roughriders 27 (October 7): Mike Pringle rushed for 179 yards, including several key yards late to help set up a game-winning field goal by Carlos Huerta with five seconds remaining before 31,421 fans at Memorial Stadium. The game was one of the more dramatic of the season. The Stallions (13–3) trailed 10–0 after the first quarter and 17–7 at halftime. Baltimore had to overcome sloppy play, which included three turnovers in the come-from-behind victory. The comeback included an 89-yard punt return for a touchdown by Chris Wright to get the Stallions on the scoreboard in the second quarter. Huerta's foot kept the Stallions in the game with four field goals. Tracy Ham also connected on a 26-yard touchdown pass to Gerald Alphin. Warren Jones completed 29 of 40 passes for three touchdown and wideout Don Narcisse had 13 catches for 127 yards and two touchdowns in the losing effort for the Roughriders.

Stallions 28, B.C. Lions 26 (October 21): Carlos Huerta connected on a 20-yard, game-winning field goal late in the fourth quarter as Baltimore won its ninth straight game before 33,208 fans at Memorial Stadium. The Stallions played three quarterbacks in the game. Starting signal-caller Tracy Ham led the Stallions to an early 17–3 lead after tossing a 10-yard touchdown pass to Chris Armstrong in the second quarter before leaving the game with a mild concussion. The Lions pulled within 17–10 at halftime after Charles Gordon intercepted a pass from Stallions backup Shawn Jones. The Lions eventually took a 26–25 lead after Cory Philpot's second touchdown of the fourth quarter. However, Ham returned to the game in the fourth quarter and led Baltimore on a 54-yard drive with about two minutes remaining in regulation to set up Huerta's field goal. Armstrong finished the game with six catches for 120 yards and two touchdowns for the Stallions (14–3).

Baltimore Stallions 24, Hamilton Tiger-Cats 17 (October 29): The Stallions opened up a close game with two third-quarter touchdowns before holding off the visiting Tiger-Cats before 29,310 fans at Memorial Stadium. The Stallions (15–3) led just 6–3 at halftime before scoring 14 unanswered points in the third quarter. Hamilton rallied to outscore Baltimore, 14–4, in the fourth quarter, but it was too little, too late. The game represented the Stallions' final regular season game played in Baltimore.

Post-Season

Stallions 36, Winnipeg Blue Bombers 21 (November 4): Mike Pringle rushed for a season-high 211 yards and two touchdowns on 28 carries as the Stallions won in the Southern Division semifinals before 21,040 fans at Memorial Stadium. The attendance was the smallest crowd in the franchise's history. Tracy Ham completed 10 of 19 passes for 218 yards for the Stallions, who recorded their 11th straight victory. Chris Armstrong had three catches for 82 yards, while linebacker Tracy Gravely had a 95-yard interception return and O. J. Brigance added four tackles and a sack for Baltimore. The Blue Bombers scored two touchdowns in the fourth quarter to make the game appear more competitive than it actually was.

Stallions 21, San Antonio Texans 11 (November 13): Carlos Huerta provided all the offense the Stallions would need as he booted seven field goals in front of 30,217 fans at Memorial Stadium. With the win in the Southern Division finals, the Stallions advanced to the Grey Cup for the second straight year. Defense was key for the Stallions, who stifled a Texans offense that had averaged more than 40 points a game over their previous ten contests. Baltimore actually led, 15–1, at halftime before being outscored 10–6 in the second half.

Tracy Ham rushed for 72 yards on seven carries while Mike Pringle contributed 136 yards on 24 carries on the ground for the Stallions, who won for the first time in the season without scoring a touchdown. Defensively, Baltimore was led by O. J. Brigance, who had five tackles, a sack, and a fumble recovery. The Stallions recovered two fumbles by Texans quarterback David Archer. Archer's three-yard touchdown pass to Mark Stock late in the fourth quarter and Roman Anderson's 42-yard field goal in the third quarter were the highlights for the Texans. The game represented the final CFL game played at Memorial Stadium and the final game played in the league to feature two teams from the U.S.

Stallions 37, Calgary Stampeders 20 (November 19): Rookie Chris Wright had an 82-yard punt return for a touchdown, defensive back Alvin Walton recovered a block punt for a touchdown, and Mike Pringle rushed for 137 yards as the Stallions became the first U.S. team to win a Grey Cup before an announced crowd of 52,564 at Taylor Field in Regina, Saskatchewan. Wright's score put Baltimore in the driver's seat early as his Grey Cup-record return came just 2:26 into the game. Walton's touchdown occurred after a blocked punt by O. J. Brigance. The Stallions also benefited from five field goals by Carlos Huerta.

Baltimore's defense did the rest as they kept Calgary quarterback Doug Flutie in check for most of the game. Brigance paced the defense with ten tackles for Baltimore, which finished the season 18–3, winning its final 13 contests. Tracy Ham completed 17 of 29 passes for 213 yards and was named the game's Most Outstanding Player for the Stallions.

Appendix B: Where Are They Now?

Quarterbacks

- **Tracy Ham**

    With Stallions: Ham completed 512 of 914 passes for 7,705 yards, with 51 touchdowns and 27 interceptions, while rushing for 1,223 yards and eight touchdowns in 36 games.

    Career stats: Ham completed 2,670 of 4,943 passes for 40,534 yards, with 284 touchdowns and 164 interceptions, while rushing for 8,043 yards and 62 touchdowns from 1987 to 1999 for the Edmonton Eskimos (1987–1992), Toronto Argonauts (1993), Baltimore Stallions (1994–1995), and Montreal Alouettes (1996–1999). In 2007, Ham, a former Georgia Southern University standout, was inducted into the College Football Hall of Fame, and he was inducted into the Canadian Football Hall of Fame in 2010.

    Now? As of 2020, Ham was the senior associate athletics director for internal operations at Georgia Southern University.

- **Dan Crowley**

    With Stallions: Crowley completed 2 of 8 passes for 21 yards and an interception in 1995 as a rookie.

    Career stats: Crowley completed 402 of 816 passes for 4,933 yards, with 29 touchdowns and 40 interceptions, while rushing for 530 yards and five touchdowns for the Baltimore Stallions (1995), Montreal Alouettes (1996), Edmonton Eskimos (1999–2001), and Ottawa Renegades (2002–2003).

    Now? As of 2020, Crowley was the senior associate director of athletics, development for Towson University, his alma mater.

- **John Congemi**

    With Stallions: Congemi completed 18 of 49 passes for 522 yards with six interceptions in 1994.

    Career Stats: Congemi completed 440 of 846 passes for 6,180 yards, with 30 touchdowns and 48 interceptions, while rushing for 182 yards and three touchdowns for the Toronto Argonauts (1987–1990, 1992), Ottawa Rough Riders

(1991), Miami Hooters (AFL, 1992), Saskatchewan Roughriders (1993), and Baltimore Stallions (1994).

Now? Congemi works as an analyst for the Miami Dolphins and ESPN's college football coverage.

* **Shawn Jones**

    With Stallions: Jones completed 50 of 102 passes for 700 yards, with four touchdowns and six interceptions, while rushing for 49 yards.

    Career Stats: He completed 50 of 102 passes for 700 yards, with four touchdowns and six interceptions, while rushing for 49 yards combined in 1994 and 1995 with the Baltimore Stallions (1994–1995). He also played one game at defensive back for the NFL's Minnesota Vikings in 1993.

    Now? He retired from professional football after the 1995 season with the Stallions.

Running Backs

* **Mike Pringle**

    With Stallions: Pringle rushed for 3,763 yards and 26 touchdowns while also recording 79 catches for 718 yards and three touchdowns.

    Career Stats: Pringle rushed for 16,425 yards and 137 touchdowns on 2,960 carries while recording 396 catches for 3,830 yards and 12 touchdowns for the Edmonton Eskimos (1992, 2003–2004), Sacramento Goldminers (1993), Baltimore Stallions (1994–1995), and Montreal Alouettes (1996–2001).

    Now? Pringle signed a one-day contract on June 22, 2005, to officially retire as a Montreal Alouette. He retired as the all-time leader in CFL history for career rushing yards and yards from scrimmage (20,254). He was inducted into the Canadian Football Hall of Fame in 2008. He currently owns a Max Muscle Sports Nutrition Franchise in Lawrenceville, Georgia.

* **Robert Drummond**

    With Stallions: Drummond rushed for 228 yards on 45 carries and had 36 catches for 419 yards and one touchdown.

    Career Stats: Drummond rushed for 6,893 yards and 79 touchdowns and had 413 catches for 4,252 yards and 19 touchdowns over 14 seasons for the NFL's Philadelphia Eagles (1989–1991), Baltimore Stallions (1994–1995), Toronto Argonauts (1996–1997, 2002), and BC Lions (1998–2001).

    Now? Drummond retired from professional football after the 2002 season.

* **Peter Tuipulotu**

    With Stallions: Tuipulotu rushed for 57 yards on 19 carries and had 72 catches for 906 yards and three touchdowns.

    Career Stats: Tuipulotu rushed for 92 yards and three touchdowns and had 103 catches for 1,203 yards and three touchdowns in a five-year career that included stints with the Baltimore Stallions (1994–1995) and Saskatchewan

Roughriders (1996). He also appeared in six games for the NFL's San Diego Chargers in 1992.

Now? As of 2020, Tuipulotu was coaching middle school football, basketball, and soccer in North Carolina.

Wide Receivers

* **Chris Armstrong**

    With Stallions: Armstrong caught 136 catches for 2,697 yards and 29 touchdowns.

    Career Stats: Armstrong caught 486 passes for 8,996 yards and 78 touchdowns over a ten-year career that included stints with the AFL's Washington Commandos (1990), Edmonton Eskimos (1991–1992), Ottawa Rough Riders (1992), Baltimore Stallions (1994–1995), Montreal Alouettes (1996–1999), and Winnipeg Blue Bombers (1998–1999).

    Now? As of 2020, Armstrong was the head football coach at Loch Raven High School in Towson, Maryland.

* **Shannon Culver**

    With Stallions: Culver caught 42 passes for 536 yards and four touchdowns.

Fullback Peter Tuipulotu (No. 32) was one of many key players who were members of both Baltimore teams to play in the CFL (photograph by John Patrick Kelly, from the archives of John W. Ziemann)

Career Stats: Culver caught 294 passes for 3,866 yards and 67 touchdowns over a 13-year career that included stints with the Baltimore Stallions (1994–1995), Spring Football League's Los Angeles Dragons (2000), XFL's Orlando Rage (2001), and the Arena Football League's Anaheim Piranhas (1997), Grand Rapids Rampage (1998), Los Angeles Avengers (2000–2001), Dallas Desperadoes (2002–2003), Austin Wranglers (2004), and Arizona Rattlers (2006).

Now? Culver retired from professional football after the 2006 season.

- **Robert Clark**

    With Stallions: Clark caught 39 passes for 691 yards and two touchdowns.

    Career Stats: He caught 254 passes for 4,235 yards and 23 touchdowns over a nine-year career that included stints with the NFL's New Orleans Saints (1987–1988), Detroit Lions (1989–1991), and Miami Dolphins (1992), and the CFL's Toronto Argonauts (1993) and Baltimore Stallions (1994–1995).

    Now? Clark retired from professional football after the 1995 season.

- **Walter Wilson**

    With Stallions: Wilson caught 50 passes for 900 yards and four touchdowns in 1994.

    Career Stats: Wilson caught 139 passes for 1,928 yards and seven touchdowns over a six-year career that included stints with the NFL's San Diego Chargers (1990), World League of American Football's Ohio Glory (1992), and CFL's Baltimore Stallions (1994) and Memphis Mad Dogs (1995).

    Now? Wilson lives in Baltimore and is president and CEO of Project 84.

- **Mark Orlando**

    With Stallions: Orlando caught six passes for 125 yards and a touchdown in 1995.

    Career: All with the Stallions.

    Now? As of 2020, Orlando was director of consulting at CGI Technologies in Virginia.

Offensive Linemen

- **Shar Pourdanesh**

    With Stallions: Pourdanesh was a key leader up front in both 1994 and 1995. He became the first rookie in CFL history to be awarded the Leo Dandurand Award, which is given annually to the league's most outstanding offensive lineman.

    Career Stats: Pourdanesh also played for the NFL's Washington Redskins (1996–1998), Pittsburgh Steelers (1999–2000), and Oakland Raiders (2001) in his eight-year career.

    Now? As of 2020, Pourdanesh was director of business development for Applied Cardiac Systems, Inc. in Irvine, California.

- **Neal Fort**

    With Stallions: Fort helped anchor the line in 1994 and 1995 and was a CFL All-Star in his second season in Baltimore.

    Career: Fort was originally drafted by the NFL's Los Angeles Rams in 1991. After two seasons in Baltimore, he played for the Montreal Alouettes from 1996 to 2004.

    Now? As of 2020, Fort was living in Texas and was a senior project coordinator for Rigaku Americas.

- **John Earle**

    With Stallions: Earle played guard for the Stallions in 1994 and 1995.

    Career: Along with his time in Baltimore, Earle had brief off-season and/or practice squad tenures in the NFL with the Cincinnati Bengals (1992), Kansas City Chiefs (1992–1993), New England Patriots (1993), Atlanta Falcons (1994), and St. Louis Rams (1996) over his five-year career.

    Now? Earle helps operate Think Twice Ministries with his twin brother, Guy. He is also the pastor of students at First Colleyville Church in Colleyville, Texas.

- **Guy Earle**

    With Stallions: Earle played guard for the Stallions in 1994 and 1995.

    Career: Along with his time in Baltimore, Earle had brief tenures in the NFL with the Washington Redskins (1993) and Houston Oilers while also playing for the CFL's Winnipeg Blue Bombers (1996–1997) over his five-year career.

    Now? Earle operate Think Twice Ministries with his twin brother, John. He is also the executive pastor at Gracepointe Church in Corinth, Texas.

- **Nick Subis**

    With Stallions: Subis played in 31 games between in 1994 and 1995.

    Career: Subis appeared in a combined total of 61 games for the NFL's Denver Broncos (1991), and the CFL's Sacramento Gold Miners (1993), Baltimore Stallions (1994–1995), and Montreal Alouettes (1996) over the course of his six-year career.

    Now? Subis retired from professional football after the 1996 season.

Defensive Linemen

- **Jearld Baylis**

    With Stallions: Baylis had a combined 87 tackles and six sacks in 1994 and 1995.

    Career: A four-time CFL All-Star, Baylis had a combined 347 tackles and 55.5 sacks for the USFL's New Orleans Breakers (1984) and Portland Breakers (1985), the CFL's Toronto Argonauts (1986–1988), BC Lions (1991), Saskatchewan Roughriders (1992–1993), and Baltimore Stallions (1994–1995), and the Arena Football League's Milwaukee Mustangs and New York City Hawks (1997) over the course of his 14-year career.

    Now? Baylis retired from professional football after the 1997 season.

- **Elfrid Payton, Sr.**

    With Stallions: Payton finished with 67 tackles and 22 sacks in 1994 and 1995.

    Career: Payton finished with 485 tackles and 154 sacks (second highest in CFL history) playing for the Winnipeg Blue Bombers (1991–1993), Shreveport Pirates (1994), Baltimore Stallions (1994–1995), Montreal Alouettes (1996–1999), Winnipeg Blue Bombers (2000, 2004), Toronto Argonauts (2001), and Edmonton Eskimos (2002–2003) over the course of his 13-year career.

    Now? A seven-time CFL All-Star, Payton was inducted into the Canadian Football Hall of Fame in 2010. Payton's son, Elfrid Payton, Jr., is an NBA player who signed with the New Orleans Pelicans for the 2018–2019 season.

- **Grant Carter**

    With Stallions: Carter recorded 41 tackles and six sacks in 18 games in 1994 and 1995.

    Career: Carter finished with a combined 286 tackles and 43 sacks for the Baltimore Stallions (1994–1995), Montreal Alouettes (1997), Winnipeg Blue Bombers (1997–1999), and Edmonton Eskimos (1999–2000) over his seven-year career.

    Now? As of 2018, Carter lived in Johns Creek, Georgia, and is founder/manager of Declex LLC.

Linebackers

- **Alvin Walton**

    With Stallions: Walton had 82 tackles in 31 games in 1994 and 1995.

    Career: Prior to playing with the Stallions, Walton recorded 12 interceptions and won two Super Bowl rings as a member of the NFL's Washington Redskins from 1986 to 1991.

    Now? Walton lives in Las Vegas, Nevada.

- **O. J. Brigance**

    With Stallions: Brigance recorded 110 tackles and 13 sacks in 1994 and 1995.

    Career: Brigance recorded 375 tackles and 35 sacks while playing for the CFL's BC Lions (1991–1993) and Baltimore Stallions (1994–1995) before moving on to play for the NFL's Miami Dolphins (1996–1999), Baltimore Ravens (2000), St. Louis Rams (2001–2002), and New England Patriots (2002) over his 12-year career.

    Now? The only player to win a Grey Cup and a Super Bowl in the same city, Brigance founded the Brigance Brigade Foundation in Baltimore after being diagnosed with amyotrophic lateral sclerosis, also known as ALS or Lou Gehrig's disease.

- **Matt Goodwin**

    With Stallions: Goodwin recorded 132 tackles, four sacks and three interceptions in 1994 and 1995.

Career: He won the CFL's Most Outstanding Rookie Award in 1994 after he recorded 54 tackles, three interceptions, three sacks, four blocked punts, and four fumble recoveries (including three returned for touchdowns).

Now? Goodwin last played professional football in 1995 for the Stallions.

- Tracy Gravely

With Stallions: Gravely recorded a combined 159 tackles and two interceptions while appearing in all 36 regular season games.

Career: He finished with a combined 591 tackles, ten interceptions, and seven sacks while playing for the Ottawa Rough Riders (1991), BC Lions (1992–1993), Baltimore Stallions (1994–1995), and Montreal Alouettes (1996–2001) over his 11-year career.

Now? Gravely lives in West Virginia, where he is the cornerbacks coach at Concord University, an NCAA Division II school and his alma mater.

Defensive Backs

- Irvin Smith

With Stallions: Smith recorded 75 tackles, seven interceptions and a sack in 1994 and 1995.

Career: A three-time CFL All-Star, Smith recorded 329 tackles and 35 interceptions for the NFL's New York Jets (1989–1990), Washington Redskins (1993) and Minnesota Vikings (1993), the World League of Professional Football's London Monarchs (1991–1992), and the CFL's Hamilton Tiger-Cats (1991), Saskatchewan Roughriders (1992), Baltimore Stallions (1994–1995), and Montreal Alouettes (1996–2001) over his 13-year career.

Now? Smith still lives in Maryland and as of 2020 was a lieutenant for the Montgomery County Fire and Rescue Service.

- Ken Watson

With Stallions: Watson recorded 115 tackles and two interceptions in 1994 and 1995.

Career: He recorded 371 tackles and 15 interceptions for the CFL's BC Lions (1989–1991), Calgary Stampeders (1991–1993), BC Lions (1991), Baltimore Stallions (1994–1995), Montreal Alouettes (1996–1997), and Edmonton Eskimos (1999). Watson also played for the World League of American Football's San Antonio Riders in 1993 during his 11-year career.

Now? Watson lives in Alabama and is the defensive backs coach at Miles College, an NCAA Division II school.

- Michael Brooks

With Stallions: Brooks recorded 56 tackles and four interceptions and was named a CFL East All-Star in 1994.

Career: Brooks recorded 64 tackles and had four interceptions for the Baltimore Stallions (1994) and the Memphis Mad Dogs (1995). Brooks also played for the NFL's San Diego Chargers (1989–1990) and Dallas Cowboys (1990) over his six-year career.

Now? Brooks lives in Arizona and works for American Express.

• **Lester Smith**

With Stallions: Smith recorded 39 tackles and an interception and averaged 17.2 yards on kick returns and 11.2 yards per punt return in 1994 and 1995.

Career: He recorded 286 tackles and 26 interceptions and averaged 18.2 yards per kick return and 11.6 yards per punt return for the Baltimore Stallions (1994–1995), Toronto Argonauts (1996–1998), and Montreal Alouettes (1999–2001) over his eight-year career.

Now? As of 2020, Smith, who won three Grey Cup titles, lives in Michigan and works for Ford Motor Company.

• **Douglas Craft**

With Stallions: Craft recorded 18 tackles, a forced fumble, and a fumble recovery in six games in 1995.

Career: He recorded 302 tackles and 21 interceptions for the Arena Football League's Dallas Texans (1993) and the Canadian Football League's Calgary Stampeders (1993–1994), Baltimore Stallions (1995), Montreal Alouettes (1996–1998), and Saskatchewan Roughriders (1999) over his seven-year career.

Now? Craft lives in New Mexico and is director, president, and general manager of operations for Crystal Clear Maintenance Inc.

This is the 1995 Grey Cup ring given to retired Baltimore Stallions defensive back Douglas Craft (photograph courtesy of Douglas Craft).

Special Teams

• **Donald Igwebuike**

With Stallions: The placekicker connected on 43 of 53 field goal attempts and 47 of 48 point-after attempts for Baltimore in 1994.

Career: He connected on 154 of 206 field goal attempts and 212 of 225 extra-point attempts while playing for the CFL's Baltimore football club (1994) and Memphis Mad Dogs, the NFL's Tampa Bay Buccaneers

Donald Igwebuike connected on 43 of 53 field goals in his lone season with the team in 1994 (photograph by John Patrick Kelly, from the archives of John W. Ziemann).

(1985–1989) and Minnesota Vikings (1990), and the Arena Football League's Tampa Bay Storm.

Now? Igwebuike lives in Washington, D.C.

- **Carlos Huerta**

    With Stallions: The placekicker connected on 57 of 72 field goal attempts and 50 of 50 extra-point tries in 1995.

    Career: He connected on 136 of 211 field goal attempts and 189 of 196 extra-point tries with the CFL's Las Vegas Posse (1994) and Baltimore Stallions (1995), the NFL's Chicago Bears (1996) and St. Louis Rams (1996), the World League of American Football's Amsterdam Admirals (1997), and the Arena Football Leagues Florida Bobcats (1998) and San Jose SaberCats (1999–2001) over his eight-year career.

    Now? Huerta lives in Nevada and is president of Go Global Properties.

- **Josh Miller**

    With Stallions: The punter averaged more than 45 yards per attempt in 1994 and 1995, earning a CFL All-Star selection in each season.

    Career: Miller averaged 43.6 yards per punt for the CFL's Baltimore Stallions (1994–1995) along with the NFL's Pittsburgh Steelers (1996–2003), New England Patriots (2004–2006), and Tennessee Titans (2007) over his 14-year career. He won a Super Bowl ring with the Patriots in 2004.

    Now? Miller is the founder/president of Gelstx Sports.

- **Chris Wright**

    With Stallions: Wright averaged 21.9 yards per kick return and 12.4 per punt return with three touchdowns as a rooking in 1995.

    Career: Wright averaged 21.4 yards per kick return and 10.3 yards per punt return with five touchdowns while playing for the Baltimore Stallions (1995), Montreal Alouettes (1996–1998), and BC Lions 2002 over his seven-year career.

    Now? Wright was murdered in a shooting in Atlanta on July 31, 2005. He was just 32 years old.

- **Rob Davis**

    With Stallions: Davis served as the team's long snapper during the 1995 season.

    Career: He signed with the NFL's Chicago Bears in 1996 and played for the Green Bay Packers from 1997 to 2007 to close out his 13-year career.

    Now? After retiring as a player, joined Davis joined the Packers' front office as director of player development. He left the team in 2017 before become senior director of people and culture for Pierce Manufacturing in Appleton, Wisconsin.

Front Office/Head Coach

- **Jim Speros**

    With Stallions: Team owner

    Career: Speros owned the Baltimore Stallions from 1994 to 1995. In 1996, the CFL made him cancel the franchise when he moved the team from Baltimore to Montreal. There, the franchise was reborn as the Alouettes, where they reclaimed that once-dormant franchise's history of 1946 to 1986.

Now? Speros has remained involved in several business endeavors since he sold the Alouettes in 1997. Most recently, he is the owner and founder of the Velocity Five Sports Restaurant chain and chairman and chief executive office of Velocity Wings LLC.

- **Don Matthews**

    With Stallions: Matthews posted a 27–9 record during the regular season (32–10 including the post-season) in 1994 and 1995. He advanced to the Grey Cup both seasons, winning the title in 1995.

    Career: He posted a career 231–132–1 record over 22 seasons as a head coach in the CFL. His career wins are the second-most all-time in league history. During that time, Matthews coached teams to five Grey Cup victories, advanced to the championship four other times, and won 11 divisional titles with the BC Lions (1983–1987), Toronto Argonauts (1990, 1996–1998, 2008), Saskatchewan Roughriders (1991–1993), Baltimore Stallions (1994–1995), Edmonton Eskimos (1999–2000), and Montreal Alouettes (2002–2006). He was inducted into the Canadian Football Hall of Fame in 2011.

    Now? Matthews died on June 14, 2017, after a battle with cancer. He was 77 years old.

Currently Active Coaches

- **Steve Buratto**

    With Stallions: Buratto served as offensive coordinator and quarterbacks coach.

    Career: He served as offensive line coach for the Saskatchewan Roughriders (1980–1983, 1993 and 2011), head coach of the Calgary Stampeders (1984–1985), offensive coordinator for the BC Lions (1986–1987), offensive coordinator for the Baltimore Stallions (1994–1995), head coach of the BC Lions (2000–2002), offensive coordinator for the BC Lions (2003–2004), offensive line coach/associate head coach for the Calgary Stampeders (2005–2006), offensive coordinator for the Toronto Argonauts (2007–2008), special teams coordinator for the Toronto Argonauts (2009), and offensive coordinator/associate head coach for the University of British Columbia (2015–2017) over his 38-year coaching career.

- **Bob Price**

    With Stallions: Price served as defensive coordinator and defensive backs coach.

    Career: He served as defensive coordinator for Eastern Utah University (1981–1982), linebackers and special teams coach for the University of Nevada (1984–1985), defensive coordinator/secondary coach/special teams coach for UNLV (1986–1989), secondary coach for the University of California (1990), secondary coach for the Ottawa Rough Riders (1991), defensive coordinator/secondary coach for the Saskatchewan Roughriders (1992–1993), defensive coordinator and defensive backs coach for the Baltimore Stallions (1994–1995), head coach for the Montreal Alouettes (1996), and at the University of Virginia (running backs coach, 1997–1999; defensive backs coach, 2000–2004; tight ends coach/recruiting coordinator, 2005–2009; and football administrator, 2010–present) over his 38-year career.

- **Daryl Edralin**

    With Stallions: Edralin served as linebackers coach and special teams coordinator.

    Career: Edralin served as assistant coach at the University of Hawaii (1979–1991), linebackers coach and special teams coordinator of the WLAF's Orlando Thunder (1991–1993), linebackers coach and special teams coordinator for the Saskatchewan Roughriders (1992–1994), linebackers coach and special teams coordinator for the Baltimore Stallions (1994–1995), Toronto Argonauts (1996–1999), and Hamilton Tiger-Cats (2000–2002), defensive and special teams coordinator for the Toronto Argonauts (2002–2003), defensive coordinator for the Hamilton Tiger-Cats (2004–2005), assistant coach for the Montreal Alouettes (2005–2006), and teacher in the Peel District School Board (2008–present) over his 40-year career.

- **Marty Long**

    With Stallions: Long served as the defensive line coach.

    Career: He served as defensive ends coach and recruiting coordinator for The Citadel (1987–1993), defensive line coach for the Baltimore Stallions (1994–1995), defensive line coach for the University of Arizona (1996–2003), defensive line coach for the University of Nevada (2004–2006), and defensive line coach for Northwestern University (2007–present) over his 32-year career.

- **Charlie Carpenter**

    With Stallions: Carpenter served as offensive line coach in 1995.

    Career: He served as offensive coordinator for Murray State University (1987–1991), offensive line coach for the Winnipeg Blue Bombers (1992–1993), offensive line coach for the Ottawa Rough Riders (1994), offensive line coach for the Baltimore Stallions (1995), offensive line coach for the Toronto Argonauts (1996), offensive coordinator with the BC Lions (1997–1998), offensive line coach for Bethany College (2013–2014), offensive line coach for Widener College (2014–2016), and offensive line coach for the Montreal Alouettes (2017) over his 31-year career.

- **Donald Hill-Eley**

    With Stallions: Hill-Eley served as receivers coach.

    Career: After leaving the Stallions, Hill-Eley served as a guest coach with the Toronto Argonauts (1996–1997), offensive coordinator at Hampton University (1997–2000), offensive coordinator at Morgan State (2001), head coach at Morgan State (2002–2013), wide receivers coach at Norfolk State (2014), and head coach at Alabama State (2017–present) over his 25-year career.

- **Jim Popp**

With Stallions: Popp served as general manager and director of player personnel.

Career: Popp followed the franchise to Montreal and served in a similar role with the Alouettes from 1996 to 2016. During that time, the Alouettes won three Grey Cups and advanced to four others under Popp, who also served as the team's head coach on several occasions. Popp then took over as general manager of the Toronto Argonauts in 2017, where he won the Grey Cup in his first season at the helm.

Appendix C: Baltimore Football Timeline

September 7, 1947—The original Baltimore Colts of the All-America Football Conference played their first game ever, defeating the Brooklyn Dodgers, 16–7.

September 17, 1950—Now a member of the NFL, the original Baltimore Colts lost their season opener, 38–14, to the Washington Redskins. Facing financial struggles, the team folded after the season.

December 10, 1950—The Colts lost their season finale, 51–14, at the New York Yanks.

January 23, 1953—Businessman Carroll Rosenbloom bought the Dallas Texans and moved them to Baltimore, renaming the NFL franchise the Colts.

September 27, 1953—The new Baltimore Colts played their first game, defeating the visiting Chicago Bears, 13–9, before a crowd of 23,715 at Memorial Stadium.

December 28, 1958—In a game that became known as "The Greatest Game Ever Played," the Baltimore Colts defeated the New York Giants, 23–17, in overtime to capture the 1958 NFL Championship before 64,185 fans at Yankee Stadium in New York.

December 27, 1959—The Baltimore Colts defeated the New York Giants, 31–16, to capture their second straight NFL Championship before 57,545 fans at Memorial Stadium in Baltimore.

December 27, 1964—The Baltimore Colts lost to the Cleveland Browns, 27–0, in the NFL Championship Game before 79,544 fans at Cleveland Stadium in Ohio.

January 12, 1969—In what is considered one of the greatest upsets in American professional football history, the New York Jets upset the Baltimore Colts, 16–7, in Super Bowl III before a crowd of 75,389 at the Orange Bowl in Miami, Florida. The game was the final contest before the official merger of the NFL and AFL.

January 17, 1971—The Baltimore Colts defeated the Dallas Cowboys, 16–13, to win Super Bowl V before 79,204 fans at the Orange Bowl. The win marked the Colts' only Super Bowl victory while in Baltimore.

July 13, 1972—Owner Carroll Rosenbloom traded ownership of the Colts franchise to businessman Robert Irsay, who owned the Los Angeles Rams.

December 24, 1977—The Oakland Raiders defeated the Baltimore Colts, 37–31, in double overtime in an AFC Divisional Playoff game before 59,925 fans at Memorial Stadium. That was the last playoff game the Colts ever played in Baltimore.

March 29, 1984—The Baltimore Colts sneaked out of town in the middle of the night and moved to Indianapolis.

February 24, 1985—The former Philadelphia Stars of the United States Football League played their first game as the Baltimore Stars, a 22–14 loss at the Jacksonville Bulls. The team played in College Park due to legal issues with the Colts' lease at Memorial Stadium.

July 14, 1985—The Baltimore Stars defeated the Oakland Invaders, 28–24, at Giants Stadium in New Jersey to win the USFL championship. It was the last game in league history.

July 29, 1986—A federal grand jury found in favor of the USFL in its antitrust suit against the NFL. The USFL was awarded only $1 in damages, tripled to $3 under antitrust law. The league suspended operations and folded a day later.

January 15, 1988—Bill Bidwell announced that he was moving the NFL's Cardinals franchise from St. Louis to Arizona. The move came after Bidwell considered relocating the franchise to Baltimore.

August 27, 1992—More than 60,000 fans packed Baltimore's Memorial Stadium for an NFL preseason game between the Miami Dolphins and the New Orleans Saints. The theme of the day was "Give Baltimore the Ball," a rallying cry the city used to make their case for an NFL expansion team.

June 11, 1993—Businessman Jim Speros received Canadian Football League owner's registration manual. He then submitted his deposit and registered with the league for a proposed expansion franchise.[1]

July 16, 1993—Jim Speros met with CFL Commissioner Larry Smith, agreed with terms and conditions of a proposed expansion franchise for Baltimore, and affirmed that he would pursue efforts to obtain the Baltimore franchise for the 1994 season.

August 5, 1993—Jim Speros made a $100,000 non-refundable deposit for a CFL franchise in Baltimore.

August 27, 1993—Jim Speros met with Baltimore Mayor Kurt Schmoke and other city officials in regard to a proposed CFL franchise for the city.

October 4, 1993—Jim Speros met with the CFL expansion committee in Toronto.

October 26, 1993—The NFL's 28 owners unanimously voted to grant businessman Jerry Richardson an expansion team for North Carolina, beating out bids from Baltimore, Jacksonville, Florida, St. Louis, Missouri, and Memphis. The Carolina Panthers began play in 1995.

October 28, 1993—Jim Speros submitted a lease proposal and franchise agreement to Mayor Schmoke and other city officials.

November 30, 1993—In a surprising move, NFL owners voted, 26–2, to grant an expansion franchise to businessman Wayne Weaver for Jacksonville, Florida. It was believed heading into the vote that St. Louis and Baltimore were the two favorites.

December 3, 1993—The Canadian Football League owners and Commissioner Larry Smith granted Jim Speros a CFL expansion franchise for Baltimore, contingent on an approved stadium lease in the city.

December 15, 1993—Baltimore Mayor Kurt Schmoke submits a five-year stadium lease for the Baltimore CFL team to play at Memorial Stadium.

December 30, 1993—Jim Speros hired veteran CFL coach Don Matthews to coach his Baltimore expansion team.

January 9, 1994—Mayor Kurt Schmoke met with Jim Speros and CFL Commissioner Larry Smith regarding lease negotiations.

January 15, 1994—The announcement comes that the official signing of Memorial Stadium lease between the city of Baltimore and Jim Speros will be delayed 30 days at the request of Maryland Gov. William Donald Schaeffer. The governor wanted the time to ensure that Baltimore would not be granted an NFL team before supporting a CFL franchise in town.

February 1, 1994 –Baltimore's CFL team hired seven assistant coaches and 12 front office personnel.

February 3, 1994—Jim Speros met with Gov. William Donald Schaeffer to discuss potential improvements and renovations for Memorial Stadium. Schaeffer requested a proposal for construction costs.

February 11, 1994—Jim Speros met with Baltimore recreations and parks officials to finalize the five-year lease and renovations to Memorial Stadium.

February 15, 1994—Jim Speros and Mayor Kurt Schmoke signed a five-year lease for Memorial Stadium. The mayor presented Speros the keys to the stadium at a ceremony.

February 17, 1994—At a news conference, the CFL officially granted Jim Speros an expansion franchise for Baltimore. The team would become the third U.S. franchise in the CFL and the 11th franchise overall in the league's history. Speros paid a $3 million expansion franchise fee to the league.

February 20, 1994—The Baltimore CFL team signed its first player, veteran quarterback Tracy Ham.

February 25, 1994—Jim Speros moved the team's offices into Memorial Stadium.

March 1, 1994—The team officially announced the plan to name the expansion club the Baltimore CFL Colts and said the team colors would be blue, silver, white, and black.

March 3, 1994—The CFL owners met in Sacramento, California, and appointed Jim Speros to the CFL expansion television and marketing committees.

March 20, 1994—The Baltimore CFL Colts held an initial open tryout camp. About 450 athletes turned out for the event at Johns Hopkins University.

March 26, 1994—About 5,000 people came out to Memorial Stadium for the team's first Colts Fanfest.

April 18, 1994—The Baltimore CFL Colts hosted a kickoff luncheon with the CFL caravan of stars. More than 500 people attended the event.

April 28, 1994—The CFL owners met in Las Vegas, where Speros submitted a bid for Baltimore to host the 1996 Grey Cup.

April 29, 1994—The NFL sued Jim Speros and his ownership group for name and trademark infringement over the Colts name.

May 19, 1994—Jim Speros and Don Matthews drew the post positions for the 119th running of the Preakness Stakes, the second leg of horse racing's Triple Crown, held annually at Pimlico Race Course in Baltimore.

June 24, 1994—The Baltimore CFL football team played its first preseason game, a 33–18 victory at the Shreveport Pirates.

June 28, 1994—The Baltimore CFL football club held its first pep rally at the Baltimore Inner Harbor.

June 29, 1994—Baltimore hosted its first pre-season game, a 45–43 win over the Winnipeg Blue Bombers before an announced crowd of 28,798 fans at Memorial Stadium.

July 7, 1994—Baltimore played its first CFL regular season game, defeating the host Toronto Argonauts, 28–20, before 13,101 fans at SkyDome.

July 16, 1994—Baltimore lost its home opener to the Calgary Stampeders, 42–16, before 39,247 fans at Memorial Stadium. It was the first regular season professional football game played in Baltimore since the Colts defeated the Houston Oilers, 20–10, in their season finale on December 18, 1983.

November 12, 1994—Baltimore defeated the Toronto Argonauts, 34–15, in the Eastern Division semifinals before 35,223 fans at Memorial Stadium. The game was the first professional football playoff game in Baltimore since 1977.

November 27, 1994—The BC Lions upset Baltimore, 26–23, to win the 82nd Grey Cup before 55,097 fans at BC place in Vancouver, British Columbia.

June 30, 1995—The now-Baltimore Stallions lost their second season opener, 37–34, to the BC Lions before 23,999 fans at BC Place in Vancouver, British Columbia.

October 29, 1995—The Baltimore Stallions defeated the Hamilton Tiger-Cats, 24–17, before 29,310 fans at Memorial Stadium. With the win, the Stallions finished the regular season 15–3, secured the South Division regular season title, and clinched home field advantage throughout the playoffs.

November 4, 1995—The Baltimore Stallions advanced to the South Division finals with a 36–21 victory over the Winnipeg Blue Bombers before 21,040 fans at Memorial Stadium. The crowd was the smallest to watch a home game in Stallions history.

November 6, 1995—Browns owner Art Modell officially announced that he was moving his NFL franchise from Cleveland to Baltimore in time for the 1996 season.

November 12, 1995—The Baltimore Stallions advanced to the Grey Cup for the second straight season, following their 21–11 victory in the North Division finals over the San Antonio Texans before 30,217 fans at Memorial Stadium. The game was the last home contest in franchise history for the Stallions.

November 19, 1995—The Baltimore Stallions became the first U.S. team in CFL history to win the Grey Cup, a 37–20 victory over the Calgary Stampeders before 52,564 fans at Taylor Field in Regina, Saskatchewan.

November 20, 1995—The Baltimore Stallions held a championship celebration rally at the Inner Harbor in downtown Baltimore, the last time the team formally gathered in the city.

February 2, 1996—Jim Speros formally requested permission to move the Baltimore Stallions to Montreal and rename the team the Alouettes. The request was granted, and the CFL's experiment of expanding into the U.S. officially came to an end.

April 20, 1996—The Baltimore Ravens made their first ever NFL Draft selections, taking offensive tackle Jonathan Ogden at No. 4 overall and linebacker Ray Lewis at No. 26 overall. Both went on to be first-ballot Hall of Fame players.

September 1, 1996—The Baltimore Ravens defeated the Oakland Raiders, 19–14, in their first game ever before 64,124 fans at Memorial Stadium.

January 28, 2001—The Baltimore Ravens defeated the New York Giants, 34–7, to win Super Bowl XXXV before 71,921 fans at Raymond James Stadium in Tampa, Florida. Ravens linebacker O. J. Brigance became the only player in football history to win a Super Bowl ring and a Grey Cup ring with teams in the same city.

February 3, 2013—The Ravens defeated the San Francisco 49ers, 34–31, to win Super Bowl XLVII before 71,024 fans at the Mercedes-Benz Superdome in New Orleans, Louisiana.

July 26, 2015—More than 20 former Baltimore Stallions players, along with team coaches and officials, gathered in Towson, Maryland, for a reunion to celebrate the 20th anniversary of the team winning the Grey Cup over the Calgary Stampeders.

Chapter Notes

Chapter 1

1. John Steadman, *From Colts to Ravens: A Behind-The-Scenes Look at Baltimore Professional Football* (Centerville, MD: Tidewater Publishing, 1997).

Chapter 4

1. Vito Stellino, "Football Is Back in Baltimore – Even If It's Only An Exhibition," *Los Angeles Times*, August 23, 1992, http://articles.latimes.com/1992-08-23/sports/sp-7445_1_pro-football-game.

Chapter 6

1. Kevin McManus, "Jim Speros, Starting Fast in Baltimore," *Washington Post*, October 10, 1994, https://www.washingtonpost.com/archive/business/1994/10/10/jim-speros-starting-fast-in-baltimore/b9f44a20-3295-47c2-b2cf-b50f2ed19b66/?utm_term=.d183f1163c83.

2. Ken Murray, "Football Back in Baltimore, Canadian-style," *Baltimore Sun*, February 16, 1994, http://articles.baltimoresun.com/1994-02-16/news/1994047007_1_speros-tracy-ham-cfl.

3. Jonathan Elbaz, Jeremy Granoff, Israel Spencer, and Eric Morrow, "Baltimore's Forgotten Champion," *Capital News Service*, January 23, 2014, https://cnsmaryland.org/interactives/baltimore-stallions-oral-history/.

Chapter 8

1. Ken Murray, "Blocking For Pringle, CFL's Tight-Knit Line Get the Last Laugh," *Baltimore Sun*, October 28, 1994, http://articles.baltimoresun.com/1994-10-28/sports/1994301002_1_pringle-group-of-guys-subis.

2. Ken Murray, "After Travels, Travails, Armstrong Finds Home," *Baltimore Sun*, September 10, 1994, http://articles.baltimoresun.com/1994-09-10/sports/1994253080_1_armstrong-cfl-training-camp.

3. Gary Vogt, "Baltimore Just Adores Colts—the Canadian Version," *Sacramento Bee*, September 11, 1994.

Chapter 9

1. Christine Brennan, "Baltimore's Game for a Team With No Name," *Washington Post*, September 22, 1994.

Chapter 11

1. Ed Willes, "There's Never Been a Game Like the 1994 Grey Cup," *National Post*, November 25, 2011, https://nationalpost.com/sports/football/cfl/theres-never-been-a-game-like-the-1994-grey-cup.

Chapter 12

1. Canadian Football League, *First and Ten from the Fifty-Five: Canadian Football Explained* (1995).

2. Gary Lambrecht, "Stallions Ride Out Travelin' Blues," *Baltimore Sun*, August 8, 1995, http://articles.baltimoresun.com/1995-08-08/sports/1995220056_1_stallions-alberta-calgary.

Chapter 15

1. Erik Malinowski, "Wild Stallions: How a Team from Baltimore Rocked Canadian Football," *Rolling Stone,* November 18, 2015, https://www.rollingstone.com/culture/culture-sports/wild-stallions-how-a-team-from-baltimore-rocked-canadian-football-42712.

2. Ed Hinton, "Ticket to Ride: Though Baltimore Won the Grey Cup, It Must Look for a New Home." *Sports Illustrated,* November 27, 1995, https://www.si.com/vault/2016/07/07/ticket-ride-though-baltimore-won-grey-cup-it-must-look-new-home.

Chapter 16

1. Gary Lambrecht, "CFL Faces Grim Decisions After Successful Grey Cup," *Baltimore Sun,* November 24, 1995, http://articles.baltimoresun.com/1995-11-24/sports/1995328077_1_grey-cup-week-cfl-canadian-football-league.

2. Kevin Eck and Gary Lambrecht, "Stallions Seek Move to Montreal; CFL Reportedly Set to End U.S. Presence," *Baltimore Sun,* January 25, 1996, http://articles.baltimoresun.com/1996-01-25/sports/1996025019_1_speros-cfl-shreveport-pirates.

3. Kevin Eck, "Movers Pack Up Speros' Equipment, But Not His Troubles," *Baltimore Sun,* March 23, 1996, http://articles.baltimoresun.com/1996-03-23/sports/1996083062_1_speros-memorial-stadium-stallions.

4. Jon Morgan, "Money Woes Won't Dampen Speros Spirits: Undaunted by Bills, Ex-Stallions Owner Tries a New Game," *Baltimore Sun,* February 26, 1997, http://articles.baltimoresun.com/1997-02-26/sports/1997057101_1_speros-baltimore-stallions-team-members.

5. Kevin Eck, "Stallions Draw Ringing Support from Volunteers Saving Effort: Dedicated Group Solicits Season-Ticket Buyers by Phone to Help Keep the CFL Team in Town," *Baltimore Sun,* January 7, 1996, https://www.baltimoresun.com/news/bs-xpm-1996-01-07-1996007191-story.html.

Chapter 17

1. Ken Murray, "Speros Hopes for Replay In Montreal: Owner Tries to Repeat Baltimore Success," *Baltimore Sun,* June 27, 1996, http://articles.baltimoresun.com/1996-06-27/sports/1996179091_1_speros-alouettes-memorial-stadium.

2. Dan Ralph, "Legendary CFL Coach Matthews Dead at 77," *Canadian Press,* June 14, 2017, https://www.cbc.ca/sports/football/cfl/legendary-cfl-coach-don-matthews-dead-age-77-1.4160687.

3. Dan Cherry, "Retired NFL Bothers Minister at Local Jail," *Daily Telegram,* September 2, 2011, http://www.lenconnect.com/article/20110902/NEWS/309029918.

Appendix A

1. Mike Gathagan, *Baltimore Stallions 1995 Media Guide* (Baltimore: Delta Graphics and Communications, 1995).

Appendix C

1. Mike Gathagan, *Baltimore CFL Colts Magazine* (Baltimore: John D. Lucas Printing, 1994).

Bibliography

Interviews

All interviews were conducted in Baltimore by the author

Chris Armstrong (Stallions slotback), August 2018.
Rob Betz (Stallions season ticket holder), September 2018.
O. J. Brigance (Stallions/NFL linebacker), January 2007.
Leonard "Big Wheel" Burrier (Stallions superfan), October 2018.
Kevin Byrne (Baltimore Ravens Vice President of Public and Community Relations), March 2014.
Grant Carter (Stallions defensive end/linebacker), October 2018.
Glenn Clark (Baltimore area sports talk show host), October 2018.
Douglas Craft (Stallions defensive back), September 2018.
Dan Crowley (Stallions quarterback), October 2018.
Bruce Cunningham (Stallions radio broadcaster/current sports director Fox 45), September 2018.
Bonnie Downing (Stallions Director of Community Relations), August 2018.
Guy Earl (Stallions offensive tackle), September 2018.
John Earl (Stallions offensive tackle), September 2018.
Neal Fort (Stallions offensive tackle), October 2018.
Scott Garceau (Stallions TV broadcaster/current sports talk show host, 105.7 The Fan), October 2018.
Mike Gathagan (Stallions Director of Public Relations), August 2018.
Michael Gibbons (Director Emeritus of the Babe Ruth Birthplace and Museum), October 2018.
Tracy Gravely (Stallions linebacker), September 2018.
Tom Guy (Stallions special teams), September 2018.
Tracy Ham (Stallions quarterback), August 2018.
Donald Hill-Eley (Stallions wide receivers coach), September 2018.
Carlos Huerta (Stallions kicker), September 2018.
Pete Kerzel (Stallions reporter for AP/current editor for MASNSports.com), October 2018.
Roch Kubatko (former *Baltimore Sun* reporter/current Orioles reporter for MASN), October 2018.
Bruce Laird (Stallions broadcaster/Retired NFL Baltimore Colts defensive back), March 2014.
Brendan Marr (Stallions fan), October 2018.
Tom Matte (Former part-owner of the Baltimore Stallions/Retired NFL Baltimore Colts player), March 2014.

Josh Miller (Stallions/NFL punter), September 2018.
Paul Mittermeier (Stallions Assistant Director of Public Relations), October 2018.
John Moag (former Executive Director of the Maryland Stadium Authority), March 2014.
Dan O'Connell (Stallions statistician), August 2018.
Elfrid Payton (Stallions rush end), August 2018.
Shar Pourdanesh (Stallions offensive tackle), August 2018.
Bob Price (Stallions defensive coordinator), September 2018.
Mike Pringle (Stallions running back), August 2018.
Mike Rogers (Toronto-based CFL fan), October 2018.
Kevin Sherping (Canadian-based Montreal Alouettes fan), October 2018.
Irvin Smith (Stallions defensive back), September 2018.
Jim Speros (Stallions owner), September 2018.
Mark Viviano (WJZ Sports Director), October 2018.
Ken Watson (Stallions linebacker), September 2018.
Walter Wilson (Stallions wide receiver), September 2018.
Zach Wolpoff (Maryland area sports fan), October 2018.
John Ziemann (president of the Baltimore Stallions Marching Band/current president of Baltimore's Marching Ravens), August 2018.

Books and Articles

Brennan, Christine. "Baltimore's Game for a Team with No Name." *The Washington Post*. September 22, 1994.
Canadian Football League. *First and Ten from the Fifty-Five: Canadian Football Explained*. (1995).
Cherry, Dan. "Retired NFL Brothers Minister at Local Jail." *The Daily Telegram*. September 2, 2011. Accessed August 21, 2018. http://www.lenconnect.com/article/20110902/NEWS/309029918.
Eck, Kevin. "Movers Pack Up Speros' Equipment, but Not His Troubles." *The Baltimore Sun*. March 23, 1996. Accessed November 1, 2018. http://articles.baltimoresun.com/1996-03-23/sports/1996083062_1_speros-memorial-stadium-stallions.
Eck, Kevin. "Stallions Draw Ringing Support from Volunteers Saving Effort: Dedicated Group Solicits Season-Ticket Buyers by Phone to Help Keep CFL Team in Town." *The Baltimore Sun*. January 7, 1996. Accessed November 1, 2018. http://www.baltimoresun.com/news/bs-xpm-1996-01-07-1996007191-story.html.
Eck, Kevin, and Gary Lambrecht. "Stallions Seek Move to Montreal; CFL Reportedly Set To End U.S. Presence." *The Baltimore Sun*. January 25, 1996. Accessed October 30, 2018. http://articles.baltimoresun.com/1996-01-25/sports/1996025019_1_speros-cfl-shreveport-pirates.
Elbaz, Jonathan, Jeremy Granoff, Israel Spencer and Eric Morrow. "Baltimore's Forgotten Champions." *Capital News Service*. January 23, 2014. https://cnsmaryland.org/interactives/baltimore-stallions-oral-history/.
Gathagan, Mike. *Baltimore CFL Colts Magazine*. Baltimore: John D. Lucas Printing, 1994.
Gathagan, Mike. *Baltimore Stallions 1995 Media Guide*. Baltimore: Delta Graphics and Communications, 1995.
Hinton, Ed. "Ticket to Ride Though Baltimore Won the Grey Cup, It Must Look for a New Home." *Sports Illustrated*. November 27, 1995. Accessed October 31, 2018. https://www.si.com/vault/2016/07/07/ticket-ride-though-baltimore-won-grey-cup-it-must-look-new-home.

Bibliography

Lambrecht, Gary. "CFL Faces Grim Decisions After Successful Grey Cup." *The Baltimore Sun*. November 24, 1995. Accessed November 5, 2018. http://articles.baltimoresun.com/1995-11-24/sports/1995328077_1_grey-cup-week-cfl-canadian-football-league.

Lambrecht, Gary. "Stallions Ride Out Travelin' Blues." *The Baltimore Sun*. August 8, 1995. Accessed August 13, 2018. http://articles.baltimoresun.com/1995-08-08/sports/1995220056_1_stallions-alberta-calgary.

Malinowski, Erik. "Wild Stallions: How a Team from Baltimore Rocked Canadian Football." *Rolling Stone*. November 18, 2015. Accessed July 25, 2018. https://www.rollingstone.com/culture/culture-sports/wild-stallions-how-a-team-from-baltimore-rocked-canadian-football-42712.

McManus, Kevin. "Jim Speros, Starting Fast in Baltimore." *The Washington Post*. October 10, 1994. Accessed July 25, 2018. https://www.washingtonpost.com/archive/business/1994/10/10/jim-speros-starting-fast-in-baltimore/b9f44a20-3295-47c2-b2cf-b50f2ed19b66/?utm_term=.d183f1163c83.

Morgan, Jon. "Money Woes Don't Dampen Speros' Spirits: Undaunted By Bills, Ex Stallions Owner Tries A New Game." *The Baltimore Sun*. February 26, 1997. Accessed November 1, 2018. http://articles.baltimoresun.com/1997-02-26/sports/1997057101_1_speros-baltimore-stallions-team-members.

Murray, Ken. "After Travels, Travails, Armstrong Finds Home." *The Baltimore Sun*. September 10, 1994. Accessed November 6, 2018. http://articles.baltimoresun.com/1994-09-10/sports/1994253080_1_armstrong-cfl-training-camp.

Murray, Ken. "Blocking for Pringle, CFLs' Tight-Knit Line Gets the Last Laugh." *The Baltimore Sun*. October 28, 1994. Accessed August 21, 2018. http://articles.baltimoresun.com/1994-10-28/sports/1994301002_1_pringle-group-of-guys-subis.

Murray, Ken. "Football Back in Baltimore, Canadian-style." *The Baltimore Sun*. February 16, 1994. Accessed July 25, 2018. http://articles.baltimoresun.com/1994-02-16/news/1994047007_1_speros-tracy-ham-cfl.

Murray, Ken. "Speros Hopes for Replay in Montreal: Owner Tries to Repeat Baltimore Success." *The Baltimore Sun*. June 27, 1996. Accessed November 1, 2018. http://articles.baltimoresun.com/1996-06-27/sports/1996179091_1_speros-alouettes-memorial-stadium.

Ralph, Dan. "Legendary CFL Coach Don Matthews Dead at 77." *The Canadian Press*. June 14, 2017. Accessed July 26, 2018. https://www.cbc.ca/sports/football/cfl/legendary-cfl-coach-don-matthews-dead-age-77-1.4160687.

Steadman, John. *From Colts to Ravens: A Behind-The-Scenes Look at Baltimore Professional Football*. Centreville, MD: Tidewater Publishing, 1997.

Stellino, Vito. "Football Is Back in Baltimore—Even If It's Only an Exhibition." *Los Angeles Times*. August 23, 1992. Accessed July 25, 2018. http://articles.latimes.com/1992-08-23/sports/sp-7445_1_pro-football-game.

Vogt, Gary. "Baltimore Just Adores Colts—The Canadian Version." *Sacramento Bee*. September 11, 1990.

Willes, Ed. "There's Never Been a Game Like the 1994 Grey Cup." *National Post*. November 25, 2011. Accessed July 31, 2018. https://nationalpost.com/sports/football/cfl/theres-never-been-a-game-like-the-1994-grey-cup.

Index

Alabama State University 142, 176
Alamodome 96
Alexander, Ray 90–91
All-America Football Conference 9; AAFC 9
Allen, Damon 96
Allen, Marcus 68, 96
Alphin, Gerald 162
ALS (Lou Gehrig's disease) 137
Ameche, Alan 5
American Football League 29; AFL 29
Amsterdam Admirals 174
Anaheim Piranhas 168
Anderson, Fred 122
Anderson, Roman 157, 163
Anthony, Carmelo 5
Anthony, Charles 63, 155, 160
Anthony, Karl 88, 103, 159
Archer, David 157, 159, 163
Arena Football League 54, 131, 168, 172
Arizona Rattlers 168
Armstrong, Chris 3, 43, 50, 54, 59, 63, 68, 74, 79, 80, 82, 83, 87, 94, 108, 123, 132, 144, 152, 155–159, 163, 167
Atlanta Falcons 7, 50, 53
Austin, Kent 90, 161
Austin Wranglers 168

Babe Ruth Birthplace and Museum 10, 93
Baker, Terry 157
Ballard, Keith 80
Baltimore Browns 3
Baltimore CFL Colts 33, 38, 40, 41, 42, 180–181
Baltimore CFL Football Club 42, 63, 76, 77, 181; Baltimore CFLers 42, 62, 63, 68, 69, 73, 75, 79–80, 83–87, 89, 92, 172
Baltimore CFL Special Teamers 42
Baltimore Colts 1, 5, 6, 11–16, 18–19, 22, 23, 25–26, 33, 38, 42, 65, 69, 70, 74, 82, 100, 106, 178–179; AAFC Colts 9, 178
Baltimore Colts Marching Band 13–14, 19, 22, 37, 38, 65, 125, 144, 150; Ravens Marching Band 19, 125, 150
Baltimore Inner Harbor 25

Baltimore News-American 12, 38
Baltimore News-Post 38
Baltimore Orioles 2, 5, 14
Baltimore Ravens 1, 3, 6, 20, 38, 119, 137, 151, 170, 182
Baltimore Stars 16–20
Baltimore Sun 34, 43, 48, 71
"The Band That Wouldn't Die" 22
Baumann, Charlie 157
Baylis, Jerald 50, 56–57, 59, 82; CFL Most Outstanding Defensive Player of the Year 1993 56
BC Lions 7, 40, 46, 55, 56, 58, 88, 90, 91, 93, 95, 100, 103, 140, 143, 158–159, 162, 166, 171, 174–176, 181
BC Place 88, 92, 159, 181
Beals, Shawn 80
Beatty, Ned 76
Bell, Kerwin 160
Belzer, Richard 76, 77
Bennett Williams, Edward 2
Benson, Larry 30
Benson, Tom 30
Bergamo Lions 137
Berry, Raymond 9, 70
Betz, Rob 12, 71, 80, 86, 127, 145–146, 153
Bidwell, Bill 21, 22, 179
Big West Conference 100
Birmingham Barracudas 30, 95, 101, 120–121, 133, 160–161
Birmingham Stallions 18
Boise State 59
Bowie Baysox 34
Brigance, O.J. 3, 48, 55, 82, 137–138, 142, 145, 152, 159–161, 163, 170, 182
Brigham Young University 52
Brooks, Horace 157
Brooks, Michael 171
Brown, Eddie 158
Brunning Paint Company 35
Buffalo Bills 29, 31
Buratto, Steve 52, 59, 140, 145, 175
Burgess, Tom 157, 162
Burrier, Leonard "Big Wheel" 12, 19–20, 42, 69, 71, 80, 93, 110, 126

189

Index

Byrd Stadium 16, 18
Byrne, Kevin 107, 150

Cal-Berkley 60
Calgary Stampeders 28–29, 58–59, 64, 73–75, 88, 91, 100, 103, 113–115, 147, 155, 163–164, 171–172, 175, 181–182
California State-Fullerton 50
Calvillo, Anthony 161
Camden Yards 22, 34, 77
Candy, John 28
Canley, Sheldon 156
Canton, Ohio 1
Capers, Dom 20
Carolina Panthers 18
Carpenter, Charlie 176
Carter, Grant 94, 99–100, 104, 110, 120–121, 135, 137–138, 140, 170
CFL Hall of Fame 49, 51, 95, 130–131, 133, 145, 170, 175
Chadron State University 53
Charlotte, North Carolina 6, 26, 27, 179
Chicago Bears 139–140, 174, 178
Chicago Blitz 20
Chicago Cardinals 21
Chicago Enforcers 54
Chrebet, Wayne 7, 134
Cincinnati Bengals 29
The Citadel 47, 60, 176
Clancy, Tom 22
Clark, Glenn 67, 78, 93, 124, 146
Clark, Robert 168
Clemmons, Mike "Pinball" 87, 156, 159
Clemson University 31
Cleveland Browns 1, 3, 6, 7, 12, 52, 105–108, 110, 150, 178, 182
Cleveland Indians 105
Cleveland Stadium 105, 178
Cobb, Robert 157
College Park, Maryland 16, 18, 20
Colts Corrals 37, 144
Combs, Gordy 98
Commonwealth Stadium 158, 160
Concord University 58, 134
Congemi, John 165–166
Craft, Douglas 103, 116, 120, 133–134, 172
Crowley, Dan 98–99, 136–137, 151–152, 165
Culver, Shannon 94, 95, 167–168
Cunningham, Bruce 27, 41, 62, 74, 92–93, 110, 119, 129, 146

Dallas Cowboys 10, 16, 171
Dallas Desperadoes 168
Dallas Texans (Arena Football League) 172
Dallas Texans 9, 178
Davis, Rob 97, 140
Denver Broncos 10, 29, 131
DePodesta, Paul 143
Detmer, Ty 52
Detroit Lions 168

Donovan, Art 9, 14, 67, 70, 150
Downing, Bonnie 41, 76, 124, 151
Drummond, Robert 87, 158–159, 166
Dunnigan, Matt 95, 155, 161

Earle, Guy 53, 54, 72, 89, 91, 109, 115, 135–136
Earle, John 53, 54, 73, 83, 91, 135–136
East Carolina University 55
Eastern Utah 60
Ed Block Courage Awards 37
Edmonton Eskimos 48, 50, 54, 59, 75, 88, 100–101, 114, 131, 133, 135, 142, 158, 160, 165–167, 170–171, 175
Edralin, Daryl 59, 60, 141, 176
Elway, John 10
ESPN 28, 53
ESPN 2 62, 77
ESPN's "30 for 30" 22
Evening Sun 38

Fangio, Vic 20
Fayetteville State University 54
"First and Ten from the Fifty-Five: Canadian Football Explained" 96, 97
Flacco, Joe 150
Florida Bobcats 139, 174
Flutie, Darren 90–91
Flutie, Doug 28, 73, 113–115, 155, 164
Football Writers Association of America 55
Fort, Neal 52–53, 73, 79, 82, 122, 134, 146, 169
Frank Clair Stadium 157
Frank M. Gibson Trophy 142

Garceau, Scott 11, 18, 27, 34, 64, 91, 74, 126
Garcia, Jeff 113
Gathagan, Mike 8, 46, 143
Gay, Rudy 5
George Michael Sports Machine 109
Georgia Southern 48, 52, 123, 142, 143, 165
Giants Stadium 18, 179
Gibbons, Mike 10, 12, 19, 23, 62, 71, 93
"Give Baltimore the Ball" game 23, 25–27, 74, 147, 179
Glazer, Malcolm 22
Glendening, Parris 111
Glieberman, Bernard 121
Glieberman, Lonnie 121
The Golden Arm 14
Goodwin, Matt 156–157, 161, 170–171
Gordon, Bobby 63, 155
Grambling State 56
Grand Rapids Rampage 168
Gravely, Tracy 58, 73, 94, 124, 133–134, 163, 171
Green Bay Packers 55, 140, 174
Gregg, Forrest 57

Index

Gretzky, Wayne 28
Grey Cup 2–3, 6, 46, 48, 85, 86, 88–95, 100, 103–104, 108–110, 112–120, 125–126, 129–131, 133–134, 136–138, 145–146, 148, 151–154, 158–159, 163, 170, 175, 176, 181–182; (1990) 27; (1992) 58; (1994) 88–91
Gulf South Conference 58
Guy, Tom 27, 38, 65, 124, 144

Ham, Tracy 3, 7, 43, 48–49, 59, 63, 69, 74, 79, 82–83, 87, 90–92, 100, 102, 112, 115–116, 123, 130–131, 143–145, 151, 155–165, 180
Hamilton Tiger-Cats 29, 56, 62, 79, 114, 141, 156, 161, 163, 171, 176, 181
Hampton University 61, 141
Harris, Rod 157
Hill-Eley, Donald 60–61, 73, 82, 88, 92, 103, 109, 118, 141–142, 151, 153, 176
Hinton, Chris 10
Homicide: Life on the Street 76
Horn, Joe 7, 134
Hornet Stadium 30, 86
Houston Gamblers 20
Houston Oilers 10, 29, 121, 135
Huerta, Carlos 94, 96–97, 102, 108, 115–116, 123, 139, 152, 156–157, 160–163, 174

Idaho State 60
Igwebuike, Donald 63, 74, 80, 88, 90, 155–159, 172–173
Independence Stadium 157
Indianapolis Colts 18, 40, 103; Indianapolis Colts v. Metropolitan Baltimore Football Club Limited Partnership 40
Interprovincial Rugby Football Union 28
Irsay, Robert 10, 12–14, 26, 178
Ismail, Raghib "Rocket" 28
Italian Football Federation 137
Ivor Wynne Stadium 156

Jackie Parker Trophy 97
Jacksonville, Florida 6, 26–27, 179
Jauch, Joey 156
Jews, William 35
Jones, Bert 13, 72
Jones, Kendrick 161
Jones, Shawn 157, 162–163
Jones, Terrence 155
Jones, Warren 162

Kansas City Chiefs 7, 18, 29, 68, 140
Kelly, Jim 20
Kerrigan, Mike 63
Kerzel, Pete 12, 26, 30, 33, 71, 80, 83, 122, 143, 147
Kubatko, Roch 34, 43, 71, 77, 148

Laird, Bruce 25, 26, 62, 75
Landetta, Sean 18

Las Vegas Bowl 1992 52
Las Vegas Posse 30, 46, 54, 75, 79, 80, 82, 96–97, 134, 156–158, 174
Legion Hall 160
Lewis, Ray 1, 5, 150, 182
Liberty Bowl 122, 161
Livingston University (now University of West Alabama) 58
Loch Raven High School 18, 132, 167
London Monarchs 56, 171
Long, Marty 60–61, 141, 176
Los Angeles, California 20
Los Angeles Avengers 168
Los Angeles Coliseum 19
Los Angeles Express 19
Los Angeles Kings 28
Los Angeles Rams 10, 48, 52, 169
Lucas, David 155

M&T Bank Stadium 1, 106
Mackey, John 25, 70, 150
Major League Baseball 2, 5; strike 76, 77
Marchetti, Gino 9
Marino, Dan 2
Marr, Brendan 77
Maryfield, Curtis 79
Maryland General Assembly 22
Maryland Stadium Authority 106
MASN 34
Matte, Tom 15, 18, 26, 34, 35, 41, 62, 75
Matthews, Don 6–7, 46–47, 50, 52, 54, 58–61, 82, 86, 88, 102–103, 130, 134, 139, 140, 142–143, 146, 156, 175, 180–181
Mayfield, Curtis 156
Mayflower moving vans 11
McMannus, Danny 90, 159
McNall, Bruce 28
Meadowlands, New Jersey 18
Memorial Stadium 1, 7, 10–12, 16, 18–20, 22–23, 32–35, 37, 60, 61, 64–66, 68–69, 71, 73, 75, 77, 79–80, 83, 85, 87, 100, 103–104, 106, 108, 112–113, 123, 147–148, 150, 155–163, 178–182; World's Largest Outdoor Insane Asylum 2, 23
Memphis Mad Dogs 30, 95, 96, 100, 102, 120–121, 134, 153, 161, 168, 171–172
Memphis Showboats 20, 62, 96
Meyer, Dennis 48
Meyer, Ron 54
Miami Dolphins 2, 22, 23, 27, 29, 137, 166, 168, 170, 179
Miami Seahawks 9
Michigan State 47
Mighty Morphin Power Rangers 76
Miles, Charles 161
Miles College 171
Miller, Josh 3, 50, 55, 65, 75, 89, 91–92, 113, 137, 140, 142, 145, 152, 154, 162, 174
Mills, Sam 18, 23
Mills, Troy 157
Minnesota Vikings 56, 63, 166, 171, 174

Index

Mittermeier, Paul 13, 26, 42, 76, 111, 114, 119, 130, 149, 151
Moag, John 106–107
Modell, Art 3, 20, 105–108, 111, 124, 182
Montana, Joe 68
Montgomery County, Maryland 56
Montgomery County Fire and Rescue Service 133
Montreal Alouettes 6, 28, 29, 31, 122, 123, 129, 131–135, 141, 143, 146, 148, 165–167, 169–172, 174–176, 182
Moon, Warren 28
Moore, Lenny 9, 65, 67, 70, 97, 150
Mora, Jim, Sr. 18, 20, 23
Morgan State University 141, 176
Moss, Tony 155
Muecke, Tom 155

Namath, Joe 1
Narcisse, Don 162
NBC 10, 28
Nevada 60
New England Patriots 54, 137, 140, 170, 174
New Jersey Generals 16, 18, 20
New Orleans Saints 7, 18, 22, 23, 27, 133, 168, 179
New York Giants 1, 18, 58, 137, 178
New York Jets 1, 29, 97
New York Yankees 10
NFL Europe 29
NFL expansion 6
1958 NFL Championship 1, 5, 9, 23, 178; Greatest Game Ever Played 5, 178
1959 NFL Championship Game 9, 26, 178
1977 AFC Divisional playoffs 82
1983 NFL Draft 10
1984 NFL Draft 10
1991 NCAA I-AA Football Championship 52
1991 NFL Draft 52
Norfolk State University 141, 176
Northwestern University 141, 176

Oakland Invaders 18
Oakland Raiders 10, 29, 82, 138, 168, 179
O'Connell, Dan 75, 96, 126, 143
Ogden, Jonathan 150, 182
Ohio Glory 55, 168
Oklahoma State 95
Olympic Stadium 148
Orange Bowl 178
Oriole Park at Camden Yards 2, 22, 77, 105
Orlando, Mark 98, 99, 152, 168
Orlando Rage 168
Orlando Thunder 52, 60, 176
Osbaldiston, Paul 156
Ottawa Renegades 136, 165
Ottawa Rough Riders 29, 58, 60, 62, 157, 165, 167, 171, 175–176
Owings Mills, Maryland 12

Palmer, Jim 5, 66
Parcells, Bill 54
Pardee, Jack 95
Parker, Jim 9, 100
Passaglia, Lui 90, 159
Paterakis, John 35
Patton, Martin 157
Payton, Elfrid 3, 50, 56–59, 82, 85, 91, 109–110, 116–117, 123–124, 130, 133, 145, 151, 156, 159, 161, 170; James P. McCaffrey Award Winner, 1993 56
Payton, Elfrid, Jr. 133
PBA 5
Perkins, Bruce 161
Perry, Reggie 160
Peterson, Carl 17, 18, 20
Phelps, Michael 5
Philadelphia Eagles 16
Philadelphia Phillies 16, 166
Philadelphia Stars 16, 179
Philpot, Cory 162
Pittsburgh Steelers 13, 138, 140, 168
Poolesville High School 56
Pope, Marvin 115
Popp, Jim 7, 46, 48, 50, 52, 58, 61, 75, 77, 84, 88, 94, 108, 118, 123, 129–131, 139, 142–143, 151, 176
Pourdanesh, Shar 50–52, 54, 62, 74, 82–84, 91–92, 103, 112, 114, 137–139, 142, 145, 152, 168
Pressbury, Robert 155
Price, Bob 58–60, 63, 82, 92, 102, 110, 141, 153, 175–176
Pringle, Mike 3, 6, 44, 48, 50–51, 59, 64, 71, 74, 80, 82–83, 86–87, 90, 92, 102, 109, 115–116, 130–133, 144–145, 148, 152, 155–163, 166
Professional Spring Football League 47

Rahman, Hasim 5
Reed, Ed 150
Richardson, Jerry 26, 32, 179
Richardson, Michael 157
Ring of Honor 65–68
Ripken, Cal, Jr. 5, 77
Robinson, Brooks 5, 65
Rodgers, Pepper 96, 153
Rogers, Mike 85, 129–130
Rosenbach, Tim 156
Rosenbloom, Carroll 9–10, 178
Rozelle, Pete 20

Sacramento Gold Miners 29–30, 51, 79–80, 96, 157, 166
Sacramento State University 30
Sacramento Surge 29, 50–51
St. Louis Cardinals (football) 21, 22, 179
St. Louis Rams 135, 137, 139, 170, 174
Sam Boyd Stadium 79
San Antonio Riders 29, 58, 171

Index 193

San Antonio Texans 30, 96, 100, 103, 112, 120–121, 134, 159–160, 163, 182
San Diego Chargers 10, 29, 55, 99, 168, 171
San Francisco 49ers 99
San Jose SaberCats 139, 174
Sandusky, Gerry 105
Sandusky, Jim 160
Saskatchewan Roughriders 46, 56, 59, 134, 157, 162–163, 167, 171–172, 175
Saunders, Mike 157
Save Our Stallions 124
Schaefer, Gov. William Donald 21, 32, 180
Schmoke, Kurt 32–34, 179–180
Seattle Seahawks 140
Sherping, Kevin 129
Shippensburg University 98
Shreveport Pirates 30, 62, 79, 120–121, 134, 155–157, 161–162, 170, 181
Shula, Don 22
Skydome (now known as Rogers Centre) 62, 155, 181
Smith, Irv 50, 56, 73, 76, 79, 90, 109, 123, 133, 152, 156, 171
Smith, Larry 29, 180
Smith, Lester 160, 172
Smith, Pee Wee 155
Smith, Tony 155
Southern High School (of Baltimore) 55
Southern Methodist University 57
Southern Mississippi 56
Southern University 103
Speros, Jim 2, 6, 30, 32, 34–38, 40–41, 44–47, 50, 62, 65, 67, 69, 71, 74, 76, 86, 114, 119–120, 122–125, 127, 144, 151, 153, 174–175, 179–182
The Sporting News 55
Steadman, John 12, 37, 38, 45
Stock, Mark 163
Suggs, Terrell 150
Super Bowl 1; III 1, 10, 29, 178; V 10, 16, 178; XVI 57, XXI 18; XXV 18; XXVI 67, XXXV 1, 5, 137, 182; XLVII 5, 182

Tampa Bay Buccaneers 21, 63, 172
Tampa Bay Storm 174
Tanebaum, Myles 16
Taylor Field 113, 157, 162–163, 182
Tennessee Titans 174
Thompson, Charles 157
Thompson, Chuck 13
Tisch, Bob 22
Tittle, Y.A. 9
Tobin, Vince 20
Tolliver, Billy Joe 162
Toronto Argonauts 28–29, 48, 53, 56, 62–63, 79, 85, 87, 95, 133, 139–141, 155–156, 158–159, 165, 166, 168, 170, 172, 175–176, 181
Towson, Maryland 14, 62
Towson State University 18, 97–99; Towson University 18, 97–99, 165

Trump, Donald 16, 20
Tuipulotu, Peter 157, 166–167

Under Armour Performance Center 1
Unitas, Johnny 1, 5, 9–10, 14, 65, 67–68, 70, 75, 97, 150
United States Football League (USFL) 3, 6, 16–18, 20–21, 23, 29, 96, 122, 179
University of Arizona 55, 141, 176
University of Hawaii 60, 176
University of Maryland 16, 56
University of Nevada 52, 141, 175
University of Nevada–Las Vegas 60
University of North Carolina 47
University of Pacific 99–100
University of Virginia 141
University of Washington 50

Valley Country Club 14
Vancouver, British Columbia 88
Venable LLP 45
Veterans Stadium 16
Virginia Union University 61
Viviano, Mark 105–107, 119, 147
Volpe, Jon 158

Walton, Alvin 101, 158–159, 161, 163
Washington, Joe (CFL player) 156
Washington, Joe (former Baltimore Colt) 62
Washington Commandoes 54, 167
Washington Post 22
Washington Redskins 31, 53–54, 56, 67, 138, 168, 170, 178
Watson, Ken 58, 70, 83, 91, 96, 102, 112, 115, 133, 171
WBAL-TV 105–106
Weaver, Earl 66
Weaver, Wayne 26
Weinglass, Leonard "Boogie" 22
West Virginia Intercollegiate Athletic Conference 58
Western Illinois University 53
Western Interprovincial Rugby Football Union 28
Wetenhall, Robert 123
White, Brian 162
White, Reggie 20
Williams, Art 121
Williams, Henry "Gizmo" 142
Wilson, Walter 55, 64, 82, 90, 94, 95, 153, 158, 168
Winnipeg Blue Bombers 48, 56, 59, 62, 79, 83–88, 95, 101, 104, 108, 132, 135, 155, 158, 160, 163, 167, 170, 176, 181
Wiseman, Danny 5
Withycombe, Mike 94
WJFK-AM 62
WJZ-TV 105
WMAR-TV 11, 42, 62
Wolpoff, Zach 148

World Football League 29
World League of American Football 29, 47, 50, 52, 55–56, 58, 60, 122, 168, 171, 174, 176
Wright, Chris 115, 142–143, 159–163, 174
Wynne Stadium 161

XFL 54

Young, Steve 20

Ziemann, John 13–14, 18, 22, 26, 37, 40, 65, 125, 143–144

www.ingramcontent.com/pod-product-compliance
Ingram Content Group UK Ltd.
Pitfield, Milton Keynes, MK11 3LW, UK
UKHW042009140426
5217IPUK00015B/1069